Lawrence and Women

LAWRENCE AND WOMEN

edited by
Anne Smith

VISION
and
BARNES & NOBLE

Vision Press Limited
11–14 Stanhope Mews West
London SW7 5RD
and
Barnes & Noble Books
81 Adams Drive
Totowa, N.J. 07512

ISBN (UK) 0 85478 364 4
ISBN (US) 0 389 20055 7

© 1978 by Vision Press
First published in the Vision/Barnes & Noble
Critical Studies series 1978
Paperback edition 1980

Printed and bound in Great Britain
MCMLXXX

Contents

Introduction

It is a truism of criticism that each generation will re-interpret the great literature of the past according to its own needs, but the implications of this for the subjective element in all criticism is largely ignored. Yet it is precisely this failure on the part of the critic to respond to the personal reality of the reading experience that prompts the disillusioned author to believe, like Sartre, that "most critics are men who have not had much luck and who, just about the time they were growing desperate, found a quiet little job as cemetery watchmen." Lawrence is virtually the only novelist who makes this approach impossible; he is still "an *experience, not a classic*", and at a distance of fifty years, he still provokes an urgent and personally profound reaction in his readers. It is not so long ago that hidebound old ladies were carrying copies of *Lady Chatterley's Lover* out of bookshops with tongs, to burn it on the pavement, and now liberated young women are all but doing the same. Perhaps the day will come when we will be able to dismiss Lawrence's work contemptuously, like Norman Douglas, who said that he had merely "opened a little window for the bourgeoisie", but it is a long way off. In the meantime we have to acknowledge Lawrence's passionate sincerity, and meet it with a sincerity of our own. The essays in this book constitute an attempt to do just that, to understand the experience of the relationship between men and women as Lawrence presents it in his work, and to respond to it honestly. Perhaps they will be seen as a contribution to this most vital of all debates, which he began: what is woman, and what is man.

A.S.

Edinburgh, 1977

1

A New Adam and a New Eve — Lawrence and Women: A Biographical Overview

by ANNE SMITH

1: *Prometheus Bound*

Oedipus is the finest drama of *all* times.
(*Letters*, 26 April 1911, p. 76, to Mrs S. A. Hopkin)[1]

The last thing we should expect to emerge from an overall view of Lawrence's attitude to women is consistency, or even a steady, forward development from his oedipal, Victorian beginnings to the patchily mature, liberated tenderness of *Lady Chatterley's Lover*. It would be something of an insult to women, for it would imply that they do not change, that all the years of Lawrence's life the women he knew stood still, like a series of Patiences on monuments, to be related to. And it would be an insult to Lawrence, who believed so utterly in spontaneity, in responding with the fullness of his emotional self to "the quick of life" in everything. Frieda gives us our cue in *"Not I, But The Wind . . ."* (1935):

> He'd have quick changes of mood and thought. This puzzled me.
> "But Lawrence, last week you said exactly the opposite of what you are saying now."
> "And why shouldn't I? Last week I felt like that, now like this. Why shouldn't I?"
>
> (pp. 40–41)

Lawrence wasn't a Priest of Love to whom some dark god had handed the tablets with the Law ready written on them, coming down from Mt. Frieda to lead the people back into Paradise:[2]

he was a novelist, who began by seeing his life's work as "sticking up for the love between man and woman" (*Letters*, Christmas Day 1912, p. 171, to Mrs S. A. Hopkin). He had none of the intellectual's fear of inconsistency—a small thing to fear, considering that he faced, repeatedly, throughout the whole of his life, that greatest thing a human being has to fear: the contents of his own unconscious. Frieda wrote:

> To grow into a complete whole out of the different elements that we are composed of is one of our most elemental tasks. It is a queer story and it frightened me at the time of the dark corners of Lawrence's soul, the human soul altogether. But his courage in facing the problems and horrors of life always impressed me.
>
> ("*Not I, But the Wind . . .*", p. 62)

But the journey into the subconscious is never a tour, it is a quest. What Lawrence sought was his own sexual identity, and what his genius made of the quest was a tentative, pilgrim's map of one area of the relationships between men and women, as they are, and as they could be, for he saw that "The whole course of life now lies in the relation between man and woman, between Adam and Eve. In this relation we live or die" (*Letters*, 11 November 1916, p. 484, to Lady Cynthia Asquith).

Lawrence wrote of himself as a child, "I was a delicate pale brat with a snuffy nose."[3] The delicateness had been there from his infancy: William Edward Hopkin recalled seeing him, "a puny, fragile little specimen" in his pram, and Mrs Lawrence's expression of doubt "about being able to 'rear' him".[4] Even without the failure of her marriage, Mrs Lawrence's battle for her child's life must inevitably have strengthened the bond between them, in the way Lawrence described in *Sons and Lovers*: "Paul was rather a delicate boy, subject to bronchitis . . . so this was another reason for his mother's difference in feeling for him" (ch. 4, p. 5).[5] But the details of his oedipal attachment to his mother have been so often and so well described that they may be taken for granted here.

What is not so often noticed is the evidence that his physical weakness as a child caused him to be cast in a feminine rôle, by himself perhaps as much as by others. His sister Ada wrote that he "preferred the company of girls", and William Edward Hopkin was more explicit: "Young Lawrence was very sensitive, or as his school-fellows said, 'Mardy,' which is a term used to signify a sort of babyish disposition . . . in his elementary school days he did not get on with other boys" (*op. cit.*, p. 23). "Mardy Lawrence" seems to have been a nickname that stuck in his early years; a childhood friend, Mabel Thurlby Collishaw, recalls her mother using it quite casually and if we are to believe her, with good reason, for she writes: "Many times I had to tell him, 'Stop snivelling! you are a baby' " (*Nehls,* I, p. 30). The similarities between the young Lawrence and Dickens's Paul Dombey are perhaps unconsciously acknowledged in Lawrence's choice of name for the hero of *Sons and Lovers,* but it was one thing for a middle-class boy to be physically weak and emotionally precocious, and another thing altogether for a working-class boy—especially a working-class boy in a mining village at the end of the nineteenth century, where physical strength and hence potential earning power were the measures of manliness.

A great many of Lawrence's feminine accomplishments probably stemmed in the first place from his need to be useful in some way compatible with this physical weakness—to justify his existence, in chapel terms—and from his mother's vague knowledge of the customs of the bourgeoisie, with its less physical delineations of sexual rôles. Hence Jessie Chambers can write: "I heard father say what a rare good lad Bert was to his mother. He would black-lead the grate and scrub the floor . . ."[7] From an earlier period, Mabel Collishaw recalls Lawrence helping her to make bread, and his sister Ada presents a picture of him in childhood play which shows how naturally he slipped into the feminine rôle; and indeed, shows how he identified with his mother: "One night . . . he decided that we should make potato cakes. . . . Bert, arrayed in mother's blue checked apron, worked at the flour with the rolling-pin."[8] The last word on his childhood girlishness is surely given by the local grocer, whom May Chambers Holbrook reports as having said:

> "Do you know another lad as 'ud stand and talk like a woman about groceries? Do you ever see him with a gang of lads? Do you ever see him without two, three girls? You can't tell me he's right in his head."[9]

The way in which Lawrence did most of the housework at least in the early years of his marriage is well-known, as is the pleasure he appeared to take in it. He wrote to Will Holbrook in 1913,

". . . I . . . made some marmalade. It's amazing how it cheers one up to shred oranges or scrub the floor" (*Letters*, p. 179). Scrubbing floors was often a man's task in working-class houses in these days, but not the making of marmalade, which belongs quite definitely to the side of Lawrence which took pleasure in doing "feminine" creative things—the side which is apparent in a letter to Mary Canaan, where he exclaims ". . . I made *heavenly* chocolate cakes and *dropped* them . . . also exquisite rock cakes, and forgot to put the FAT in!!" (*Letters*, 12 December 1920, p. 637). This was as much a source of unease and amusement to the middle-class friends of his later life as it had been to his schoolfellows in the "Mardarse" days. Middleton Murry wrote of the "acute unease" he felt "when, during a whole evening, Lawrence sat trimming a hat for Frieda".[10] Hilda Brown Cotrell reported that her mother remembered Lawrence, in the war years, "designing and making an evening dress for his sister" (*Nehls*, I, p. 455). During the same period he "embroidered a little cotton frock in red and black cross-stitch" for Catherine Carswell's new baby. But this is to anticipate, for these references cluster most thickly around the war years when Lawrence's sexual identity was most threatened. The extent to which his friends were impressed by Lawrence's domestic abilities is best shown in a comment on Frieda by Hilda Brown Cottrell: "I can see her now . . . sitting back on a low arm chair, purring away like a lazy cat and showing a great deal of plump leg above her knee encased in calico bloomers probably made by D.H. himself" (*ibid.*, p. 465). Not that we should believe that he *did* make Frieda's knickers: there is evidence in the *Letters* that he didn't, in a letter to his sister Emily in which he asks her to send "for Frieda",

> 2 large meridian undervests
> 2 knickers

(*Letters*, 30 November 1929, p. 1219)

There are undeniable elements of the simplicity of the naturally liberated couple in all this too; Lawrence and Frieda must have been among the earliest "hippies", and it is always hard to tell where the female side of Lawrence's nature is uppermost because he is emotionally at a low ebb, and has regressed to his oedipal conflicts, and where he and Frieda are just being entirely unselfconscious about sexual rôles. Certainly Frieda's daughter, Barbara Weekley Barr, saw Lawrence's "feminine" achievements in this light. She wrote, "He did not have the ordinary man's domineering dependence on his womenfolk, but could mend, cook, and find his own possessions."[11]

Yet there is evidence to show that in his earlier years at least he *was* conscious of, and embarrassed about, any of his activities which could be seen as "feminine". Jessie Chambers wrote in her *Personal Record* that "he never minded father seeing him with a coarse apron tied round his waist, but if he heard my brother's step in the entry he whipped it off on the instant, fearing he would despise him for doing housework" (p. 31). The picture that emerges of him in these days is of a "mother's boy", a boy who was constantly with women. And the closeness of his union with his mother (he wrote to a friend of this, "We have been like one . . . ," *Letters*, 3 December 1910, p. 69) must have given him a precocious knowledge of women, but the wrong sort of knowledge, an over-intimate sympathy with their feelings and more especially, their sufferings. He wrote to Jessie Chambers in 1910, ". . . I have always believed it was the woman who paid the price in life. But I've made a discovery. It's the man who pays, not the woman" (*Letters*, p. 61). In his own case, in his relationship with his mother, this was undeniably true, for, over a long period, he lacked a healthy sense of the "otherness" of women, and for the whole of his life he could not reconcile an intimate knowledge of a woman's mind with sexual attraction towards her.

The negative side of this picture is the absence of his father, or of a male figure with whom he could identify. In an earlier letter he had written to Rachel Annand Taylor, "I've never had but one parent" (*Letters*, 3 October, 1910, p. 65). Because he was artistic and sensitive, there was no man in his environment with whom he could identify: the men he knew—his own and Jessie's brothers —were more different from him than he was from women, so that in the crucial years of puberty he had to define himself against a background of women.

Lawrence's adolescent quest for his sexual identity must have been made all the more difficult by the shattering experience at sixteen in the Haywood factory where the girls cornered him "in a downstairs store room, pounced on him, and tried to expose his sex. He fought free of them, but was left breathless and disgusted and retching."[12] What with his possessive mother, the hothouse spirituality of Jessie Chambers, and the crudely aggressive bawdry of the factory girls, he can have had little chance of wholeness and if the early novels, *The White Peacock* and *The Trespasser*, display a defensive attitude to women, or even, as Frank Kermode says of *The Trespasser*, present women as "refined vampires in the last throes of the romantic agony,"[13] we must bear in mind Jung's comment that "an immature man is quite right to be afraid of women, because his relations with women are generally disastrous."[14] As late as 1908 we have Lawrence's own testimony to his immaturity: ". . . to be sure, I am very young—though twenty-two; I have never left my mother, you see" (*Letters*, 15 April 1908, p. 6). Jessie Chambers recalled in her *Memoir* that "Lawrence was loath to admit that boyhood was over. He was most reluctant to begin shaving, and was hurt when people chaffed him about the pale hairs on his chin" (p. 43). As she discovered to her cost, his most vital relationship at this time was his relationship to his own self.

The parting from his mother to go to Croydon seems to have thrown Lawrence quite violently into a delayed adolescence. His letters for the period May 1908 to January 1910 at least, betray an overwhelming confusion, stemming from a need that is all the more urgent because it *is* so late, first to find his sexual identity, then to define to himself what kind of a man he was to be, and the search for the latter often threw doubt on the findings of the former, because he was to be unlike any other man he knew. It was a struggle which persisted all his life, not just because of his own complexes, and hyper-sensitivity, but also because of the failure of the men in his world to be men, and the women to be women. To what extent this failure was real, and to what extent Lawrence created it to cover his own inadequacy we cannot know, but it was surely magnified by the fact that the middle-class intellectuals of his adult experience never could have conformed with an image of men and women based on his working-class childhood. Certainly the failure of adult relationships in his work has an element of this in it, of a judgement on his part based upon irrelevant criteria. For the only successfully "blood-conscious" men in his novels are healthy versions of himself, and it is odd, for instance, that the sensitive Birkin is so drawn to Gerald, who is as deadly in his way as Hermione is in hers, right to the end. Birkin is so deeply endorsed by Lawrence, and so clearly his mouthpiece, that this ambivalence weakens one of the main themes of the novel, and brings us near to concluding that although he was physically heterosexual, emotionally Lawrence was homosexual.

This is foreshadowed in the letters of 1908, to Blanche Jennings, who was a friend of Alice Dax, four years older than himself and an active feminist. These are among the most self-revealing letters Lawrence ever wrote (and conversely, no clear picture of Blanche Jennings herself emerges from them). He seems to have used her as a mirror, a surrogate mother, and a sexually safe woman on whom he could, not without patronage, try his young man's charms without ever running the risk of being accepted as a lover. It was to her that he confessed his immaturity, and it is in these letters that he shows it most: they are amazingly adolescent. Their predominant tone is narcissistic: after working at the harvest for example, he writes to Blanche Jennings,

> My hands are brown, hard and coarse, my face is gradually tanning. Aren't you glad? I have really worked hard, I can pick alongside a big experienced man; indeed I am fairly strong; I am pretty well developed; I have done a good deal of dumbell practice. Indeed, as I was rubbing myself down in the late twilight a few minutes ago, and as I passed my hands over my sides where the muscles lie suave and secret, I did love myself. I am thin, but well skimmed over with muscle; my skin is very white and unblemished, soft, and dull with a fine pubescent bloom, not shiny like my friend's. I like you because I can talk like this to you.   (*Letters*, 30 July 1908, pp. 21–2)

In the same letter there is a kind of phallic narcissism, when he writes ". . . you could have seen me . . . on the stack, like a long mushroom in my felt hat, sweating, my shirt neck open" (p. 24). Yet he could be more natural, or modest, in writing to Louie Burrows the day before this: ". . . I have been in the hay . . . my exquisite accent . . . is gone; as the corns rose on my hands so grew gruffness in my speech. You will like me, you hussy."[15] That phrase, "you hussy", is a telling one: at this period Lawrence seems to have just discovered that he was a man, and from this point onwards he tried the rôle in its every possible aspect, most especially in these letters to Blanche Jennings.

There is the patronizing male chauvinist of "I *do* like babies! You needn't groan when a girl is born—she may in time be the mother of a man!" (*Letters*, 13 May 1908, p. 10), or "With a true womanliness, you fell out with details that didn't matter" (*Letters*,

11 November 1908, p. 36), and "Don't make foolish, feminine insinuations" (*Letters*, 15 December 1908, p. 39); then there is the corresponding smugness, when he was about to leave for Croydon, of "Seven girls are coming to tea today to weep a farewell tear into our best saucers . . . seven other girls will be left weeping at home" (*Letters*, 9 October 1908, p. 28), and later, "I am having one or two delightful little flirtations—quite little, but piquant" (*Letters*, 6 March 1909, p. 52), or "It is surprising, too, how women—one woman—yearns to nurse me and soothe me. But I will not have it" (*Letters*, 17 July 1908, p. 59). Again, there is the mixture of patronage and self-pity of "I am always opening my heart to some girl or woman, and they wax sympathetic, but they are fools with no alloy of wisdom" (*Letters*, 4 May 1908, p. 10), and "you women, when you turn, you are like Lot's wife, pillars of salt, immutable; you can never turn again and look with calm generous eyes on a thing that has disappointed and disillusioned you" (*Letters*, 15 December 1908, p. 39). At another time we have Lawrence as the gauche provincial, walking in London's Piccadilly on a Saturday morning and being over-awed by the sophisticated women he sees there: "There are women such as I've never seen before, beautiful, flowing women, with a pride and grace you never meet in the provinces. The proud, ruling air of these women of the stately West is astounding; I stand still and stare at them" (*Letters*, 16 February 1909, p. 49, to May Chambers Holbrook). Occasionally he plays the school-teacher, commenting primly "Real independence and self-responsibility are terrifying to the majority; to *all* girls, I think" (*Letters*, 17 July 1908, p. 19), and in the same letter, the wise old man, ". . . a woman can always read a man through and through—through and through." Helen Corke remembers him posing as the dissolute poet: "He tells me once that he writes half-drunk, but this I discount as a touch of the pose which, evident a year ago, has almost disappeared."[16]

Just occasionally there is a note of insecurity, as in ". . . I cannot tell a 'femme perdue' by the look of her, as most men seem to be able to do" (*Letters*, 31 December 1908, p. 41). A similar note can be heard, rather touchingly, when he sends Blanche Jennings a photo of himself with the comment: "It represents me in gross, it has no subtlety; there is no insight in it; I like myself rather bluff, rather ordinary, fat, a bit 'manly' " (*Letters*, 31 December 1908, p. 44). This is all the more poignant when we put it

alongside Barbara Weekley Barr's anecdote in her "Memoir" of
Lawrence. She and Lawrence had been looking through an old
Italian opera brochure in 1928, and came across a portrait of "a
full-looking man with a big moustache": " 'I should like to be
that man. Yes, I really would like to be just like him,' he said wist-
fully" (*op. cit.*, p. 301). His weak physique seems to have always
been a source of annoyance to him: physically—and this is nothing directly to do with his illness—he never was the man he would
like to have been. Even during his premature honeymoon, he
could write to Edward Garnett about his son David, who was
staying with Lawrence and Frieda and went bathing with them:
"He simply smashes his way through the water, while F. sits on
the bank bursting with admiration, and I am green with envy"
(*Letters*, 4 August 1912, p. 136). The narcissism of the letter to
Blanche Jennings, quoted at length above, can be seen in the light
of this as a need for reassurance. (See cover for 1908 photo.)

This is apparent even in his most complacent letters. On sending Blanche Jennings the ms. of *Laetitia* (ultimately *The White
Peacock*) for her opinion, he takes the opportunity of asking for
her opinion of his other "work", Alice Dax:

> . . . don't be afraid of my feelings. If you say something
> violently nasty I shall say 'Dear me, the woman's taste and judg-
> ment are not yet well cultivated'—and I shall become quite fond
> of you, seeing in myself the person meet to cultivate in you the
> requisite amount of good taste and discrimination.
>
> I have not showed the stuff to Mrs Dax. It is remarkable how
> sensitive I am on her score. You know, or you will know—or per-
> haps you will never discover it—my fondness for playing with the
> 'Fine Shades,' for suggesting rather than telling, for juggling with
> small feelings rather than dashing in large ones—this Mrs Dax
> would at one time entirely have scorned, and even now I am not
> sure of her. Do you not notice a change in her?—a softness,
> an increasing aesthetic appreciation of things instead of mere
> approval on utilitarian grounds, or because of appeal to a strong,
> crude emotion? . . . I attribute it to maternity—she attributes
> it to me. Are you interested?
>
> (*Letters*, 15 April 1908, p. 5)

The ill-concealed defensiveness and coy desperation of this aside,
Lawrence portrays Alice Dax here as a rather "masculine" personality. His remarks on her scorn for "Fine Shades" seem to
place her for him in the same category as his male friends, of whom

he wrote: "Give a man that damned rot *Laetitia?* I'm not such a fool. I told you most men had only about four strings to their souls; my friends are such" (*Letters,* 1 September 1908, p. 27, to Blanche Jennings).[17] She seems to have taken the traditionally masculine rôle in their relationship,[18] but at the same time to have been a surrogate mother to Lawrence. The two rôles are not incompatible, since Lawrence's mother herself seems to have assumed many of the more traditionally masculine functions in her family in the working-class way described in *The Rainbow* (ch. 1): it was she who laid down the law, she who was ambitious for the sons, and so forth. Earlier, Lawrence had written to Blanche Jennings of Alice: ". . . she carefully criticises, like a mother who reads her son's school essay" (*Letters,* 13 May 1908, p. 12). Certainly his relationship with her mirrored his oedipal situation at home—she was a wife and mother, older than him, with a strong personality. The situation is repeated in the short story of this period, "The Old Adam", in which the landlady over whom her husband and her young lodger struggle silently, is "a strong woman", "eight years older than he".[19]

Lawrence often seems at this time to have been casting about him for a mother-substitute, onto whom he might displace his oedipal feelings for his actual mother. He wrote to Blanche Jennings:

> For myself, if there were any woman to whom I could abandon myself, I should find infinite comfort if she would nurse me, console me, soothe me, and tell me I should soon be better. I miss religion for this only: that I have now no season when I can really 'become again as a little child'—and make my querulous little complaint into the ear of deep sympathy. This is a confession for a man to make, is it not?

> (*Letters,* 17 July 1908, p. 19)

His women friends during this period—Jessie Chambers, Louie Burrows, Alice Dax, Helen Corke and Blanche Jennings—were all, as Harry T. Moore has pointed out, connected with the suffragette movement: women who wished to share what had been exclusively masculine jobs and rôles. The image of the mother is identified for Lawrence with that of the "strong woman", and both inevitably shade into that of the "masculine" woman, who takes the sexual initiative. He wrote to Blanche Jennings, in an apparently casual aside, "By the way, in love, or at least in love-

making, do you think the woman is always passive . . . enjoying
the man's demonstration, a wee bit frit—not active? I prefer a
little devil—a Carmen—I like nothing passive" (*Letters*, 31 December 1908, p. 44). There is a curious remark, too, in a letter to
Louie Burrows at a later date: "But why did you cut your 'soup-
çon de moustache?'—I liked it" (*Lawrence in Love*, p. 60). Perhaps most telling of all, is Harry T. Moore's description of
Lawrence's sexual encounter with Alice Dax:

> [William] Hopkin once inadvertently heard Mrs Dax tell Mrs
> Hopkin:
> 'Sallie, I gave Bert sex. I had to. He was over at our house,
> struggling with a poem he couldn't finish, so I took him upstairs
> and gave him sex. He came downstairs and finished the poem.'
>
> (*op. cit.*, p. 149)

But even when we see her as the "onlie begetter" of the poem, in
the male rôle with Lawrence as the receptive, creative "female"
who needed fertilization before he could bring forth his little piece
of immortality, we must not lose sight of the fact that she was a
woman, and that this in itself represents a significant achievement
for Lawrence, teetering always on the edge of homosexuality,
searching so much of the time for the male in woman and the
female in man. His close contact with the suffragette movement
shows how near to his heart their debate about sexual rôles came.
And in these letters to Blanche Jennings, beyond the adolescent
posturings is a struggle to transcend his own sexual insecurity
by defining afresh what is a woman and what is a man. He wrote
to her:

> Set a woman's soul vibrating in response to your own, and it is
> her whole soul which trembles with a strong, soft note of uncer-
> tain quality. But a man will respond, if he be a friend, to the very
> chord you strike, with clear and satisfying timbre, responding
> with a part, not the whole, of his soul. It makes a man much
> more satisfactory . . . But better a woman vibrating with inco-
> herent hum than a man altogether dumb, eh? So to make a Jona-
> than for me, it would take the natures of ten men such as I
> know to complete the keyboard . . . To make a real wife for me
> would need a woman with a great range of swift and subtle feel-
> ing . . . Women can feel, but often, very often, they do not un-
> derstand, understand in their souls, I mean.
>
> (*Letters*, 30 July 1908, pp. 23–4)

It would be easy to see symptoms in this of the depressed bisexuality of the *Aaron's Rod* and *Kangaroo* years, but it would be fairer to Lawrence to say that he looked on men and women both, and found them wanting. To him, the fact that he could not give *The White Peacock* to his men friends was not a criticism of the novel, but of the men themselves.

His comments on men at this time would bear this out. He wrote to Blanche Jennings:

> You tell me I have no male friends. The man [Alan Chambers] I have been working with in the hay is the original of my George, —lacking, alas, the other's subtlety of sympathetic discrimination which lent him his nobility. But I am very fond of my friend, and he of me. Sometimes, often, he is as gentle as a woman towards me. It seems my men friends are all alike; they make themselves, on the whole, soft-mannered towards me; they defer to me also. You are right, I value the friendship of men more than that of women. Do not suppose I have no men friends. I could show you two men who claim me as their heart's best brother; there is another, home for the vacation, who has been with me every available moment—till I am tired, I confess. But of David and Jonathan—it is as impossible as magnificent love between a woman and me.
>
> (*Letters*, 30 July 1908, p. 22)

Clearly, men treated Lawrence more or less like a child—a precocious, clever child, but a child. In *The Savage Pilgrimage* Catherine Carswell wrote of S. S. Koteliansky's attitude of "jealously protective tenderness" to Lawrence (p. 23). When he waited for Frieda in Germany Lawrence wrote to her of the manager of his hotel: "He would do what my men friends always want to do, look after me a bit in the trifling, physical matters" (*Letters*, ?9 May 1912, p. 115). And again, this is mirrored in the landlord's attitude to the lodger in "The Old Adam", "playing the protector's part".[20]

The initial definition of the Lawrentian hero seems to have been reached by a negative process, a desperate paring-down. He wrote to Blanche Jennings: "Surely, surely you are Brontë-bitten in your taste in heroes; you cannot have got over the 'Rochester-Moore' stage (I presume you are well acquainted with *Shirley* and *Jane Eyre*, two of my favourite English books).[21] Strong stern men bore and irritate me; their strength lies in their insusceptibility to half the influences that deflect mortality . . . Pah—I hate women's heroes. At the bottom men love the brute in man best, like a great shire stallion makes one's heart beat." (*Letters*, 4 November 1908, p. 34). In women, too, it is the animal that excites him most: Carmen or Bernhardt. He wrote to Blanche Jennings, after seeing Sarah Bernhardt perform in *Manon Lescaut*: "Oh, to see her, and hear her, a wild creature, a gazelle with a beautiful panther's fascination and fury . . . there she is, the incarnation of wild emotion which we share with all live things . . . I could love such a woman myself, love her to madness, all for the pure wild passion of it. Intellect is shed as flowers shed their petals" (*Letters*, 25 June 1908, p. 17).[22]

There is a darker side to this worship of the animal in man and woman of course, one that Jessie Chambers, who has never been given enough credit for her knowledge of Lawrence's character, touched on in her last letter to Helen Corke. One part of this letter, Lawrence's impatient "With *should* and *ought* I have nothing to do", is quoted everywhere, with admiration. But there is more to it than the emphatic denial of the conventional moral law by the liberated artist, and Jessie Chambers put her finger on it in a letter which contains some of the deepest insights into Lawrence that were ever made:

> I said: "You ought not have involved X in the tangle of our relationships." D.H.L.'s reply took my breath away; he said, "With should and ought I have nothing to do." If you will think out the implication of that statement you will see what was the nature of D.H.L.'s bondage; he was the measure of his own universe; his own god—and also his own hell. He deliberately (or perhaps he couldn't help it)—anyhow he regarded himself as exempt from the laws that hold mankind together (I am not referring to conventional morality) and when a human being does that, he is of necessity cut off from contact with his fellows . . . At the end of that same walk, as we stood within a stone's throw of the house where his mother lay dead, he said to me:
>
> "You know, J., I've always loved mother.'
>
> "I know you have," I replied.
>
> "I don't mean that," he answered. "I've loved her—like a lover —that's why I could never love you."
>
> Then he handed me the three poems he had written since she died. I think this partly explains why he had placed himself beyond ordinary human sanctions. He was, as it were, driven out

of the land of the living into a fearful wilderness of egoism. It explains, too, why, as you remark in your book, he looked in woman only for the animal—female—qualities. It made his dilemma a cruel one, because it compelled him to deny what was best in himself. Consequently his prison was also a terrible battle-ground where his two selves were constantly fighting each other.

(*The Croydon Years*, pp. 40–41)

Virtually all the women he knew at this time—Jessie Chambers, Alice Dax, and Louie Burrows in particular—were casualties in that battle. Lawrence used them mercilessly: certainly then, and, arguably, later in his life if not his work, Lawrence's way of love is best summed up in Goldsmith's definition, "an abject intercourse between tyrants and slaves".

Yet Jessie Chambers was able to write in the same letter of 1933 to Helen Corke: "You see that in essentials my feeling has not changed in spite of other deep affection. What he has said about the indestructibility of love is quite true, on a particular plane" (p. 43). When Alice Dax's relationship with Lawrence finished, she "went through a hell of a sort we can barely imagine" and "never let another man touch her, not even her husband" (Moore, *op. cit.*). She wrote to Frieda in 1935 "I thank him always for my life though I know it cost him pains and disappointments."[23] Louie Burrows, not having seen him since she met him after he had broken their engagement—on which occasion, according to Lawrence, "she was rather ikey (adj.—to be cocky, to put on airs, to be aggressively superior)" and gave him one of those gloriously apt snubs which sometimes come as an inspiration to women scorned, when they visited an Art Exhibition: "She stared at the naked men till I had to go into another room" (*Letters*, 12 February 1912, p. 100, to Edward Garnett)—twice visited his grave.

On Lawrence's side then, we should perhaps believe these "loyal cantons of contemned love" that survive; and believe him too when he wrote to Jessie Chambers in the spring of 1911, "You say you died a death of me, but the death you died of me I must have died also, or you wouldn't have gone on caring about me. . . . They tore me from you, the love of my life. . . . It was the slaughter of the foetus in the womb" (*Letters*, p. 78). But his imagery here implies that *Lawrence* was the foetus "torn" from Jessie Chambers, that he had hoped to be "born" from her, but was aborted.

"They" here can only mean his mother—but even of her he
wrote: "I had a devil of a time, getting a bit weaned from my
mother, at the age of 22. She suffered and I suffered, and it all
seemed for nothing" (*Letters*, 11 March 1913, p. 194). Lawrence
himself was, as he wrote of Forster, "bound hand and foot
bodily" like Prometheus, trapped within the oedipal triangle,
consoling himself with a tortured narcissism, as the poem of this
period, "Virgin Youth," plainly shows. His only hope of escape
was not just in the death of his mother, but in the killing of his
mother, which he accomplished symbolically in the writing of
Sons and Lovers, and perhaps in reality, by giving her the over-
dose as described in the novel. In death, she was given back to the
Father, as the poem of this time, "Monologue of a Mother", makes
plain:

> Death, in whose service is nothing of gladness, take me;
> For the lips and the eyes of God are behind a veil.
> And the thought of the lifeless voice of the Father shakes me
> With dread and fills my heart with the tears of desire,
> And my heart rebels with anguish, as the night draws nigher.[24]

2: The Rainbow and After

> It is part of my riches, my glory, my deepest conviction that I
> was part of his work as I was of his life and a vital part. . . .
> You can read it in his work everywhere.
>
> (*Memoirs and Correspondence*, p. 308)

Critics of Lawrence tend, openly or implicitly, to take the death
of his mother as a "watershed" in his life, and to believe him,
by and large, when he wrote that in *Sons and Lovers* he had
"shed" the "sickness" of his oedipus complex. But demonstrably
this isn't true: Helen Corke affirmed that "His mother's death,
while leaving him without direction, had not freed him from
maternal compulsions" (*The Croydon Years*, p. 28), while just
before his mother's death he himself wrote to Rachel Annand
Taylor that his love for his mother had made him "in some respects, abnormal" (*Letters*, 3 December 1910, p. 69).[25] Frieda had
this to contend with, openly in the first year of their union, and
implicitly throughout their life together, and naturally she resented it bitterly—as Harry T. Moore shows, quoting the marginal

comments Frieda made "in one of Lawrence's college exercise books, next to a poem to his mother":

> I hate it—good God ! ! ! ! I hate it! Yes, worse luck! What a poem to write! Yes, you are free, poor devil, from the heart's home life free, lonely you shall be, you have chosen it, you chose it freely! Now go your own way—Misery, a sad old woman's misery you have chosen, you poor man, and you cling to it with all your power. I have tried. I have fought, I have nearly killed myself in the battle to get you in connection with myself and other people, early I proved to myself that I can love, but never you—
>
> (*op. cit.*, p. 212)

Something of this appears in the poem "First Morning" too:

> The night was a failure
> but why not ——?
>
> In the darkness
>   with the pale dawn seething at the window
>   through the black frame
>   I could not be free,
>   not free myself from the past, those others—
>   and our love was a confusion,
>   there was a horror,
>   you recoiled away from me.
>   (*Complete Poems*, I, p. 204)

Who "those others" were is perhaps indicated in a letter from Frieda to Edward Garnett, not long after she and Lawrence had gone away together, in which she says "He really loved his mother more than anybody, even with his other women, real love, sort of Oedipus" (*Memoirs and Correspondence*, p. 173).

Before he met Frieda, Lawrence knew that his attachment to his mother was abnormal, but he was, to a great extent, martyred, self-pitying, and only half articulate about it. Frieda gave him a prespective, enough at least so that he could write in the Foreword to *Sons and Lovers*:

> But the man who is the go-between from Woman to Production is the lover of that woman. And if that Woman be his mother, then is he her lover in part only; he carries for her, but is never received into her for his confirmation and renewal, and so wastes himself away in the flesh. The old son-lover was Œdipus. The

name of the new one is legion. And if a son-lover take a wife, then is she not his wife, she is only his bed. And his life will be torn in twain, and his wife in her despair shall hope for sons, that she may have her lover in her house.[26]

It is here that he first came up with his Queen Bee image of woman: "Yea, like bees in and out of a hive, we come backwards and forwards to our woman . . . we are bees that go between, from the flower home to the hive and the Queen; for she lies at the centre of the hive, and stands in the way of bees for God the Father, the Almighty, the Unknowable, the Creator. In her all things are born, both words and bees" (*ibid.*, p. 100). It might be an over-simplification, but still it wouldn't be far from the truth, to say that Lawrence's God was Woman, Woman, more-over, as Magna Mater. This was the resolution of his oedipus com-plex, and only Frieda—whom Catherine Carswell described as "rather a force of nature—a female force—than a woman" (*op. cit.*, p. 74)—could have helped him to achieve it even temporarily. In a very real way, Lawrence's writing was, as Frieda said, "the outcome of their life together". Because of this, I believe, it is as necessary to know Frieda's character as it is to know Lawrence's.

In his *The von Richthofen Sisters, The Triumphant and The Tragic Modes of Love* (1974), Martin Green argues most con-vincingly that the world of Frieda's childhood and adolescence was, because of Frieda's mother, "a matriarchal world, in the service of life and love, which she created around her" (p. 15). The background of this was a rebellion against the predominantly male world of Prussian militarism, in the form of the "erotic movement", which Green analyses, and relates to the von Richt-hofens' situation:

> Max Weber[27] defines eroticism as that glorification of love which arises wherever love "collides with the unavoidably ascetic trait of the vocational specialist type of man. . . . This boundless giv-ing of oneself is as radical as possible in its opposition to all functionality, rationality, and generality. . . . The lover realizes himself to be rooted in the kernel of the truly living, which is externally inaccessible to any rational endeavor. He knows him-self to be freed from the cold skeleton hands of rational order, just as completely as from the banality of everyday routine." Eroticism of this sort is a religious faith . . . the erotic move-ment . . . carried both von Richtofen sisters with it for a time

and Frieda for all her life. . . . Most notably in Bavaria and
Munich, there arose a matriarchal rebellion which expressed itself
in behavioral terms by idealizing the Magna Mater or Hetaera
role, a role in which a woman felt herself "religiously" called to
take many lovers and bear many children without submitting
to a husband/father/master. This matriarchal rebellion was one
of the most sharply characterized forms of the erotic movement. . . .

(op. cit., pp. 10–11)

Frieda's mother was a matriarch—the original for Anna, the
matriarch of *The Rainbow*, to whom "the outside, public life was
less than nothing", while her father was the original for Will
Brangwen. Frieda's account of her attitude to her parents in *"And
the Fullness Thereof ..."* (*Memoirs and Correspondence*, pp. 3–123)
instantly brings the mature Ursula to mind: "She had always
battled with her parents and their shallow, cynical outlook on
life. In spite of their vitality they had failed intrinsically and
obstinately, perversely made the best of things" (p. 70). Like
Ursula as a child, Frieda thought her father "perfection on earth",
and again like Ursula, she sided with him against her mother:
when they argued, she writes, she "often thought, 'You don't
handle him right, I would know better than you how to do it' "
(p. 9).

Frieda's father's weakness was the same as Will's. He was "not
at ease" in the "big world", just as Will was "wrong" in the
"outside, upper, world". The consequence in both cases was a
matriarchal reaction, given such strong women as Frieda's mother
and Anna. As Frieda grew up in this atmosphere, she became
"from a small child instinctively sorry for all men" (p. 9). It was
this that made her so suitable a wife for Lawrence in the first
place—he himself was the product of a matriarchy, if a much
narrower, meaner one—but which ultimately underlay the element
of hatred that there always was in him for her: Frieda's matriarchal, Queen Bee assumptions, combined with her aristocratic
background, of which he was naturally always aware, could exas-
perate him beyond endurance, and at the same time intimidate
him. For in effect, the new wife was the old mother writ large,
and Jessie Chambers read him aright when she wrote to Helen
Corke after his death, that he was a 'caged panther lashing himself into a fury to find some way out of his strait prison" (*The*

Croydon Years, p. 40). Frieda herself wrote to F. R. Leavis in 1956, to assert that she *was* "maternal" (*Memoirs and Corres-pondence,* p. 374). It is true, both in the ordinary sense and in the "matriarchal" sense.

Before she met Lawrence, this side of Frieda had already been powerfully endorsed by Otto Gross, who had been her lover for awhile in Germany, while she was still married to Ernest Weekley. Gross was at the same time the lover of her sister Else, an intellectual who had been "the first woman ever to be appointed by the state of Badenia to protect the rights of women factory workers" in 1900 (Green, *op. cit.,* p. 16). Green describes the gentle rivalry between the two sisters, and sums up their modes of life thus:

> Else von Richthofen entered . . . the world of academia and social reform, in her protest against patriarchy; Frieda tried academia but fled it to espouse the world of peasants and "primitive" cultures, where men live in the female mode of being.
>
> (p. 5)

Gross was a brilliant disciple of Freud, whom Freud had eventually cast off when he took a new direction in his thinking, towards eroticism, of which Freud did not approve. Gross and the erotic movement were rooted in the Cosmic Circle, a group of men who met in Germany between 1897 and 1903, and who stood for, in Martin Green's words, "life-values, for eroticism, for the value of myth and primitive cultures, for the superiority of instinct and intuition to the values of science, for the primacy of the female mode of being" (p. 73). As we have seen, Lawrence was already predisposed towards the erotic philosophy by the circumstances of his upbringing. The impetus which Frieda must have added can be partly guessed when we read the ideas of Gross. Gross believed that

> To love erotically is not to feel identified with the other person, but with the third being, the relationship itself. Erotic love alone can finally overcome man's loneliness. Relationship understood as the third thing, worshipped as a supreme value, will allow the lover to combine an erotic union with an uncompromised drive to individuality.
>
> (Green, *op. cit.,* p. 70)

This is a perfect description of the relationship Lawrence needed at the time he met Frieda, one which would satisfy him physically, and at the same time give him the comfort of a high-flown philosophical justification for not "sacrificing" his individuality to a woman. That this is how he came to Frieda in their early days is made clear in the short story of that time, "New Eve and Old Adam", in which the wife ("Paula": obviously Frieda) complains to the husband, "I pour myself out to you, and then—there's nothing there—you simply aren't there." The matriarch in Frieda is criticized when the husband mourns "She's got a big heart for everybody, but it must be like a common-room. . . . She was full of generosity and bigness and kindness, but there was no heart in her, no security, no place for one single man" (*The Mortal Coil and Other Stories*, *op. cit.*, pp. 166–195). The erotic philosophy was a sword that cut two ways, to Lawrence's eternal chagrin. Gross's influence stayed with Frieda all her life, it seems: even when she left Weekley to go with Lawrence it was, significantly, Gross's letters which she sent him to explain why.

It was Gross, then, who discovered the "New Eve" in Frieda, as his letters to her make clear. He writes, for example: "The woman that I have dreamed of for coming generations I have known and loved. . . . It is like a miracle, like a greeting from the future that you have come to me" (*Memoirs and Correspondence*, p. 84). He speaks of "the wave of happy, liberating bliss" that Frieda gives him, tells her "I need you because you make me sure and great" (*ibid.*, p. 89), and insists that Frieda free herself from Weekley and come to him, in the most modern terms:

> You say as you did before that you have no right to destroy the existence of a good man. But don't you see that you destroy your own right of self-determination, this right that can never be lost either through pact or sense of duty? How can you overlook that, if you don't want to overlook it?
>
> (*ibid.*)

Yet although Frieda was obviously ready to give Weekley up, she still felt tied by her love of her children and "the fun she had with them". She wrote that it was "not true" when Gross wrote to her that she was "free and harmonious": "—far from it. Chaos reigned in her soul", and she couldn't go against "all the millions of other people, their weight and power" (p. 88). She was torn: "He had wakened up her soul in her, that had lain coiled up and asleep, and now it had become a frightening tiger and she had it on her hands" (p. 90). A superior common sense won; she saw that "The everyday life he ignored. On visions alone you can't live" (*ibid.*) and stayed in Nottingham. Gross gave Frieda a rôle and an image of herself that suited her perfectly: she was the female catalyst—for her, it became enough just to *be*. It was at this point that Lawrence came into her life "naturally and inevitably as if he had always been there" (p. 92).

Yet if Frieda was the New Eve already, there was still a lot of the old Oedipus in Lawrence. In the first place, it seems, Frieda became more of the "classic displacement object" for his complex, than the New Eve to him: she was older than he; she was married to a man in a position of authority—authority of a semi-paternal kind over Lawrence as a student, at that; she was foreign; she was an aristocrat, and she was a mother. It appears to have presented an ideal solution to Lawrence, just how ideal is shown in the mirror situation of the first great love story of *The Rainbow*. There, Tom Brangwen's shattering experience of duality—confusion between the mother who was "the symbol for that further life which comprised religion and love and morality" (ch. 1, p. 19) and the prostitute who seduced him "upstairs in a public house" and left him disillusioned "of his first carnal contact with women" (*ibid.*, p. 20) somewhat echoes Lawrence's own, for Jessie Chambers and Louie Burrows had been, respectively, like a mother and a sister to him, and Alice Dax, one suspects, had given her favours rather too easily to satisfy his Puritan conscience. He was still left after his experiences with each of them, like Tom Brangwen, with an "innate desire to find in a woman the embodiment of all his inarticulate, powerful religious impulses" (*ibid.*). The woman he found was externally like Brangwen's Lydia, but internally far more like Anna, and the religion she brought him was the religion of Eros, whose Supreme Being was Woman. According to Mabel Dodge Luhan, Frieda was "the Mother of all orgasms"; according to Middleton Murry, the Magna Mater. But because of this, she did not release him from his oedipal compulsions, she only cured him of the uncomfortable guilt which attached to them.

Lawrence's three great novels, *The Rainbow*, *Women in Love*, and *Lady Chatterley's Lover*, are undoubtedly the "work" of both Frieda and himself, in the truest sense. When he came to her, he was still very immature for a man of his age, as the naïve enterprise of, and premature complacency with, his letters to her husband show. After his mother's death and his own serious illness, he was drifting. The first draft of *Sons and Lovers* had been written, but the book was far from its final version. His genius had come through in the two early novels, *The White Peacock* and *The Trespasser*, only in a partial way: it had not yet flowered. Frieda brought him in these early days to fullness of life, by the generous way in which she gave herself to him. He wrote during that period the jubilant "I Am Like A Rose":

> I am myself at last; now I achieve
> My very self. I, with the wonder mellow,
> Full of fine warmth, I issue forth in clear
> And single me, projected from my fellow.
> (*Complete Poems*, I, p. 218)

And he transferred this to Tom in *The Rainbow*:

> And she put her arms round him as he stood before her, round his thighs, pressing him against her breast. And her hands on him seemed to reveal to him the mould of his own nakedness, he was passionately lovely to himself.
> (ch. 3, p. 84)

Prometheus was unbound at last, and no longer had to be ashamed of his body, as Lawrence had clearly been during his engagement to Louie Burrows and, indeed, with his mother. Still, he was far from healthy—he still needed to be *given to himself* by a woman.

During their first stay in Germany, Lawrence lived up to Frieda's "New Eve" with all his strength. Asking Edward Garnett then "if anyone will have a short story", he added "But, under the influence of Frieda, I am afraid their moral tone would not agree with my countrymen" (*Letters*, 29 June 1912, p. 132). He confessed that he was beginning "to feel quite a man of the world . . . with this wickedness of waiting for another man's wife in my heart" (*Letters*, 8 May 1912, p. 114, to Frieda). When Frieda suspected that she was pregnant to him, he wrote to her:

> Never mind about the infant. If it should come, we will be glad, and stir ourselves to provide for it—and if it should not come, ever—I shall be sorry. I do not believe, when people love each other, in interfering there. It is wicked, according to my feelings. I want you to have children to me—I don't care how soon. I never thought I should have that definite desire.
> (*Letters*, ? 15 May 1912, p. 120)

But virtually the next day another problem had arisen; they were apart while Frieda stayed with her family, and we find him writing:

> If you want H——, or anybody, have him. But I don't want anybody, till I see you. But all natures aren't alike. But I don't believe even you are your best, when you are using H—— as a dose of morphia —— he's not much else to you. But sometimes one needs a dose of morphia. I've had many a one. So you know best. Only, my dear, because I love you, don't be sick, do will to be well and sane.
>
> (*Letters*, 16 May 1912, p. 122)

Whether or not Frieda *did* take the "dose of morphia" we shall never know, but she seems to have needed to fight against being wholly possessed by Lawrence. Probably because she had sacrificed so much for the freedom she gained in herself by going away with him, she wouldn't simply hand that freedom straight off to another man, even Lawrence. David Garnett recalled of that summer, in his "Frieda and Lawrence," that after she and Lawrence had had a row, Frieda "had gone down to the Isar and swum over to where a woodcutter was working, had made love with him and had swum back—just to show Lawrence she was free to do what she liked."[28] There is probably a basis in fact for the cloying nature of the man's love in "New Eve and Old Adam". Helen Corke wrote of Lawrence before he met Frieda that he demanded "the absorption of my being in his" (*The Croydon Years*, p. 12), an observation which is echoed by Lawrence's friends all down the years, but most powerfully by his own creation "Paula" (clearly Frieda) in this story:

> "You who use a woman's soul up, with your rotten life. I suppose it is partly your health, and you can't help it," she added, more mildly. "But I simply can't stick it—I simply can't, that's all."

Like Paula in this story, Lawrence, according to Frieda, couldn't "bear to be away from me, hardly for hours" (*Memoirs and Correspondence*, p. 197), and, again like Paula, Frieda felt the need to get away. She wrote to Edward Garnett "I ran away from L. for two days after having broken a plate over his head" (*ibid.*). In an article she wrote after Lawrence's death, "Lunch With Mr and Mrs Bernard Shaw," Frieda revealed why she broke the plate over his head in the first place: "Lawrence said to me women had no souls and couldn't love. So I broke a plate over his head' " (*ibid.*, p. 148). More poignantly, she wrote:

> . . . Lawrence *is* wear and tear. I am cross with him just at present, he chases my poor emotions till they drop like panting hares [Here Lawrence has scrawled 'bleeder!'] and if I feel an emotion coming miles away I am all of a tremble . . . fancy marrying again, it gives me creeps. [Here Lawrence has scrawled across the page 'Stinker'] . . . There are two sides to human love, one that wants to be faithful, the other one wants to run; my running one was uppermost . . . I used to think I should never have enough love, now I think I have got as much as I can swallow.
>
> (*ibid.*, p. 190, to Edward Garnett)

Earlier she had complained to Garnett that Lawrence "always wants to treat women like the chicken we had the other day, take its guts out and pluck its feathers sitting over a pail" (*ibid.*, Autumn, 1912, p. 158). Sometimes, though, Frieda accepted this happily, as when she wrote to Garnett about *Sons and Lovers*: "I feel quite responsible for 'Paul'. I wrote little female bits and lived it over in my own heart" (*ibid.*, p. 186). She goes on in this letter with an image that ironically foreshadows a line from "Old Adam and New Eve": "I am sure he is a real artist; the way things pour out of him, *he* seems only the pen." In the short story Paula, cloyed and trapped by love, sometimes "thought he was a big fountain pen which was always sucking at her blood for ink".

Lawrence depended on Frieda, and so often as not, he hated her for it: witness the poem "Humiliation":

> And God that she is *necessary!*
> *Necessary* and I have no choice!
> (*Complete Poems*, I, p. 215)

or the later poem "Tortoise Gallantry":

> Self-exposure, hard humiliation, need to add himself on to her
> (*ibid.*, I, p. 362)

or "The Mess of Love":

> The moment I swear love to a woman, a certain woman, all my life
>
> that moment I begin to hate her. (*ibid.*, I, p. 472)

It is a spoiled child's resentment of its own dependence.

And a spoiled child is what Lawrence seems to have resembled only too closely, when it came to the chief bone of contention between him and Frieda, Frieda's children. Lawrence was jealous of them, with a jealousy that had as much of the sibling rivalry as of the lover in it. He adopted a variety of postures towards Frieda over this. First, there was the subtle, love is all and children don't matter theme of the poem "Rose of All The World":

> How will you have it?—the rose is all in all,
> Or the ripe rose-fruits of the luscious fall?
> The sharp begetting, or the child begot?
> Our consummation matters, or does it not?
>
> To me it seems the seed is just left over
> From the red rose-flowers' fiery transience;
> Just orts and slarts; berries that smoulder in the bush
> Which burnt just now with marvellous immanence
>
> Blossom, my darling, blossom, be a rose
> Of roses unchidden and purposeless; a rose
> For rosiness only, without an ulterior motive.
>
> (*ibid.*, I, p. 219)

There there is the contempt of the Great Genius:

> And serve now, woman, serve, as a woman should,
>   Implicitly.
> Since I must serve and struggle with the imminent
>   Mystery.
>
> Serve then, I tell you, add your strength to mine,
>   Take on this doom.
> What are you by yourself, do you think, and what
>   The mere fruit of your womb?
>
> (*ibid.*, I, pp. 234–235)

In "She Looks Back", a biblical curse emerges, still with the poet as the visionary prophet distracted by maternal trivia:

> Nevertheless the curse against you is still in my heart
> Like a deep, deep burn.
> The curse against all mothers.
> All mothers who fortify themselves in motherhood, devastating
> the vision.

> They are accursed, and the curse is not taken off;
> It burns within me like a deep, old burn,
> And oh, I wish it was better.
>
> (ibid., I, pp. 206–7)

Most subtle of all are the poems in which he becomes Frieda's mother, or she his. In "Birth Night" he writes:

> You are born again of me.
> I, Adam, from the veins of me
> The Eve that is to be
>
> . . . .
>
> This is Noël for me.
> Tonight is a woman born
> Of the man in me.
>
> (ibid., I, p. 240)

And in "Wedlock":

> Cherish me, my tiny one, cherish me who enfold you.
> Nourish me, and endue me, I am only of you,
> I am your issue.
>
> (ibid., I, p. 246)

Lawrence was taking the biggest gamble of his life in fighting Frieda about her children, and he knew it. He wrote to Edward Garnett:

> She lies on the floor in misery—and then is fearfully angry with me because I won't say 'Stay for my sake.' I say 'decide what you want most, to live with me and share my rotten chances, or go back to security, and your children—decide for yourself—choose for yourself.' And then she almost hates me, because I won't say 'I love you—stay with me whatever happens.' I *do* love her. If she left me, I do not think I should be alive six months hence.
>
> (Letters, 3 July 1912, pp. 133–4)

Frieda's comment to David Garnett on Lawrence's play of this period, *The Fight for Barbara* is appropriate here: "he makes himself the strong, silent man, the *wretch*" (*Memoirs and Correspondence*, p. 187). For in the account she gives of their struggle over the children in her novel, Lawrence doesn't emerge quite as he portrayed himself to Garnett:

> Anaesthetized with suffering Paula went on for two or three days thinking of the children. She was one great wound where her children had been bleeding her to death.

Andrew was getting beside himself. He was a delicate man always. On the third day he developed a bad cold and had to stay in bed. Absently, mechanically, Paula looked after him. At last in self-preservation, knowing that they could neither of them bear this, he said to her in a detached voice from his bed, 'Paula, we really cannot go on like this. You see for yourself that it makes me ill; if things are as they are between us, if you behave like that, I think you had better leave me, go to the children altogether and leave me.'

Paula was stung into reality for the first time for days. 'Oh,' she wailed, 'don't say it, don't. Don't leave me in the lurch now, don't send me away. You know I love you, you know I can't leave you. But can't you see what it means to me, the children?'

'No,' he said quickly, 'no man can understand it.'

'Oh, but you won't try,' she cried, 'you are jealous of them . . .'

(*Memoirs and Correspondence*, pp. 97–8)

In *"Not I But The Wind . . ."* Frieda surmised that he could blackmail her so confidently because "Perhaps he, who had loved his mother so much, felt, somewhere, it was almost impossible for a mother to leave her children" (p. 38).

She was in an impossible situation: to wish to see the children was to be disloyal to Lawrence—she wrote to Edward Garnett that he "dreads my seeing the children" (*Memoirs and Correspondence*, p. 191); to abandon all hope of seeing them was to be branded by Lawrence as an unnatural mother. When they went back to England, and had to stay because of the war so that Frieda was always tempted to try to see her children, Lawrence's jealousy flared up even more strongly. David Garnett summed it up:

For though we all loved Lawrence, or were fascinated by him, it was difficult not to be shocked by his jealousy of Frieda's love for her children. The more unhappy she became, the more mean and spiteful was Lawrence's behaviour to her . . . Lawrence never showed her a grain of sympathy, or of gratitude, for what she suffered on his account.

("Frieda and Lawrence", *op. cit.*, p. 41)

Although he made out in his letters to Edward Garnett that Frieda's desire to have her children threatened their union, because it meant that she was not permanently committed to him, even after she had clearly made that commitment—"I have at last nailed F.s nose to my wagon. At last, I think, she can't leave me—at least for the present: despite the loss of her children" (*Letters*, 1 August 1914, p. 137, to Edward Garnett)—he continued to be bitterly jealous of them. And Frieda continued to fight for her own rights.

It would be presumptuous to try to judge how selfish Frieda was in the pursuit of her children, and how selfish Lawrence was in persecuting her for it. For us, perhaps, it is enough to say that their opposing attitudes seemed to be vital to the equilibrium of their relationship, and probably underlay a good deal of Lawrence's emphasis on polarity—for he invariably transformed his worst struggles, by a creative optimism, into necessary steps towards the ultimate goal, wholeness. That he needed Frieda's cooperation to keep a healthy balance in his novels is unquestionable. She wrote to Edward Garnett about the first draft of *The Rainbow*, it's like his impudence, they are *me*, these beastly, superior, arrogant females! Lawrence *hated* me just over the children . . . so he wrote this!" (*Letters*, May/June 1913, p. 207).[29] She went on, "The book will be all right in the end, you trust me for my own sake, they will have to be women and not superior flounders" (*ibid.*, p. 208). In the same letter Lawrence added: "it did me good to theorise myself out, and to depict Frieda's God Almightiness in all its glory" (*ibid.*). Frieda's "God Almightiness" seems to refer to her behaviour over her children, for she wrote to Edward Garnett:

> I hadn't cared twopence about L.'s novel. Over the children I thought he was beastly; he hated me for being miserable, not a moment of misery did he put up with; he denied all the suffering and suffered all the more, like his mother before him; how we fought over this. In revenge I did not care about his writing. If he denies my life and suffering I deny his art, so you see he wrote without me at the back to him.
>
> (*Memoirs and Correspondence*, p. 202)

How much their relationship affected the composition of *The Rainbow* becomes even more clear when we set her letters to Garnett side by side with Lawrence's letter to him of 22 April 1914. Frieda criticized *Sons and Lovers* as "an irreligious book", on these grounds:

> It does not seem the deepest and last thing said; if for instance a man loves in a book the pretty curl on the neck of 'her', he loves it ever so intensely and beautifully, there is something

behind that curl, more than that curl; there is she, the living, striving she.

(ibid.)

This "living, striving, *she*" of Frieda's letter becomes, in Lawrence's letter, "woman becoming individual, self-responsible, taking her own initiative" (*Letters*, 22 April 1914, p. 273), and Frieda's idea of religion, "the deepest and last thing" is taken up in Lawrence's "primarily I am a passionately religious man, and my novels must be written from the depths of my religious experience" (*ibid.*). In the same letter he writes to Garnett: "I am sure of . . . this novel. Before, I could not get my soul into it. That was because of the struggle between Frieda and me. Now you will find her and me in the novel, I think, and the work is of both of us" (*ibid.*). Earlier, he wrote to Middleton Murry: "now, thank God, Frieda and I are together, and the work is of me and her, and it is beautiful, I think" (*Letters*, 3 April 1914, p. 269). Two months later he had brought this into the philosophy of the New Adam and the New Eve, in a letter to A. W. McLeod. He wrote:

> I think the only re-sourcing of art, revivifying it, is to make it more the joint work of a man and woman. I think the one thing to do, is for men to have courage to draw nearer to women, expose themselves to them, and be altered by them: and for women to accept and admit men.
>
> (Letters, 2 June 1914, p. 280)

This was in every sense the healthiest period in Lawrence's life, the period of his struggle to be "re-born". Frieda wrote confidently in *"Not I But The Wind . . ."*: "I think a man is born twice: first his mother bears him, then he has to be reborn from the woman he loves" (p. 52). Yet on the same page she wrote: "In his heart of hearts I think he always dreaded women, felt that they were in the end more powerful than men": the seeds of the wartime and post-war disintegration of Lawrence's personality were always there, and the matriarchal Frieda was powerless to stop it without compromising her own faith. At the end of 1913 he wrote to Henry Savage that the poet Middleton "would have loved a man more than a woman: even physically: like the ancients did" and went on to explain at length:

> I believe it is because most women don't leave scope to the man's imagination—but I don't know. I should like to know why nearly

every man that approaches greatness tends to homosexuality, whether he admits it or not; so that he loves the body of a man better than the body of a woman—as I believe the Greeks did, sculptors and all, by far. I believe a man projects his own image on another man, like on a mirror. But from a woman he wants himself re-born, re-constructed. So he can always get satisfaction from a man, but it is the hardest thing in life to get one's soul and body satisfied from a woman, so that one is free from oneself. And one is kept by all tradition and instinct from loving men, or a man—for it means just extinction of all the purposive influences. And one doesn't believe in one's power to find and to form the woman in whom one can be free.

(Letters, 2 December 1913, pp. 251–2)

There is a world of timorous resentment behind that ideal of the late Victorian male chauvinist, to "find and form" his own woman. And it is obvious that even at the height of the *Rainbow* period with Frieda, narcissism was never very far away.[30] It is evident, too, in both *The Rainbow* and *Women in Love*. In *Women in Love*, before the real nightmare of wartime began, he was still capable of qualifying his idealized self-image with an objective view of the increasingly strident reality. Ursula (with whom Frieda delightedly identified) thinks:

> There was his wonderful, desirable life-rapidity, the rare quality of an utterly desirable man; and there was at the same time this ridiculous, mean effacement into a Salvator Mundi and a Sunday-school teacher, a prig of the stiffest type.
>
> (ch. 11, p. 144)

Yet he is never so charitable to the women in his novels; they are never physically attractive in such a basic way, nor do they ever combine priggishness with physical attraction as Birkin does here: in fact Lawrence usually describes the physiques of his heroes, but the clothes of his heroines. The most attractive male bodies in the novels, moreover, are those which mirror his own and which have, in addition, the delicate pallor of the miner's body.

It is indeed remarkable how many of Lawrence's ideals of manhood are characteristic of miners as a group: most particularly camaraderie and insouciance. He recognized this in a letter to Kyle Crichton fairly late in life, when he described the atmosphere of the mines: "The darkness, the mystery, the otherworldness, the peculiar camaraderie, the sort of naked intimacy: men as gods in the underworld, or as elementals" (*Nehls*, II, p. 422). No-one who has any intimate knowledge of miners will dispute the truth of this. The "peculiar camaraderie" is one which *is* peculiar to miners, probably unique in fact, and the nearest any other group of men has come to it has been in wartime, when the common factor is the closeness of death, the interdependence of the members of a team in the face of death. This suggests one reason why the war shattered Lawrence, and by renewing his uncertainty of his sexual identity drove him closer to homosexuality than he had ever been before: there was, once more, in the war situation as in his childhood, male camaraderie in which he had no part.[31] There were other reasons of course: he was to some extent identified with the woman again, being married to Frieda and suspected of being a spy; he couldn't earn enough to keep himself and her, and the alternative feminine creative way of life, the "new heaven and new earth" which he thought he and Frieda had begun to build, was suddenly swept away. Perhaps, too, returning to England and the middle-class social life with which he could not cope was a contributory factor.

His letters to Bertrand Russell during the war are the most pathetically naïve he ever wrote, in their assumption that he would ever have the power to shape events. They are also, ironically, far ahead of their time in their discussion of the rôle of women in the new society which he and Russell were to build:

> Every woman shall have her wage to the day of her death, whether she work or not, so long as she works when she is fit—keeps her house or rears her children.
>
> (*Letters*, 12 February 1915, p. 320)

> There must be women governing equally with men, especially all the inner half of life . . . The women's share must be equal with the men's.
>
> (*ibid.*, 15 July [1915] p. 354)

> And as the men elect and govern the industrial side of life, so the women must elect and govern the domestic side. And there must be a rising rank of women governors, as of men, culminating in a woman Dictator, of equal authority with the supreme Man.
>
> (*ibid.*, 26 July 1915, p. 356)

Frieda's reaction to the naïve side of the Russell/Lawrence political alliance gives a humorously accurate idea of it, and of how patronizing she could be to him:

> The one time I did not believe in Lawrence's activities (he was very young then) was when he and Bertrand Russell planned to make some reform in English government. I had listened to talk on politics at my uncle Oswald Richthofen's in Berlin (he was then Minister of Foreign Affairs), and what Lawrence and Bertie discussed did not seem like politics to me . . .
> (pp. 142–43)[32]

When this fell through, it left Lawrence lower than he had ever been, as an alarmed letter from Frieda to Russell shows. She asks Russell to visit Lawrence in Cornwall because "He might just die because everything is too much for him" (*Memoirs and Correspondence*, p. 209).

This was the beginning of his *Blutbruderschaft* phase, and the beginning of Frieda's private hell, for he rejected and humiliated her, inevitably blaming her for his wretched situation. She wrote to S. S. Koteliansky:

> You think I do not count besides Lawrence, but I take myself, my ideals and life quite as seriously as he does his. It hurts me very much when you think I do not count as a human being . . . But you see I am also his wife on this earth, the wife to the man as distinguished from the artist; to that latter I would always submit but, you see, some things I just know and he doesn't. Don't talk as if I were such a bad wife and he a blooming angel.
> (*ibid.*, pp. 206–207)

An outside view of their relationship at this time, showing that there were faults on both sides which we shall probably never understand, is given by Katherine Mansfield in a letter, also to Koteliansky:

> It is degrading—it offends one's soul beyond words. I don't know which disgusts me worse—when they are very loving and playing with each other or when they are roaring at each other and he is pulling out Frieda's hair and saying 'I'll cut your bloody throat, you bitch' . . .
> When he is in a rage with Frieda he says it is she who has done this to him and that she is 'a bug who has fed on my life'. I think that is true. I think he is suffering from quite genuine

monomania at present, through having endured so much from her.[33]

Much later Frieda wrote to Middleton Murry about this period "I know you and K. blamed me a lot, but I had to throw myself against that elemental Lawrence and fight him" (*Memoirs and Correspondence*, p. 342).

One serious aspect of "that elemental Lawrence" which threatened Frieda in Cornwall was his homosexuality. It was then that he offered Murry *Blutbruderschaft* and was rejected, after which he seems to have sought relief in a relationship with a local farmer. Frieda summed it up tersely in a letter she wrote to Murry in 1953: "I think the homosexuality in him was a short phase out of misery—I fought him and won" (*Memoirs and Correspondence*, p. 332).

Yet there was still a healthy side to the battle—or perhaps, a series of false dawns. He wrote to Murry in 1916

> Frieda and I have finished the long and bloody fight at last, and are at one. It is a fight one has to fight—the old Adam to be killed in me, the old Eve in her—then a new Adam and a new Eve. Till the fight is finished, it is very honourable to fight. But, oh dear, it is very horrible and agonising.
>
> (*Letters*, 11 October 1916, p. 479)

At least the battle of the sexes was still a valid one for Lawrence, and we should probably be grateful to Frieda for the fact that it was, and that it was never finished. In a letter to Katherine Mansfield, returning a "Jung book", he gives his version of what he was fighting against:

> Beware of it—this mother-incest idea can become an obsession. But it seems to me there is this much truth in it: that at certain periods the man has a desire and a tendency to return into the woman, make her his goal and end, find his justification in her. In this way he casts himself as it were into her womb, and she, the Magna Mater, receives him with gratification. This is a kind of incest . . . I have done it, and now struggle with all my might to get out. In a way, Frieda is the devouring mother. It is awfully hard, once the sex relation has gone this way, to recover.
>
> (*Letters*, ? 21 November 1918, p. 565)

This is all very reasonable, but he goes on to report that "Frieda says I am antedeluvian in my positive attitude", because

> I do think a woman must yield precedence to a man, and he must take this precedence. I do think men must go ahead absolutely in front of their women, without turning round to ask permission or approval from their women. Consequently the women must follow as it were unquestioningly. I can't help it. I believe thus. Frieda doesn't. Hence our fight.
>
> (*ibid.*)

It seems that he had searched Jung and come up with new authority to support his old need, that of the spoiled child, to domineer and possess. And Frieda, rejected some of the time by Lawrence and most of the time by his friends, was too insecure in herself to give him the reassurance he had to have. Clearly he felt himself to have been let down by her love in the war years, and love seems to have faded somewhat on her side too, for she wrote to Middleton Murry in 1951, "I believe my deepest feeling for L. was a profound compassion. He wanted so much that he could never have with his intensity. I felt so terribly sorry for him or I could never have stood it all" (*Memoirs and Correspondence*, p. 312).

In the post-war years Lawrence was perhaps, as Jessie Chambers had predicted, too isolated. His voice too often has the tone of a child who has first been spoiled and then ignored; one who knows that his spoiling is brought about by self-indulgent women, and has no reference to his personal qualities. Turning against Frieda—"hating" her, in her own words—he sought reassurance from all the women he knew at this time, and flirted impotently with them all, but especially with Mabel Dodge Luhan and Dorothy Brett. These were for Lawrence years of a grim struggle to recover the balance and the wholeness of the pre-war phase, years in which self-pity and an absurd egomania as often as not won the day. The author of *Aaron's Rod* and *Kangaroo* is easily recognizable in a letter to Mabel, when he writes, "One day I will come and take your submission. When you are ready. . . . I will take a submission from you one day, since it is still yours to give" (*Letters*, 8 November 1923, p. 761), or when he says to Dorothy Brett "You have no idea, Brett, how humiliating it is to beat a woman; afterwards one feels simply humiliated."[34] Frieda's response to Lawrence's attitude in this period comes through very plainly in a conversation reported by Brett, about *The Boy in the Bush*:

[Brett:] ". . . I don't like the end. He should have died. . . ."

[Lawrence:] "I know . . . I made him die—only Frieda made me change it."

[Frieda:] "Yes . . . I made him change it. I couldn't stand the superiority of the man, always the same self-importance. 'Let him become ordinary,' I said. Always this superiority and death."

(*ibid.*, *Nehls*, II, p. 355)

The whole tone of the curious spinster-and-curate-ish ménage at Taos is neatly suggested by a passage from Mabel's book:

One evening when I needed my hair trimmed, I mentioned it, saying how I hated the town barber. What I really wanted was to have Lorenzo suggest that he do it for me. I longed to have him shear me. But he didn't say anything, and instead Brett said, brightly:

'I'll do it! Run along and fetch me a little shears. I always snipped Katherine's for her.'

I made a face for Lawrence's benefit that she didn't see, and brought the scissors and sat down, grim. Lorenzo hovered round and began to direct her, and Brett slashed into my hair. I could hear her panting a little. She slashed and slashed and suddenly cut the end of my ear off!

The blood ran down and Lawrence palely offered me his handkerchief. I looked at Brett in amazement and, I must admit, in some admiration! She was half snuffling, with tears in her eyes, and laughing too.

'Why you cut my ear off!' I exclaimed. I couldn't get over it. [She] hated me, and she was deaf, and she tried to mutilate my ear! That seemed so interesting that I forgot to be indignant. However, I didn't forget to make a good deal of it to the tenderhearted Lorenzo.[35]

Lawrence played them off against Frieda in a way that was as cruel as it was ludicrous. And it is surely significant that when he finally attempted to be physically unfaithful to her, with Brett, it was after Frieda's daughters, now grown up, had come for a holiday with her. First he got his sister Ada to join them. Then when he got tired with his sister he joined Brett.

Yet it was all part of his struggle for independence, a struggle to achieve something immeasurably higher than this side of the story suggests. From the misery and disappointment of the war years he had, characteristically, managed to extract a desperate, profound and positive vision:

> . . . life's the only thing that matters, not love, not money, not anything else—just the power to live and be one's own self. Love is heavily over-weighted. I'm going to ride another horse. I mean love in general—humanity and all. Life let us cherish.
>
> (*Letters*, 1 July 1919, p. 589, to Cynthia Asquith)

> One has to learn that love is a secondary thing in life. The first thing is to be a free, proud, single being by oneself: to be oneself free, to let the other be free: to force nothing and not to be forced into anything.
>
> (*Nehls*, I, p. 500)

But it was a vision that he could only intermittently sustain, and the three violent novels of the post-war years, during which he plainly suffered from physical weakness and nervous exhaustion, give weight to Jessie Chambers' comment to Helen Corke, that Lawrence was "a man in bondage, and all his theorisings and philosophisings only bear witness to his agony" (*The Croydon Years*, p. 40). The frustration of his failure to control his world, or just to control Frieda, had its oblique expression in the "male Cranford" of *Aaron's Rod* ("When a woman's got her children, by God, she's a bitch in the manger"), the near-fascism of *Kangaroo* with its tired, superfluous prose, and the hysterical posings of *The Plumed Serpent*. All three novels have a powerful homosexual bias; Lawrence in his shattered state still sought the "short phase out of misery", but their pointless violence shows that his escape route was just a blind alley, and that Lawrence, with all the neurotic obsessiveness of an exhausted man, kept banging his head on the wall at the end of it.

When his new vision finally did find its way into his work, in *Lady Chatterley's Lover*, he had carried it much further than the first expression in these letters of the end of the war, to a new capacity for tenderness, and a more mature faith in the future of the love relationship. After the publication of this novel he wrote to Aldous Huxley: "I'm reading Beethoven's letters—always in love with somebody when he wasn't really, and wanting contacts when he didn't really—part of the crucifixion into isolate individuality" (*Letters*, ?14 November 1927, p. 1020). The agonies of the years between were not wasted; the crucifixion into isolate individuality is the supreme human achievement, light years ahead of the crucifixion into sex of the "Tortoise" poems. Yet it seems it was only achieved when Lawrence had become as sexually impo-

tent as Clifford Chatterley. Impotence, and Frieda's continuing
to care for him, was the ideal, final solution for Lawrence's complexes: invalid and impotent he was as safe as a child. In his last
novel he succeeded in splitting this part of himself off from the
vital, potent male who had been struggling to emerge from the
damaged, oedipus-ridden reality all Lawrence's life and who had
figured in his greatest novel, *Women in Love*, as the physically
frail and emotionally self-absorbed Birkin. Frieda summed up the
personal achievement which *Lady Chatterley's Lover* represented
in Lawrence's life in a letter to Harry T. Moore thus: "The terrible
thing about Lady C. is that L. identified with both Clifford and
Mellors; that took courage, that made me shiver, when I read
it as he wrote it" (*Memoirs and Correspondence*, p. 352).

Yet *Lady Chatterley's Lover*, with its suggestion that love heals
the wounds of experience suffered in a cold world, was really only
a beginning. Behind the tenderness and the realism of pregnancy
and work and property there is still an element of adolescent
fantasy (much stronger in the final version than in the earlier ones),
with the working-class gamekeeper pouncing out from behind
trees to have his way with the lady of the manor, and behind *this*
lies Lawrence's inability to come to terms with women as full
human beings, and his inability to show a satisfactory, fulfilling
marriage between two articulate people. Even when we allow that
he was right about the need for a vital relationship that goes beyond mere consciousness and social compatibility, the fact remains
that such a relationship in itself could not be fulfilment, and that,
for example, the semi-comatose acquiescent stupor of March at
the end of *The Fox* presents woman as the "gentle domestic
beast" so dear to the hearts of the Victorians.

Yet Lawrence's "sickness" was, as he himself often wrote, one
which is characteristic of twentieth-century man, and if he had
not fought against it with such courage all his life, the twentieth
century would have been much the poorer. Nonetheless, his contribution has not been an unmixed blessing. Donald Davie wrote
of his own generation that "some of us . . . tried to conduct our
marriages on Lawrentian principles, with touching and comical consequences" (*TLS* 1 October 1977, p. 1233), and it seems only too
often that the Lawrentian—i.e. perfect—marriage could not work
unless the man were another Lawrence, and the woman another
Frieda. Perhaps we have trusted the teller too much, and too

readily taken the tales as allegories of an abstract ideal relationship, quasi-Biblical parables of the New Adam and the New Eve, rather than as the specific re-creation of Lawrence and Frieda's own "savage pilgrimage"—for ultimately, Lawrence was a pilgrim, the first, which made him also something of an explorer. But his journey was unfinished; the map he has left us is a terrifying one, full of areas of darkness, and no-one has tried, it seems, to complete it, although he pointed towards the route—and was unequivocal about the sacred necessity of the journey:

> One must learn to love, and go through a good deal of suffering to get to it, like any knight of the grail, and the journey is always *toward* the other soul. . . . To love, you have to learn to understand the other, more than she understands herself, and to submit to her understanding of you. It is damnably difficult and painful, but it is the only thing which endures.
>
> (*Letters*, 7 July 1914, p. 288 to Sir Thomas Dacre Dunlop)

NOTES

1 *The Collected Letters of D. H. Lawrence*, ed. Harry T. Moore (1962). Hereafter referred to in the text as *Letters*.

2 Yet Frieda wrote to Edward Garnett in May or June 1913, about Goethe's Iphigenie "I'll be hanged if any man wants to love her, as well as [be] married to the tablets of the ten commandments, though mind you a man looks for that in a woman too! " (*Letters*, p. 208).

3 "Autobiographical Sketch" quoted in *D. H. Lawrence: A Composite Biography*, gathered, arranged and edited by Edward Nehls (hereafter *Nehls*), I, p. 8.

4 "D. H. Lawrence: A Personal Memoir." Original publication of a BBC recording (17 August 1949) quoted in *Nehls*, I, p. 21.

5 Penguin edition. All subsequent refs. to Lawrence's novels and short stories are to the Penguin editions.

6 *D. H. Lawrence: Reminiscences and Correspondence* (1934) quoted in *Nehls*, III, p. 132.

7 "E.T.", *D. H. Lawrence: A Personal Record* (1935), p. 30.

8 Ada Lawrence and G. Stuart Gelder, *Early Life of D. H. Lawrence: Together with Hitherto Unpublished Letters and Articles* (1932), p. 31.

9 *Nehls*, III, ch. 6 "The Chambers Papers", p. 571.

10 *Between Two Worlds: An Autobiography* (N.Y., 1936), p. 246.

11 "Memoir of D. H. Lawrence", in *D. H. Lawrence Novelist, Poet, Prophet* ed. Stephen Spender (1973) pp. 26–7. Hereafter *Spender*.

12   Harry T. Moore; *The Priest of Love: a life of D. H. Lawrence* (Penguin, 1974) p. 64.

13   "The Novels of D. H. Lawrence," in *Spender* (pp. 77–89), p. 79.

14   *Two essays on Analytical Psychology*, trans. R. F. C. Hull (Princeton U.P., Bollingen Series XX, 1972), p. 106.

15   *Lawrence in Love: Letters to Louie Burrows* ed. James T. Boulton (Nottingham 1968), p. 16 (2 September 1908). Hereafter *Lawrence in Love*.

6   *D. H. Lawrence: The Croydon Years* (Austin, Texas, 1965) p. 9. Hereafter *The Croydon Years*.

17   Yet he wrote to his sister Ada about the reviewers of *The White Peacock* "They amuse me highly by wondering if I'm a woman" (*Letters*, 9 February 1911, p. 72), and Catherine Carswell wrote in *The Savage Pilgrimage* (1932) "To Lawrence's amusement his work was taken for a woman's in several quarters" (p. 6).

18   Enid Hilton wrote of Alice Dax: ". . . most of the men of her generation feared her . . . she could and did contradict their statements and words of wisdom, and she *dared* to be right" (Moore, *op. cit.*, p. 156).

19   In *The Mortal Coil and Other Stories*, pp. 67–87.

20   The friends of Lawrence who treated him like a child had obviously never encountered Burns's warning about "the chiel' among ye, takin' notes".

21   In passing it is interesting to note a parallel between the new woman, Ursula, in *The Rainbow*, and Jane Eyre. Ursula struggles against "the close, physical, limited life of herded domesticity" (ch. 13, p. 354); Jane says "I desired liberty; for liberty I gasped; for liberty I uttered a prayer" (Penguin ed., ch. 10, p. 117). Ursula feels this after her affair with Winifred Inger, her schoolmistress: Jane after her former schoolmistress and companion, Miss Temple, gets married.

22   He admired *Hedda Gabbler* immensely too: he sent Louie Burrows a copy of it, recommending Hedda's "new-fangled madness".

23   See *Frieda Lawrence: Memoirs and Correspondence* ed. E. W. Tedlock (1961), p. 245. Hereafter *Memoirs and Correspondence*.

24   *The Complete Poems of D. H. Lawrence*, ed. Vivian de Sola Pinto and Warren Roberts, vol. 1, p. 47. Hereafter *Complete Poems*.

25   Daniel Weiss makes an excellent case for Lawrence's having suffered from the oedipus complex all his life, and argues that "*Sons and Lovers* is a coin whose reverse is the remainder of Lawrence's works" in his *Oedipus in Nottingham: D. H. Lawrence* (Seattle: University of Washington Press, 1962).

26   Foreword to *Sons and Lovers*, in *The Letters of D. H. Lawrence*, ed. Aldous Huxley (1932) p. 100.

27   Max Weber was the lover of Frieda's sister Else.

28   "Frieda and Lawrence" in *Spender*, (pp. 37–41) p. 39.

29   Confirmation of Frieda's influence comes in an interesting echo of the powerful cathedral scene in *The Rainbow* when she writes to David Garnett early in 1913, "L. approaches all people (women specially) as

if they were Gothic cathedrals, then he finds that they are little houses and hates them for it" (*op. cit.*, p. 192).

30   For an interesting discussion of this letter, see Jeffrey Meyers, "D. H. Lawrence and Homosexuality" in *Spender*, pp. 135–158.

31   His ambivalent attitude to this is perfectly summed up in a letter to Dollie Radford, written just after an army physical: "And even this terrible glamour of camaraderie, which is the glamour of Homer and all militarism, is a decadence, a degradation, a losing of individual form and distinction, a merging in a sticky male mass. It attracts me for a moment . . ." (*Letters*, 29 June 1916, p. 456).

32   "Apropos of Harry T. Moore's Book, *The Intelligent Heart*" in *Memoirs and Correspondence*, pp. 142–143.

33   *The Letters and Journals of Katherine Mansfield* ed. C. K. Stead (Penguin, 1977) p. 79.

34   Dorothy Brett, *Lawrence and Brett* (1934), quoted in *Nehls*, II, p. 31.

35   Mabel Dodge Luhan, *Lorenzo in Taos* (1932), quoted in *Nehls*, II, pp. 335–6.

2

Lawrence's Treatment of Women in *Sons and Lovers*

by FAITH PULLIN

> It is not of love that we are fulfilled, but of love in such in-
> timate equipoise with hate that the transcendence takes place.[1]

Lawrence is a ruthless user of women; in *Sons and Lovers*, the
mother, Miriam and Clara are all manipulated in Paul's painful
effort at self-identification, the effort to become himself. In many respects, Lawrence never emerged from the infantile state in which
other people are merely instruments. This leads him to make con-
fusing and contradictory demands on his characters, as well as on
the women with whom he interacted in his real life. Paul Morel
is a curiously passive figure. The other children make lives for
themselves outside the home, especially William, who, until his
death, is *the* lover and of whom Paul is jealous. But Paul, at the
age of fourteen, when he is expected to go out into the world and
make his living, has no higher aim than the regressive one of living with his mother:

> His ambition, as far as this world's gear went, was quietly to
> earn his thirty or thirty-five shillings a week somewhere near
> home, and then, when his father died, have a cottage with his
> mother, paint and go out as he liked, and live happily ever after.[2]

This wish-fulfilment is actually expressed by Lawrence himself in
a letter to Ernest Collings (17 January 1913) when he said

> It is hopeless for me to try to do anything without I have a
> woman at the back of me . . . I daren't sit in the world without a
> woman behind me.[3]

Lawrence is an extremely egotistical writer. In his portraits of women, he is usually defining some aspect of himself, rather than attempting the creation of the other sex. Many critics have argued that Lawrence (whether homosexual or bisexual in fact himself) was the true androgynous artist and therefore attuned to the inner experience of both sexes. My purpose here is to emphasize the point that Lawrence's main object was always to examine the male psyche and to use his women characters to that end. Indeed, even when a character like Ursula in *The Rainbow* is given a female name, she is merely a vehicle for the Lawrentian autobiography. When Ursula reappears, in *Women in Love*, she is a much lesser figure, since Lawrence, in Birkin, is able to present himself as a man. Lawrence's women are allowed their liberty only in so far as they will always, finally, acknowledge him the master. Lawrence remained deeply bound to his early Eastwood life, in that his later relations with women were determined by his privileged mother's boy status and his taking over many feminine characteristics (*becoming* his mother). Lawrence's later longing for a tender male friendship comes from the nurturing companionship between his father and his father's male friends at the pit; a community life, from which the women were rigorously excluded. Morel's ineffectual attempts to control his wife and to dominate her, by physical means if necessary, were later mirrored in Lawrence's struggles with Frieda. However much these difficulties are the result of cultural conditioning, in that working class patriarchy insists on the pre-eminence of the male (husbands in *Sons and Lovers* are called masters), they are equally the result of Lawrence's own personal psychic conflicts. Clever dodges such as presenting a female critique of his overbearing views, wrapped up in a fake abstract system, through the mouths of women characters (as in *Women in Love*) do not succeed in masking the fact that Lawrence must always have the last word. Lawrence was not really interested in his woman characters, or only for as long as they supported and encouraged the male. Lawrence isn't concerned with women as themselves, but only as examples; he has a marked tendency to undervalue individuality in women (clever women he distrusted and hated). Mrs Morel is much more of a stereotype than her husband. Indeed, it's clear that to Lawrence, Morel himself is a more compelling figure and the one on whom he was to base the positive values of his later life. As a child Lawrence himself was unable to appreciate his father's qualities, since this would have been seen as treachery by his mother (on whom he depended for emotional security and self-esteem). May Holbrook, Jessie Chambers' elder sister, noted at the time that Lawrence was afraid to reveal any similarities between himself and his father or any understanding or liking for him:

> Next time Bert was at our tea table, I offered him the cream.
> "You know Bert doesn't take cream," remarked Mother, But I pressed it on him till he said:
> "I don't like it, I like the taste of the tea." And I informed my family, "Those are the very words his father used when I passed him the cream jug!"
> Bert reddened. "Yes, he doesn't take it." And I followed up: "Fancy you inheriting his taste!" For I couldn't forget the waves of hate that came from him as he humped himself up.[4]

On another occasion, there is an argument about some mushrooms. It turns out that Lawrence wanted them for his father's tea:

> "Well!" I cried in sheer surprise, "and you hating him as you hate him! You don't hate him as you pretend you do, or you'd never make trouble with your friends to take their mushrooms for him!"
> "I have to hate him for Mother's sake," he replied. "But I can take mushrooms home when I find them, and they'll be for his tea because he loves wild things you find."[5]

It's because Lawrence is afraid that he is like his father that he presents Paul as a male version of Mrs Morel. He even looks like her:

> Paul was now fourteen, and was looking for work. He was a rather small and rather finely-made boy, with dark brown hair and light blue eyes.
>
> (p. 112)

There is a great deal of class antagonism here. Paul, through his mother, is determined that he will not be a common labourer. Upward social mobility demands that he take on the characteristics of Mrs Morel's lower middle class status. The children refuse to speak in dialect and they read books. In real life, this worked against both Lawrence and his mother since Lawrence rose a little too high and found that his mother was not pleased when he put

The White Peacock into her dying hands. She would have preferred him to have written a romance.

Paul and his father are unable to talk to each other, since the
father has been cast as the enemy. The only time when contact is
possible is when Morel works about the house. Then the children
can come to terms with him: "they united with him in the work,
in the actual doing of something, when he was his real self again."
Significantly, Morel is the storyteller, the creator. He comes into
his own when he tells the children tales of the pit ("Morel had a
warm way of telling a story. He made one feel Taffy's cunning").
Morel, too, is the dancer of the family, whereas Mrs Morel is unable to dance, even if her Puritan principles would let her:

> "You don't dance yourself, do you missis?", asked her nearest
> neighbour, in October, when there was great talk . . .
> "No—I never had the least inclination to", Mrs Morel replied.
> "Fancy! An' how funny as you should ha' married your Mester.
> You know he's quite a famous one for dancing."
>
> (p. 22)

What emerges from all this (and Lawrence himself realized it later)
is that the true love in *Sons and Lovers* is between Paul and his
father. His deepest adolescent desire is to be a painter, a creator
and celebrator of life, like his father. His mother, on the other
hand, thinks in terms of material advancement. She wishes to
impose herself on the world through her sons (William was like
her knight who wore *her* favour in the battle), she is not interested in the thing itself—only in the recognition that achievement
will bring (p. 113).

All through his life, Lawrence found it hard to resist the temp-
tation of blaming women. For coming too close and impinging on
his divine selfhood or for being too detached and daring to have
a life of their own. The subtext of *Sons and Lovers*, the novel
Lawrence actually produced, rather than the one he thought he
was writing, is concerned with condemning Mrs Morel for her
stifling hold on Paul. He is presented as a mere victim on whom
her view of the world is forcibly branded. As Jessie Chambers
pointed out,[6] the climactic rejection of Miriam does not come about
because Paul has made a conscious decision, but because he cannot successfully resist his mother. In other words, Paul is an object
over whom two strong women are struggling. In actual fact,
Lawrence gave Jessie Chambers up at his mother's bidding; in the

novel, he attempts to justify this action by insisting on Miriam's inadequacies, both as a personality and, specifically in sexual terms. It is easy to appreciate Jessie Chambers' bitterness at this picture, and to condemn Lawrence for projecting his own problems on to the Miriam character. However, as Lawrence himself said, "one sheds one's sicknesses in books."[7] One of the main sicknesses has been pointed out by Helen Corke. She, with Jessie Chambers, is one of the most perceptive of Lawrence's early critics. This fault in *Sons and Lovers*, and in many other works of Lawrence, comes from his habit of generalizing. Mrs Morel is a *type* of woman, so is Miriam and so is Clara. Lawrence's error was to talk in terms of Man and Woman; whereas, as Helen Corke says, there is no such abrupt and total distinction between the sexes. Lawrence then "tends to perpetuate the old semitic racial error symbolised in the story of the creation of Eve".[8] In his fear of the power of women ("But no—women, are more passionate than men, only the men daren't allow it"[9]), Lawrence reacts into a desire for a tension free sensuous life with men. Obviously this archetype derives from his remembrance of his father, and from what was in fact his only successful relationship in his early life, the friendship with Jessie Chambers' brother, Alan.

Paul Morel's efforts to emancipate himself from the influence of women often make him very cruel. In spite of his deep involvement with his mother, he is determined to get away from her and his passion for her in the end is unreal and self-indulgent, in line with his self-dramatizing desire to join her in death. All this is healthy in the sense that, in the natural course of events, Paul *must* separate himself from his mother in order to survive. Yet there is real resentment and spite in his attitude to his mother as she is dying. She must get it over as quickly and with as little pain to him as possible (can one deny that there is real sickness, even necrophilia in some of the poems written at this period). It can be argued that this intensity is simply a mask for Paul's terrible pain, and yet, there is also a very real sense in which Paul wants to see his mother off, since she has ended her usefulness to him. According to Lawrence's gloss on the novel, in the Garnett letter,[10] Mrs Morel realizes that she is an obstacle to Paul's sex life and so decides to die. There is truth in this view, but it also indicates that Paul was never able to develop an adult relationship with his mother. In his own life, Lawrence often showed a chilling resentment of other people's injuries and sorrows, for example his jealous frenzies over Frieda's children; and, surely, the emotions expressed in the poem "Mutilation" are more those of an abandoned child than of an adult, male lover.

It seems clear from the records of Jessie Chambers and May Holbrook that Lawrence's mother was a much less formidable and distinguished figure than she appears in the novel. My point is that, in order to make sense of his story, Lawrence had to create women characters who are not really credible so that he could avoid guilt and responsibility. And, in this case, the relationship with the mother, who is presented as an almost magical figure, literally breathing life and purpose into her son, and, on at least one occasion, saving him from death, is the basis on which Lawrence was later to found his theory of the man/woman relationship. This theory, as stated in *Fantasia of the Unconscious*[11] is little different from the ideal life of Paul Morel when he works at the factory and comes home to be restored by the admiration of his mother.

> Primarily and supremely man is *always* the pioneer of life, adventuring onward into the unknown, alone with his own temerarious, dauntless soul. Woman for him exists only in the twilight, by the camp fire, when day has departed.

and again, in the unpublished foreword that Lawrence wrote to *Sons and Lovers*:

> Now every woman, according to her kind, demands that a man shall come home to her with joy and weariness of the work he has done during the day: that he shall then while he is with her, be re-born of her; that in the morning he shall go forth with his new strength.[12]

Later, in the same foreword, a note of foreboding is sounded as to what this exemplary woman will do, if she finds the man weak and unsatisfactory (a foreshadowing of Lawrence's fear that he cannot satisfy Frieda—or any woman—sexually?).

The same pattern of passive male, victimized by representative Woman, appears in *The Trespasser*, in which Siegmund kills himself because he cannot resolve the situation between himself and two women. Lawrentian self-pity appears in the final chapters, where the women concerned are shown crassly getting on with life after Siegmund has hanged himself. But, here again, in spite of Lawrence's evident insights into the weaknesses of his hero, women are blamed. Helena obviously suffers from the same kind of sexual repression as the wretched Miriam: "she belonged to that class of 'dreaming women' with whom passion exhausts itself at the mouth."[13] Siegmund's wife, on the other hand, is a bad housekeeper. It's clear too that Siegmund is very much the swooning kind of lover who feels inadequate to the women's demands.

> He lay still on his back, gazing up at her, and she stood motionless at his side, looking down at him. He felt stunned, half-conscious. Yet as he lay helplessly looking up at her some other consciousness inside him murmured: "Hawwa-Eve-Mother!" She stood compassionate over him. Without touching him she seemed to be yearning over him like a mother.[14]

He is as ineffectual and victimized by Helena (sexually) and Beatrice (in practical life) as Skrebensky in *The Rainbow*. Finally, Siegmund is destroyed by the two women. Lawrence's basic sickness, which paradoxically provided much of the most compelling material in his work, is a series of conflicts aroused by his Oedipal situation with his mother. It is often, as here, conceived of as a battle to the death between Man and Woman. Siegmund is killed, but, in *Sons and Lovers* Paul Morel manages to kill his mother, or at least, hasten her death.

Throughout *The Trespasser* Siegmund is very much concerned with his own body and its beauties, and a lot less concerned with Helena's, except in so far as it manifests her self-sufficiency, which he resents. This narcissistic concern with the male body is also very evident in *The White Peacock* in which the true love affair is between George and Cyril; and again, the women only serve to underline the varying stages of the relationships between the men. And, here, too is found an archetypal statement of misogyny in the destructive words of Annable the gamekeeper.

An important and instructive scene as regards Lawrence's attitude to women in *Sons and Lovers* is the episode in which Paul breaks Annie's doll. Although deeply upset at the pain he has caused Annie, Paul gives the doll a strangely vindictive funeral:

> 'Let's make a sacrifice of Arabella," he said. "Let's burn her." She was horrified, yet rather fascinated. She wanted to see what the boy would do. He made an altar of bricks, pulled some of the shavings out of Arabella's body, put the waxen fragments

into the hollow face, poured on a little paraffin, and set the whole thing alight. He watched with wicked satisfaction the drops of wax melt off the broken forehead of Arabella, and drop like sweat into the flame. So long as the stupid big doll burned he rejoiced in silence. At the end he poked among the embers with a stick, fished out the arms and legs, all blackened, and smashed them under stones.

"That's the sacrifice of Missis Arabella," he said. "An' I'm glad there's nothing left of her."

Which disturbed Annie inwardly, although she could say nothing. He seemed to hate the doll so intensely, because he had broken it.

(pp. 75–6)

In just the same way, Paul hates Miriam because he has broken her. Although we hear no more of the fictional Miriam after she has failed to rise to Paul's requirements and deserves to be discarded, we know that Jessie Chambers herself was appalled by what she took to be Lawrence's betrayal, in his distortion of their relationship as it appeared in the novel. A very important aspect of this is that Jessie Chambers launched Lawrence on his career and was responsible for the rewriting of *Sons and Lovers*, encouraging Lawrence to be more attentive to actual events; to cultivate what A. Alvarez considers the characteristic of Lawrence's poetry, emotional realism, thus avoiding the literariness and artificiality of *The Trespasser*.

What is particularly significant about the passage quoted above is the language used to describe Paul's emotional response to the situation, "wicked satisfaction", the "stupid" doll, the gratuitous smashing of the already burned arms and legs. And then, so typical of Lawrence, the summing up with the clinching insight, "he hated the doll so intensely, *because he had broken it*." This ominous passage can only be compared with George's cruelty in drowning the injured female cat in *The White Peacock*. It is as if these men, so passive in their relations with actual women, will revenge themselves on female substitutes when they think they can get away with it.

Lawrence uses Annable in *The White Peacock* to voice the most overtly misogynistic statement to be found in his early work. As has been noted, structurally, there is no reason for Annable's story being included in the novel (though it was a story Lawrence wanted to tell since it forms the basis of *Lady Chatterley's Lover*). The logic of the novel as a whole is that George must degenerate as a result of his weakness in not seizing the woman of his choice, regardless of the consequences (like Siegmund, but unlike Lawrence himself); and yet, George's failure is presented implicitly as in some profound way, the fault of the women around him. Again, the definitive statement is made by Helen Corke:

> These three women are fully drawn, but Lawrence is not interested in them as individuals. He sees them only in relation to their men. "Take," he would seem to say to his reader, "a male creature! We shall now study its reactions to the various forms of feminine stimuli".
>
> Of the men, George Saxton alone is fully realised. Leslie Tempest is only visible when Lettie iluminates him. Annable the keeper is not so much a man as an incarnate indignation. But one sees the whole George.[15]

Very familiar elements from Lawrence's later work appear in *The White Peacock*. Emily is the sexless, soulful woman who drives Cyril to rebellion because of her "gift of sorrow". The kind of dialogue we are familiar with in *Sons and Lovers* appears also in this earlier work, "You have always got your soul in your eyes, such an earnest, troublesome soul . . . You think the flesh of the apple is nothing, nothing. You only care for the eternal pips."[16] It seems that to Lawrence here, Woman equals defilement. Annable states this when a peacock perches on a gravestone "The proud fool!—look at it! Perched on an angel, too, as if it were a pedestal for vanity. That's the soul of a woman—or it's the devil":

> "Just look!" he said, "the miserable brute has dirtied that angel. A woman to the end, I tell you, all vanity and screech and defilement".[17]

Annable describes his humiliation in being played with and then rejected by a lady (in the repeat situation, Mellors has his revenge). Annable too (like George and Siegmund) is a remarkable physical specimen.

> "I was Greek statues for her . . . Croton, Hercules, I don't know what! She had her own way too much—I let her do as she liked with me."[18]

That, of course, was his cardinal error. It should have been the other way round. As Lawrence counselled Middleton Murry in a

letter (dated Thurs 1913) on his dealings with Katherine Mansfield:

> Satisfaction is never accomplished even physically unless the
> man is strongly and surely himself, and doesn't depend on any-
> thing but his own *being* to make a woman love him. . . . Make
> her certain—don't pander to her—stick to *yourself*—do what
> you *want* to do—don't *consider* her—she hates and loathes being
> considered.[19]

Here Katherine is reduced to the status of mute Woman. One
wonders why any human being should have it thought of them
that they hated and loathed being considered. Annable's reaction
to his casting off is paralleled in the case of George; both work
out their fury on "inferior" animal-like women whom they breed
from; and, in Annable's case, treat very sadistically. Having made
his statement, Annable suffers a symbolic death in nature. After
Annable's funeral, Cyril is glad.

Annable is explicitly remembered in the bathing scene with
George, when Cyril is full of reverence (like Annable's lover) for
the beauty of George's naked body. So many points relevant to
my argument are made here that the passage must be quoted in
full:

> We stood and looked at each other as we rubbed ourselves
> dry. He was well proportioned, and naturally of handsome
> physique, heavily limbed. He laughed at me, telling me I was
> like one of Aubrey Beardsley's long, lean ugly fellows. I referred
> him to many classic examples of slenderness, declaring myself
> more exquisite than his grossness, which amused him.
>
> But I had to give in, and bow to him, and he took on an
> indulgent, gentle manner. I laughed and submitted. For he knew
> not I admired the noble, white fruitfulness of his form. As I
> watched him, he stood in white relief against the mass of green.
> He polished his arm, holding it out straight and solid; he rubbed
> his hair into curls, while I watched the deep muscles of his
> shoulders, and the bands stand out in his neck as he held it
> firm. I remembered the story of Annable.
>
> He saw I had forgotten to continue my rubbing, and laughing
> he took hold of me and began to rub me briskly, as if I were a
> child, or rather, a woman he loved and did not fear. I left myself
> quite limply in his hands, and, to get a better grip of me, he put
> his arm round me and pressed me against him, and the sweetness

of the touch of our naked bodies one against the other was superb. It satisfied in some measure the vague, indecipherable yearning of my soul; and it was the same with him. When he had rubbed me all warm, he let me go, and we looked at each other with eyes of still laughter, and our love was perfect for a moment, more perfect than any love I have known since, either for man or woman.[20]

In the context of the novel, this passage rings true in a way the more theoretical experiences with women simply do not. The trouble with the women is that they think and breed, both inconveniences. But in the confrontation described above, there is no barrier to the rapturous contemplation of the mirror image. The obvious physical desire mediated through the biblical language is, to Cyril, a purer and more valuable sensation than any that the men and women of the novel manage to have together. George's own marriage is marred by Meg's inappropriate pleasure in her children. Cyril comments sourly on a similar propensity in Emily:

> A woman is so ready to disclaim the body of a man's love; she yields him her own soft beauty with so much gentle patience and regret; she clings to his neck, to his head and his cheeks, fondling them for the soul's meaning that is there, and shrinking from his passionate limbs and his body. It was with some perplexity, some anger and bitterness that I watched Emily moved almost to ecstasy by the baby's small, innocuous person.
>
> "Meg never found any pleasure in me as she does in the kids," said George bitterly, for himself.[21]

Miriam is condemned in the same way for showing excessive love for her small brother. But it's notable that Lawrence himself felt a deep affection for young children, as expressed in the poem, "A Baby Running Barefoot" (in actual fact, the child of his London landlady). Apparently, this was acceptable; what was not acceptable was children coming between the male protagonist and Woman.

It is the story of Paul's abortive relationship with Miriam that is at the centre of *Sons and Lovers*. Although Lawrence tries, within his psychic limitations, to be just in his assessment of the failure of the affair and indicates Paul's contribution to that failure, there is again a strong sense that both Miriam and his mother are to blame, Paul is not. Again, he is acted upon, rather than active. He tells Miriam that they shouldn't meet so often because *they* say so. Paul feels torn between Miriam and his family and bitterly resents the emotional hold that both sides have on him. He seems to have no adult sense that he can choose for himself. Similarly, he doesn't really choose Clara: he tentatively presents the idea to his mother and goes ahead with the new friendship when his mother has given permission. Throughout the conflict with Miriam, Paul ascribes feelings to the girl which are not very convincing, and which are designed basically to elucidate Paul's attitudes and sense of the situation. One can argue that this is justified by the fact that the novel is Paul's story (the original title was *Paul Morel*). However, Lawrence implicitly claims that he is presenting Miriam's inner consciousness, just as much as he does Paul's. We know, from *A Personal Record*, that Jessie Chambers was much more dominant in the relationship than Lawrence is willing to allow and that she never really expected him to leave her, since she fully understood how necessary she was to his work. This factor is very much played down in the novel, where Miriam is cast as the dazzled disciple, rather than any kind of intellectual equal. Paul's brutal insensitivity to Miriam, in his totally egocentric response to their situation, often repels even the mild creature Lawrence wishes to recast Jessie as.

> Miriam was the threshing floor on which he threshed out all his beliefs. While he trampled his ideas upon her soul, the truth came out for him. She alone was his threshing floor. She alone helped him towards realization. Almost impassive, she submitted to his argument and expounding. And somehow, because of her, he gradually realized where he was wrong. And what he realized, she realized. She felt he could not do without her.
>
> (p. 279)

Paul wants to maintain a sexless companionship with Miriam so that he can continue to have her help with his work, without giving anything in return. His cruelty consists in the fact that he has no sense of her as a human being with needs of her own (Clara has to point out to Paul that he may be wrong about Miriam's not wanting him physically). Of course it is Paul's own sexual inhibition that causes the terrible tensions between them. On occasions he is able to acknowledge this, but then, transfers the blame to his mother. *Sons and Lovers* has been described as a novel of adolescent love;[22] virginal hesitations can perhaps be

successfully subsumed in the portrait of a tentative, exploratory
young man; but this defence does not hold up in view of the fact
that such attitudes towards sexual experience and the demanding
female are characteristic of many of Lawrence's other books. And
of the poetry too, in the neurotic self-consciousness about the
body expressed in "She Said As Well To Me":

> Don't touch me and appreciate me.
> It is an infamy.
> You would think twice before you touched a weasel on a fence

Obviously, the problem here is that the male body is being admired
by a woman. This passage compares oddly with the lyricism of
Cyril's contemplation of the nude George in *The White Peacock*.
    Paul's defensiveness with regard to Miriam leads to many dis-
tortions when he tries to examine what their relationship actually
is.

> "We agreed on friendship, he went on in a dull, monotonous
> voice. How often *have* we agreed for friendship! And yet — it
> neither stops there, nor gets anywhere else . . .
>   I can only give friendship—it's all I'm capable of — it's a flaw
> in my make-up."
>
> (p. 271)

It is clear that it is Paul's deficiencies that are being discussed
here. Instead of examining this more comprehensively, Lawrence
immediately transfers to Miriam's thoughts and what emerges is
that it is Miriam who is to blame because of her lack of self-
confidence. Incidentally, this lack of confidence has never actually
been demonstrated in the text. In many ways, Miriam appears to
be a strong figure with a secure sense of herself and of her
superiority to her surroundings. But in this, she is merely being
manipulated as a mirror image of Paul. He wants her to write,
though she shows no real aptitude for it and he wants her to have
his own interests. What she must not do is compete with him.

> Perhaps he could not love her. Perhaps she had not in herself
> that which he wanted. It was the deepest motive of her soul,
> this self-mistrust.
>
> (p. 271)

One of the things wrong with Miriam as far as Paul is concerned
is that she is not the passive, all accepting fantasy figure he would
like her to be. Lawrence's method, whenever Miriam as a char-

c

acter becomes real in any sense, is to reduce her to size, destroy her before she becomes too much of a threat.

> "You'd far better not talk," he said.
> "But I wish to know"—she replied.
> He laughed resentfully.
> "You always do," he said.
>
> (p. 270)

A typical movement in the dealings between man and woman in Lawrence's work occurs at the beginning of this scene between Paul and Miriam. Paul is complaining that Miriam is making extortionate, unnatural demands on him which he is right to refuse to fulfil.

> "You don't want to love—your eternal and abnormal craving is to be loved. You aren't positive, you're negative. You absorb, absorb, as if you must fill yourself up with love, because you've got a shortage somewhere."
>
> (p. 268)

This statement is irrelevant to the situation. Paul is really talking about his mother. Her demands on his love are excessive and unnatural; but he has allowed them to be so. ("somewhere in his soul, he was at peace because he still loved his mother best", p. 264). Paul wants to maintain his relationship with the Leivers family because they provide him with what he does not get at home. His mother appreciates his art work for the money and recognition it brings, but Miriam and her mother have some sense of its intrinsic value. Paul is so self-indulgent and unaware of the reality of other people that he doesn't stop to consider what effect his continued presence, unattainable as he has made himself, would have on Miriam. He is well aware that she loves him, but it's not convenient for him to admit it. In his immaturity Paul thinks that he can continue to have all the privileges of a relationship without the responsibility. When Miriam is cold at the end of their interview, he is offended. He does not expect her to behave as an autonomous individual; her rôle is simply to accept the situation that he has laid down. For relief from this impasse— and the pain he has caused himself—he turns to Edgar in order to punish Miriam and to boost himself with a relationship which, whatever its disturbing undertones, is, on the face of it, no threat. Incidently, the incipient priggishness in Paul, which Mrs Morel notes and attributes to Miriam's influence, is well brought out in the gauche manner in which Paul deals with the ended friendship: "Two days later he sent up a book and a little note, urging her to read and to be busy." The combination of conceit and insensitivity contained in this and the following sentence "At this time he gave all his friendship to Edgar" is hard to credit. It is no wonder that Jessie Chambers herself came to despise Lawrence for his weakness; and her family to feel great anger at his treatment of her.

Miriam shows no lack of self-confidence when she brings about the first meeting between Paul and Clara Dawes. According to Lawrence, she sees it as a test, in which Paul must choose the higher (herself) over the lower (Clara). Again, this does not quite convince. It is Mrs Morel who has led Paul to "refine" himself, though it is never really implied that *she* has any problems about sexuality herself. Here again, Paul is using women to explain his own personal problems. It is possible that Miriam might want to force the issue by indicating the existence of other kinds of women. But the imputation of Miriam's spirituality is entirely Paul's own. Physically, Miriam is described as fully mature; and there are many occasions when she is expecting an "animal" response from him. Notably, during the holiday at Mablethorpe:

> He turned and looked at her. She stood beside him, for ever in shadow. Her face, covered with the darkness of her hat, was watching him unseen. But she was brooding. She was slightly afraid — deeply moved and religious. That was her best state. He was impotent against it. His blood concentrated like a flame in his chest. But he could not get across to her. There were flashes in his blood. But somehow she ignored them. She was expecting some religious state in him.
>
> (pp. 220)

Lawrence's following interpretation is that Miriam "could scarcely stand the shock of physical love". In the circumstances, one wonders whether this is not true of Paul, rather than of her. The references, in the above passage, to Miriam's religious quality seem more like special pleading to disguise Paul's own ineffectuality.

The transference of Paul's interest from Miriam to Clara, as one who might help him to solve his immediate sexual problem, is indicated at the point where the three meet Limb with the stallion. Miss Limb's overt admiration for the masculinity of the horse embarrasses both Paul and Miriam, but Clara goes to the heart of the problem by asserting that Miss Limb wants a man. Paul insists that "it is the loneliness sends her cracked"—in other words, lack of companionship is more important than lack of sex. Yet, immediately, Paul forgets Miriam and turns his attention towards Clara. Significantly, he shows the same desire to control, through pity, that he had always demonstrated in his previous attitudes.

> Rather than walking, her handsome body seemed to be blundering up the hill. A hot wave went over Paul. He was curious about her. Perhaps life had been cruel to her.
>
> (p. 290)

There is an inescapable sense here that what arouses Paul in his dealings with women is a prurient pleasure in their suffering or physical ineptitude. Miriam is often described as clumsy and her lack of ordinary physical dexterity is insisted on rather gloatingly in contrast to Paul's own neatness and competence in everyday domestic affairs. What comes over powerfully at such moments in the narrative is the idea that Paul considers himself a better woman than any of the actual women that he encounters. His intensely critical attitude to women is literally deadly. Clara is able to point out some confused elements in Paul's response, but he avoids the issue by treating her remarks as a form of love-play.

> "I have no doubt," said Clara, "that you would much rather fight for a woman than let her fight for herself."
> "I would. When she fights for herself she seems like a dog before a looking-glass, gone into a mad fury with its own shadow."
> "And *you* are the looking-glass?" she asked, with a curl of the lip.
> "Or the shadow," he replied.
> "I am afraid," she said, "that you are too clever."
> "Well, I leave it to you to be *good*," he retorted, laughing "Be good sweet maid, and just let *me* be clever."
>
> (p. 286)

Paul is able to ignore the real meanings of this, and the implications of Clara's participation in the struggle for women's rights, by noting immediately after this dialogue that "the upward lifting of her face was misery and not scorn". Lawrence may have thought that he was revealing an underlying tenderness for all women on Paul's part (stemming from his love for his mother), but what such episodes truly indicate is that a perverse kind of sexual feeling is at work here. One which rejoices in failure, unhappiness and physical suffering in woman; all states that allow the male to dominate. Needless, to say, any reciprocal move on the part of women to comfort men is seen as stifling and destructive. When he is twenty-one (and therefore legally an adult) Paul writes to Miriam a very literary letter which only serves to demonstrate yet again his lack of awareness about himself. Yet again, he describes himself as merely reacting to a quality he finds in her; though it has long been obvious to the reader (if not to Lawrence himself) that this is a case of projection.

> See, you are a nun. I have given you what I would give a holy
> nun—as a mystic monk to a mystic nun.
>
> (p. 307)

The affectation of style in this extract conveys clearly the unreality of the emotion. In any case, what had the non-conformist Paul Morel to do with mystic nuns? Later, there is an important conversation between Paul and his mother on the subject of his happiness and what he ought to do to attain it. Paul rejects his mother's formula for settling his life with a good woman who would enable him to do his work:

> "You mean easy, mother," he cried. "That's a woman's whole
> doctrine for life—ease of soul and physical comfort. And I do des-
> pise it."
>
> (p. 314)

Nevertheless, it's obvious that his own ideas about battling and suffering are little more than adolescent self-dramatizing.

In many ways, the Clara episode is redundant in the scheme of *Sons and Lovers*. It begins as a re-run of the Miriam relationship and Lawrence appears to have intended it merely to show that Paul was capable of successful sexual relations (and that Clara, in spite of the fact that she was seven years older than Paul and an experienced woman, would be swept away by his expertise). The episode's only function seems to be like that of Annable in *The White Peacock*, to justify Lawrentian prejudices in some way, to demonstrate a theoretical position that does not arise naturally from the material of the novel. Once Clara has fulfilled her purpose of vindicating Paul sexually, she can be casually handed back to her husband, in whom Paul is actually much more interested.

At the start of the affair, Paul is outraged by Clara's lack of approval for his work.

> "H'm!" She made a small doubtful sound. "It doesn't interest me much."
>
> "Because you don't understand it," he retorted.
>
> "Then why ask me about it?"
>
> "Because I thought you would understand."
>
> She would shrug her shoulders in scorn of his work. She maddened him. He was furious. Then he abused her, and went into passionate exposition of his stuff. This amused and stimulated her. *But she never owned that she had been wrong.*
>
> (p. 323; my italics)

A piquant element in the situation is that Paul is literally Clara's boss. This means that, in spite of her attempt to appear superior, she is in fact subject to his will. A very titillating situation, and one that, no doubt, Lawrence would have liked to get every woman into.

> "Here, I say, you seem to forget I'm your boss. It just occurs to me."
>
> "And what does that mean?" she asked coolly.
>
> "It means I've got a right to boss you."
>
> (pp. 325–6)

When they discuss her marriage, it's clear that Paul is fascinated by Clara's view both of her own and her husband's attitudes. Yet he is more interested in her husband's and tries to make a case for him, which is odd since he is obviously considering seducing Clara himself. However, it would, and does, cover the situation where Paul will eventually return a refurbished wife to Dawes.

> "Did you leave him out of count all along?"
>
> "He left me," she said.
>
> "And I suppose he couldn't *make* himself mean everything to you?"
>
> "He tried to bully me into it."
>
> (p. 336)

This passage is a foretaste of the efforts of Lawrence's later protagonists to impose themselves on their women. In itself it mirrors his own struggles to escape from his mother, as he described them in a letter to Garnett:

> I had a devil of a time getting a bit weaned from my mother, at the age of 22. She suffered, and I suffered, and it seemed all

for nothing, just waste cruelty. It's funny. I suppose it is the final breaking away to independence.[23]

Lawrence, understandably fearing the rôle of the helpless victim, and engaged in a lifelong struggle for self-assertion, nevertheless found opposition from the woman intolerable. The effort to assert himself as a man was too great for him to be able to attain the security of accepting the individuality, sexually and in all other respects, of the woman. Lawrence inevitably imposed this struggle motif on all relationships and elevated it into a general truth, indeed *the* truth about life. As he said in a letter to Garnett in 1912:

> I don't think the *real* tragedy is in dying, or in the perversity of affairs. . . . I think the real tragedy is the inner war which is waged between people who love each other.[24]

And yet, often, Lawrence with his great powers of insight saw the truth about his own view, but attributed it to someone else. Here, he writes to Garnett later the same year:

> It seems to me queer you prefer to present men chiefly—as if you cared for women not so much for what they were themselves as for what their men saw in them. So that after all in your work women seem not to have an existence, save they are the projections of the men. That is, they seem almost entirely sexual answers to or discords with the men. No, I *don't* think you have a high opinion of women . . . It's the *positivity* of women you seem to deny—make them sort of instrumental. . . . You really study the conflict and struggles of men over women: the women themselves are inactive and merely subject.[25]

The Clara/Dawes/Paul triangle is a clear case of this kind of manipulative interest on the part of an author. In spite of their initial passion, Paul soon loses interest and Clara asks the perceptive question: "is it *me* you want or is it *It?*" When Lawrence (in the poems), or his male protagonists, feel themselves reduced to objects by their sexual partners, they are filled with righteous indignation. Yet what Paul does to Clara is worse than mere reification. She does not exist, even as an object. During their climactic sexual experience (the peewits screaming in the field), Paul feels an impersonal emotion (just as he had during the period of his brutal using of Miriam, merely to gain sexual experience): "then Clara was not there for him, only a woman . . . it was not

Clara, and she submitted to him." The situation has been put on a right footing previously; Clara has no claim on him and can make no demands since she is, after all, a married woman. Miriam's great failing had been to refuse this grand impersonality and to insist on their individuality as lovers:

> Never any relaxing, never any leaving himself to the great hunger and impersonality of passion; he must be brought back to a deliberate, reflective creature. As if from a swoon of passion she called him back to the littleness, the personal relationship. He could not bear it. "Leave me alone—leave me alone!" he wanted to cry.
>
> (p. 347)

It is hard to see how it would be possible to engage in a love affair that was not "personal"; unless, as is in fact the case, Paul does not really want a woman at all. There is a strange passage at the very beginning of the Clara affair when Paul is still fascinated by the idea of himself sleeping with this sophisticated woman (who is, at the same time, a non-threatening mother figure). His obsession takes a nightmarish form when, in the theatre, he feels that nothing exists but Clara's eyes and "her bosom coming down on his . . . Then he felt himself small and helpless, her towering in her force above him" (p. 403). Paul experiences Clara's growing love for him as an impertinence, a nagging desire to get at him and possess him. After the major experience of passion, it is clear that Clara has fulfilled her purpose:

> He felt more and more that his experience had been impersonal, and not Clara . . . He had wanted her to be something she could not be.
>
> (p. 431)

Paul begins to give Clara instruction as to her relationship with Dawes and deduces general statements about women from the evidence—Clara and all other real women are made to illustrate an evolving theory. When Paul tells Clara that she has treated her husband rottenly, he expects a reprimand and is "surprised" that his view is taken seriously. A typical Lawrentian projection is going on here. Paul had wanted Clara to be something other than she was; now he imputes this response to Clara and blames her for it.

> "I suppose you thought he was a lily of the valley, and so you put him in an appropriate pot, and tended him according. You

made up your mind he was a lily of the valley, and it was no
good his being a cow-parsnip. You wouldn't have it."

"I certainly never imagined him a lily of the valley."

"You imagined him something he wasn't. That's just what a
woman is. She thinks she knows what's good for a man, and she's
going to see he gets it; and no matter if he's starving, he may
sit and whistle for what he needs, while she's got him, and is
giving him what's good for him."

(p. 438)

It's all right for Paul to leave Clara because he has relieved her
of her self-mistrust and had given her herself (though, of course,
"the rest of her life would be an ache after him"), but now their
"missions" were separate. The mission of Lawrence's heroes from
now on seems largely to consist of withdrawing love from a series
of women and criticizing and rejecting them. There is much more
sexual tension in the ensuing fight with Baxter Dawes than there
ever was in the descriptions of physical love between Paul and
Clara. At the end of it, all Paul wants to do is to get to his mother.
The repetition emphasizes the urgency: "he wanted to get to his
mother—he must get to his mother—that was his blind intention." When Clara and Miriam visit him on his sick-bed, he rejects them both. The moral seems to be not just that being
involved with women is dangerous, but the physical contact with
men is infinitely more exciting. When Paul visits Dawes in Hos-
pital, "the two men were afraid of the naked selves they had
been." After the interview, "the strong emotion that Dawes
aroused in him, repressed, made him shiver." Interwoven with this
new concern with a man is the actual death of Mrs Morel and the
symbolic death of the relationship with Clara. Paul almost consciously uses the horror of his mother's death to drive Clara away
from him. He tells her that he grudges the food his mother wants
to eat. He condemns his mother for wanting to live, for wanting
to continue to be with him. His attitude to her is vindictive; and
the reader is not made to feel that this is simply a reaction to his
mother's unbearable pain. It is expressed in too crude and un-
modulated a fashion for that. Paul's feelings are summed up in his
short, brutal sentences, "she won't die," "I don't want her to
eat," "I wish she'd die." In the end, Paul literally kills his mother,
and, whatever the conscious motivation, it's clear that they are
both aware that this will happen and are engaged in a terrible
battle. It is the mother's will that is intolerable to Paul; but, as

soon as she has been overcome by death, he falls into a sentimental loverlike relationship with her. She becomes the young girl he would always have liked her to be. This has been explicitly stated in the instructive exchange between them on the trip to Lincoln: "why can't a man have a *young* mother? What is the old for?" The final scene between Paul and his mother is definitive:

> She lay like a maiden asleep . . . She lay like a girl asleep and dreaming of her love. The mouth was a little open, as if wondering from the suffering, but her face was young, her brow clear and white as if life had never touched it. He looked again at the eyebrows, at the small, winsome nose a bit on one side. She was young again. Only the hair as it arched so beautifully from her temples was mixed with silver, and the two simple plaits that lay on her shoulders were filigree of silver and brown. She would wake up. She would lift her eyelids. She was with him still. He bent and kissed her passionately.
>
> (p. 485–6)

The sleeping beauty connotations of this make clear the acknowledged fact that Paul was his mother's true husband ("I've never had a husband—not really"). It is a symbolic picture of the essence of their relationship, but purified and idealized. The reality is that Paul has ruthlessly despatched his mother because her continued existence, and his inability to resolve the situation, had become unbearable to him.

Paul's continuing self-deceptions lead him to rearrange the destinies of Clara and Dawes. Dawes and Paul have become fraternal in their attitude to each other, now Paul wants to escape from Clara. He encourages Dawes to repossess her; meanwhile, the real emotion in the situation continues to be between the two men:

> The eyes of the two men met. They exchanged one look. Having recognised the stress of passion each in the other, they both drank their whisky.
>
> (p. 490)

Lawrence makes Clara feel hatred for Paul since she feels that "their three fates lay in his hands"; not only that, but Paul has already decided what is to happen. He intends to withdraw from the situation. "He was a mean fellow, after all, to take what he wanted and then give her back." This, of course, is what Paul has actually done. However, Lawrence must have the last word and justify the proceedings:

She did not remember that she herself had had what she wanted, and really, at the bottom of her heart, wished to be given back.

(p. 495)

There is no real evidence in the text that Clara ever feels this at all. What does come over is that she is fully conscious that Paul will never be committed to her. When Paul leads her to say that she doesn't want a divorce, it is clear (since she is still deeply in love with him) that her response comes from self-protectiveness and is not what she would really wish. Paul is simply concerned with releasing himself since he has failed to make a relationship with her.

Paul's final failure with Miriam—he can't take her even after his mother's death—is the last scene of the novel. Throughout, this fatal inability to come to terms with Miriam as a person, has been the indicator of Paul's immaturity and narcissism.

Paul summed up the problem himself when he spoke to his mother of his inability to relate to his lovers as people:

"You know, mother, I think there must be something the matter with me, that I *can't* love. . . . Sometimes, when I see her just as *the woman*, I love her, mother; but then, when she talks and criticizes, I often don't listen to her."

(p. 426)

It is a response that Lawrence exploited in many of his later novels, usually to the detriment of women in general. The truth is that the Lawrence hero can't cope with women except in their maternal aspect or as faceless objects of passion. His descriptions of intercourse rely heavily on the pleasures of a descent to the unconscious and obviously contain an incipient death-wish. All idea of a woman as a thinking being, operating in any but a supportive and reinforcing manner with her mate, is rejected. A woman, after all, can only give the unimportant part of herself to work, the rest must be available for the use of the man. It's no wonder that Miriam remarks, in one of the truest sentences in the novel, "I have said you were only fourteen—you are only four!" Yet again, Lawrence makes Paul project his own feelings onto Miriam, to escape guilt:

She knew she felt in a sort of bondage to him, which she hated because she could not control it. She had hated her love for him from the moment it grew too strong for her. And, deep down, she had hated him because she loved him and he dominated her. She had resisted his domination. She had fought to keep herself free of him in the last issue.

(pp. 361–2)

This passage describes Paul's emotional situation, surely, not Miriam's. All the evidence points to the fact that Miriam loves Paul and wants a lifelong relationship with him. The refusal and hesitation is all on his side. Similarly, at their last meeting, the end of the relationship is brought about by Miriam's inability to claim her mate. Miriam can't win; had she tried to claim him she would have been thrown off as a dominating, stifling female intent on her prey. What is going on in this scene is that Paul is condemning Miriam for not taking the active rôle, the rôle appropriate to himself as the male partner:

> She felt that now he lay at her mercy. If she could rise, take him, put her arms round him, and say, "You are mine", then he would leave himself to her. But dare she? . . . It lay there, his body, abandoned. She knew she ought to take it up and claim it, and claim every right to it.
>
> (p. 507)

Granted that Paul is in a debilitated state, of almost clinical depression, it yet seems odd that he should react with such extreme passivity in this decisive encounter. His basic emotional response is fear of Miriam because she has forced him into the realization of "the hate and misery of another failure".

The final pages of the novel concern Paul's determination to go on alone. As has often been noted, the "healthy" aspects of his mental state at this point are his urge to go towards the town (life) and reject the darkness (death); and the final word of the text is "quickly", used in both its senses. However, the mystical solution which Lawrence presents is not very satisfactory. Paul's mother, like Wordsworth's Lucy, has become part of the universe:

> Who could say his mother had lived and did not live? She had been in one place, and was in another; that was all. . . . Now she was gone abroad into the night, and he was with her still.
>
> (p. 510)

Yet this is no real consolation since what Paul wants is the actual physical presence of his mother, and he wants this much more than he ever wanted Miriam or Clara. The desolation expressed in this final passage is infinitely greater than that that should attend the death of a parent, however beloved. Paul has never become adult—he has never emerged as a separate human being. What Lawrence presents here is a false situation and a false resolution of it. In his letters, and in *Fantasia of the Unconscious*, he writes about the Paul Morel kind of dilemma, and, as usual, generalizes it into a common problem of the time.

> You have done what it is vicious for any parent to do; you have established between your child and yourself the bond of adult love. . . . When Mrs. Ruskin said that John Ruskin should have married his mother she spoke the truth. He *was* married to his mother.[26]

Lawrence's own attachment to his mother, from which he was never able to release himself, meant that he was unable to relate to women as people. Given that he took the man/woman relationship as his great theme, this is rather a serious limitation. Insisting as he had to do because of his theoretical views, on total polarity of the sexes, he fell into the trap of producing diagrams, rather than portraits. Lawrence's psychic history meant that, in spite of his often brilliant insights, he was unable to represent women as they are. Frieda Lawrence has given a succinct summary of Lawrence's own sense of his dilemma:

> In his heart of hearts I think he always dreaded women, felt that they were in the end more powerful than men. Woman is so absolute and undeniable.[27]

The result was that, instead of examining the interactions of real men and women, what Lawrence actually wrote about was the relationship between man and a series of female stereotypes.

NOTES

1 *Phoenix*, ed. E. D. McDonald (1936), p. 693.
2 Penguin edition of *Sons and Lovers* (1977), p. 113. All subsequent references to Lawrence's works are from the Penguin editions.
3 *The Letters of D. H. Lawrence*, ed. A. Huxley (1932), p. 93. Subsequent references are to this edition.
4 *Selections from the May Chambers Holbrook Papers*, quoted in

Twentieth Century Interpretations of Sons and Lovers, ed. Judith Farr (1970), p. 111.

5   *Ibid.*, p. 113.
6   In *A Personal Record* by E.T. (1935).
7   "I felt you had gone off from me a bit, because of Sons and Lovers. But one sheds one's sicknesses in books—repeats and presents one's emotions, to be master of them." Letter to A. D. McLeod, 27 October 1913, *Letters*, p. 150.
8   Helen Corke, *Lawrence and Apocalypse* (1933), p. 93.
9   Letter to Ernest Collings, 7 November 1912, *Letters*, p. 71.
10 14 November 1912, *Letters*, pp. 76–7.
11 P. 109.
12 Letter to Garnett, *Letters*, pp. 101–2.
13 *The Trespasser*, Heinemann Phoenix Edition (1970), p. 23.
14 *Ibid.*, pp. 60–1.
15 *D. H. Lawrence, The Croydon Years* (1965), p. 52.
16 *The White Peacock* (1976), p. 86.
17 *Ibid.*, pp. 174–5.
18 *Ibid.*, p. 177.
19 *Letters*, p. 159.
20 *The White Peacock*, p. 257.
21 *Ibid.*, p. 317.
22 Alan Sillitoe, "D. H. Lawrence and His District", in *D. H. Lawrence*, ed. S. Spender (1973), p. 49. "There he meets Miriam the daughter, and his description of their long association makes *Sons and Lovers* the finest novel of adolescent love in the English language."
23 Letter to Garnett, 11 March 1913, *Letters*, p. 112.
24 Letter to Garnett, 29 June 1912, *Letters*, p. 44.
25 Letter to Garnett, Autumn 1912, *Letters*, pp. 74–5.
26 Pp. 120, 121.
27 Frieda Lawrence, *"Not I But The Wind . . ."* (1935), pp. 52–3. In the same passage she recalls: "Towards the end of *Sons and Lovers* I got fed up and turned against all this 'house of Atreus' feeling, and I wrote a skit called: 'Paul Morel, or His Mother's Darling'. He read it and said, coldly: 'This kind of thing isn't called a skit.' "

3

Mothers and Daughters in D. H. Lawrence: *The Rainbow* and Selected Shorter Works

by LYDIA BLANCHARD

> Look out, Persephone!
> You, Madame Ceres, mind yourself, the enemy is upon you.
> ("Purple Anemones", *Birds, Beasts and Flowers*)

During the first months of 1914, while D. H. Lawrence was working in Italy on the novel that he would later split into *The Rainbow* and *Women in Love*, he wrote to Edward Garnett about the many ways in which he saw his work changing radically from *Sons and Lovers*. "I have to write differently," he told Garnett,[1] and the earlier style of *Sons and Lovers* was increasingly altered and discarded as Lawrence moved further into the new work. As he experimented with language, however, his thematic concerns remained very similar to those of the earlier novel. Lawrence's preoccupation, in all the fiction, is with the relationship between man and woman, but *Sons and Lovers* and *The Rainbow* also simultaneously explore the relationship between parent and child, particularly mother and child. They are the only two of Lawrence's major works in which he is significantly concerned with the extent to which the coming together of men and women is influenced by their functioning as parents or, earlier, as children.

In *Sons and Lovers*, the marriage of Walter and Gertrude Morel is defined through Mrs Morel's obsessive love for her sons, and Paul's unsatisfactory encounters with Miriam and Clara are subsequently determined by his relationship with his mother. The importance of this mother-son relationship has its counterpart in *The Rainbow*, where Lawrence considers the marriage of Lydia and Tom Brangwen, and then that of Anna and Will Brangwen, as well as the relationship between Ursula and Skrebensky, in part through an examination of the connection between mothers and daughters—a cathexis Adrienne Rich recently described in *Of Woman Born* as "the great unwritten story" in art.[2] If, as Lawrence has told us, *Sons and Lovers* is "the tragedy of thousands of young men",[3] then *The Rainbow* is the story of thousands of young women who, like Ursula, have struggled to define themselves in terms of, as well as in reaction against, their mothers and their mothers' values.

In these terms alone, *The Rainbow* would be an extraordinary achievement, for, as Rich argues, the significance of the mother-daughter relationship has been generally "minimized and trivialized", not only in art but in theology and sociology and psychoanalysis as well, in favour of an examination of the mother-son relationship. "Small wonder," Rich says, "since theology, art, and social theory have been produced by sons. Like intense relationships between women in general, the relationship between mother and daughter has been profoundly threatening to men."[4] It is a relationship that Lawrence pursues exhaustively in *The Rainbow*, however, and if the literature describing mother-daughter relationships is indeed slim, this "big and beautiful work" by Lawrence,[5] as well as some of the shorter fiction, is as important a contribution to its study as *Sons and Lovers* is to an examination of the mother-son relationship. In a variety of situations—Lydia's sending Anna away in favour of the husband; Anna's crying out for her mother in labour; Anna's later momentary feelings of disappointment when her first-born is a daughter and not a son; Ursula's striking out against the overwhelming fecundity of her mother's life—in situations like these in *The Rainbow*, Lawrence shows the complexity of the feelings mothers and daughters share. Further, this mother-daughter connection determines the central theme of the novel, Ursula's coming to maturity. As with Paul Morel, Ursula must come to terms with her mother before she can make her full commitment to life.

As Lawrence described the germ of the work to Garnett, *The Rainbow* is the story of "woman becoming individual, self-responsible, taking her own initiative."[6] Such coming to perfection of the individual was for Lawrence the goal of life, a development, he thought, that came only through contact, often conflict, with others—through polarized relationships. The importance of the connection between polarity and individual development is one of the elements that remain consistent throughout all of Lawrence's frequently contradictory exposition. Generally, of course, as Lawrence wrote in "Morality and the Novel", of the various relations which establish the polarity necessary for development, "the great relationship, for humanity, will always be the relation between man and woman. The relation between man and man, woman and woman, parent and child, will always be subsidiary."[7] And the canon of Lawrence's fiction traces the myriad ways in which this polarity between man and woman can be worked out— in conflict, in submission, in destruction, ideally in balance.

But often Lawrence also recognized that the central relationship between man and woman was developed in and determined by more complex family relationships, by what Lawrence called, in *Fantasia of the Unconscious*, "the family connection".

> The connection is as direct and as subtle as between the Marconi stations, two great wireless stations. A family, if you like, is a group of wireless stations, all adjusted to the same, or very much the same vibration. All the time they quiver with the interchange, there is one long endless flow of vitalistic communication between members of one family, a long, strange *rapport*, a sort of life-unison. It is a ripple of life through many bodies as through one body. But all the time there is the jolt, the rupture of individualism, the individual asserting himself beyond all ties or claims. The highest goal for every man is the goal of pure individual being. But it is a goal you cannot reach by the mere rupture of all ties. A child isn't born by being torn from the womb. When it is born by natural process that is rupture enough. But even then the ties are not broken. They are only subtilized.[8]

In his non-fiction, particularly in *Fantasia*, Lawrence argues that mother and father are equally important in formation of the child. But in the fiction, particularly *Sons and Lovers* and *The Rainbow*, his concern is primarily with the mother. Lawrence wrote in *Fantasia* about the womb:

> This is the great centre, where, in the womb, your life first sparkled in individuality. This is the centre that drew the gesta-

ting maternal blood-stream upon you, in the nine-months lurking, drew it on you for your increase. This is the centre whence the navel-string broke, but where the invisible string of dynamic consciousness, like a dark electric current connecting you with the rest of life, will never break until you die and depart from corporate individuality.[9]

In *Sons and Lovers* this "invisible string of dynamic consciousness" is destructively close and tight—not only for the children, but also for the mother and father. The crippling effects of Gertrude Morel's love for her sons result, of course, from societal restrictions on her opportunities, restrictions that force her to make her mark in the world through her children, once her love for the husband is gone. Her only identity is through the children, particularly the boys, and her warping of them comes not only because she uses them as lovers, as replacements for the hated father, but also because they serve as surrogates for the work she is unable to do in a world in which jobs for women are sweated. And because she feels so constrained, Gertrude Morel has a moment of agony when her husband threatens, child-like, to run away. "She sat trembling slightly, . . . her heart brimming with contempt. What would she do if he went to some other pit, obtained work, and got in with another woman?"[10] Her economic existence depends on his wages, meagre as they are. Although *Sons and Lovers* records moments of great beauty in the life of the Morels, the family relationships are basically destructive; the invisible string chokes.

Perhaps the most significant difference between Gertrude Morel, very much a woman of the nineteenth century, and Ursula Brangwen, often identified as our first modern woman, is in their understanding of family inter-dependence. For all her hatred of Walter Morel, Gertrude needs him economically: "Ah, wouldn't I, wouldn't I have gone long ago, but for those children. Ay, haven't I repented not going years ago, when I'd only the one" (pp. 22–3). Further, she sees an inadequate father as better than no father at all: "These were the happy moments of her life now, when the children included the father in her heart" (p. 48). But Ursula sees family ties in a different way at the end of *The Rainbow*.

As Ursula lies ill, feverish, it is primarily future family connections with which she is tormented. Recognizing even in her delirium the falsity in her attraction to Skrebensky, recognizing that he has not touched her innermost sense of self, she is consequently tormented in her fever by the question of why she still feels bound to him.

> What extraneous thing bound her to him? There was some bond put upon her. Why could she not break it through? What was it? What was it?
> In her delirium she beat and beat at the question. And at last her weariness gave her the answer—it was the child. The child bound her to him. The child was like a bond round her brain, tightened on her brain. It bound her to Skrebensky.[11]

But Ursula, in her delirium, does not accept that the child *must* bind her to Skrebensky. She may be pregnant by Skrebensky, but she need not be *bound* to him. It is a radical departure from the attitude of Gertrude Morel, who feels she must tolerate Walter Morel for the sake of the children. Instead Ursula asks, "But why, why did it bind her to Skrebensky? Could she not have a child of herself? Was not the child her own affair? all her own affair? What had it to do with him? Why must she be bound, aching and cramped with the bondage, to Skrebensky and Skrebensky's world?" (p. 491). And so, recognizing that it is the pregnancy which establishes her connection with Skrebensky, nevertheless accepting that the child is her own affair, Ursula begins the fight in her delirium to free herself. The fight becomes larger, one to free herself "from all the vast encumbrances of the world that was in contact with her, from her father, and her mother, and her lover, and all her acquaintance." She must break out of her world, "like a nut from its shell" (pp. 491–2).

And Ursula succeeds. She *does* see herself cut free, becoming "the naked, clear kernel thrusting forth the clear, powerful shoot".

> The world was a bygone winter, discarded, her mother and father and Anton, and college and all her friends, all cast off like a year that has gone by, whilst the kernel was free and naked and striving to take new root, to create a new knowledge of Eternity in the flux of Time.
>
> (p. 492)

Achieving this new independence, Ursula can place down "her new root in new ground". The crisis in her illness is passed and she sleeps.

When she awakens, she knows, of course, that there will be no child. But "if there had been a child, it would have made little difference. . . . She would have kept the child and herself, she would not have gone to Skrebensky. Anton belonged to the past" (p. 493). It is an extraordinary change in attitude about the relationship between mother and father and child, and it is a change which can be traced by following Lawrence's creation of three generations of mothers, to see how Ursula's mother and grandmother prepare her to become, in turn, woman and mother.

Primarily what Ursula learns in *The Rainbow*, the great development of the novel, is not only that it is possible for a woman to be someone other than her mother, but also that such a development can come through affirmation as well as rejection. Such a realization breaks the influence of the mother in a way far more complex than Paul's turn toward the city at the end of *Sons and Lovers*. Ursula must not only, like Paul, come to terms with the emotional ties of parent-child love; she must also form a new model to organize her life, one based on grounds more satisfactory than simple acceptance or rejection of her mother's values. At the end of the novel, Ursula understands why her mother chose to devote her life to family, to raising children, to a relationship with a husband based primarily on fulfilment of sexual needs. Ursula, after a long period of rejection, sees this choice as legitimate for her mother, and even—briefly—considers it as a model for herself. But she also realizes, almost simultaneously, that she does not have to accept her mother's choice, that she can be a new person, defining herself through new relationships that grow out of her past but are different from it. It is this realization that brings Ursula to maturity, that makes her the "woman becoming individual, self-responsible, taking her own initiative" that Lawrence described in his letter to Garnett.

In working towards this realization at the end, *The Rainbow* considers a variety of relationships that can exist between mother and daughter—often troubling, sometimes destructive, finally freeing. Lydia, for example, is so self-contained that there is little overt demonstration of her love for Anna. Lydia's rôle is primarily one of protector for the child, a rôle stemming in part at least from her own precarious background, one in which her ability to provide for the physical needs of her children was often threatened. Having lost two children, she cuts herself off from any strong demonstration of love to Anna. Anna's response is first a fierce period of jealous battling with the step-father for what there is of her mother's affections.

As a young girl of four, she comes to her mother's bed, the morning after Lydia marries Tom Brangwen, to tell the step-father to leave, still asking on the second night why the mother cannot sleep with her. The battle rages between father and daughter at first, as Anna wants to take her mother away, to help her mother when she is ill or unhappy. Anna is anxiously connected —Lawrence tells us—with the mother (p. 67). After a troubling first marriage, in which attempts at combining a number of different rôles—mother, wife, patriot/rebel, nurse—did not work for her, Lydia has withdrawn into the security of a far less complicated second marriage. She is herself so calmed that she cannot see the anxiety in her daughter.

But when Lydia becomes pregnant, the pregnancy forces her apart from Tom. Memories of her earlier life with Lensky and of the death of their two children come back to haunt her, and her sadness drives Brangwen away. There is a period of silence and distance between the parents, and in the middle of the pregnancy, Tom turns to Anna: "Soon they were like lovers, father and child" (p. 60). When Lydia's labour pains begin, not only is a new child born. A new relationship also is created among the three.

As father and daughter sit listening to the cries of labour, Tom is moved out of his own pain by the child's distracted sobbing. "I—want—my—mother", over and over again she cries. In one of the most moving scenes of the novel, Brangwen wraps the little girl in his mother's silk Paisley shawl and takes her with him to help feed the cows. As they work together, in the barn, "a new being was created in her for the new conditions", almost as if Brangwen himself gives birth to a new Anna (p. 74).[12] The child's allegiance moves from mother to father, and Anna no longer fights him for the mother's love.

> [Anna] ceased to have so much anxiety for her mother after the baby came. Seeing the mother with the baby boy, delighted and serene and secure, Anna was at first puzzled, then gradually she became indignant, and at last her little life settled on its own swivel, she was no more strained and distorted to support her mother. She became more childish, not so abnormal, not charged with cares she could not understand. The charge of the mother,

the satisfying of the mother, had devolved elsewhere than on her. Gradually, the child was freed. She became an independent, forgetful little soul, loving from her own centre . . . Anna was very conscious of her derivation from her mother, in the end, and of her alienation.

(pp. 78–9, p. 82)

But then Lydia and Tom themselves realize that this shift in the father's affection away from the mother to the daughter has simply reflected their own growing apart since the birth of their first baby. Their conscious recognition of this helps them to reestablish their earlier relationship, and the mother and father are able to come together again, after two years of married life, in a connection that is "much more wonderful to them than it had been before" (p. 91). Once the mother and father have reconciled their own differences, their peace is reflected in Anna. The mother and father form, at least temporarily, that perfect balance, the arch which is the symbol in Lawrence's great middle period of the ideal human relationship—neither half too strong. And because she has seen the equilibrium established, Anna is no longer torn between attempts to protect and desires to turn away from her mother. She has learned to deal with her conflicting attitudes towards her parents, to accept them as a unit rather than as separate beings to be pitted against each other.

> Anna's soul was put at peace between them. She looked from one to the other, and she saw them established to her safety, and she was free. She played between the pillar of fire and the pillar of cloud in confidence, having the assurance on her right hand and the assurance on her left. She was no longer called upon to uphold with her childish might the broken end of the arch. Her father and her mother now met to the span of the heavens, and she, the child, was free to play in the space beneath, between.
>
> (p. 92)

As is usual in Lawrence, however, this balance is not always stable. At times Anna moves closer to one parent or the other, most often feeling the old connection with her father, and after meeting her cousin Will Brangwen, the relationship shifts dramatically again—the young people drawing together, apart from their parents. As Tom and Lydia watch this turn from them, they react ambivalently, at times almost with hatred, remembering Anna as a child, the father particularly seeing that her maturing is directly connected with his aging. It is the father who is primarily opposed to the wedding, unwilling to let the daughter go, and as in *Sons and Lovers*, this parent-child conflict-attraction is described in strongly sexual terms. However, Anna has greater inner strength than Paul, in part because the allegiance to the father is counterbalanced by strong love for the mother, and seeing the security of her parents' life, she is herself determined to marry.

The marriage between Will and Anna is not, however, a successful one. They are young, with little experience. And Anna misunderstands the strength of her parents' marriage; she tries to duplicate the close and intense family life which worked so well for Tom and Lydia without understanding the essential differences between her mother and herself, and between her father and Will. As Anna matures, she leaves her intimacy with the father. "Anna went more to her mother" (p. 240). And what emerges in the relationship between Anna and Will becomes a matriarchy. "She felt like the earth, the mother of everything" (p. 205). As Anna becomes more and more fulfilled in her rôle as mother, Will turns more and more to the children, particularly to Ursula, to his work, to the outside world, to other women. But Anna remains absorbed in her motherhood, finding herself in a way superficially reminiscent of her own mother, although Lydia, before choosing to become wife to Tom and mother of his children, had had a different earlier life in a wider environment. Anna's commitment to the children, like Gertrude Morel's, is unbalanced, turning Will away from her. It is a commitment that Ursula also comes to hate. "How Ursula resented it, how she fought against the close, physical, limited life of herded domesticity" (p. 353).

As the eldest child, she must bear the responsibility for the younger ones—and this early motherhood disturbs her. "How Ursula *hated* always to represent the little Brangwen club. She could never be herself, no, she was always Ursula—Gudrun—Theresa—Catherine" (pp. 260–61). The domestic situation for her is a nightmare. "When she saw, later, a Rubens picture with storms of naked babies, and found this was called 'Fecundity', she shuddered, and the word became abhorrent to her. She knew as a child what it was to live amidst storms of babies, in the heat and swelter of fecundity" (pp. 262–3).

Thus Ursula struggles in a number of different ways to break the tie with her mother. There is, when she is young, and then

later in adolescence, a strong connection with the father. "Her
father was the dawn wherein her consciousness woke up" (p. 218),
and particularly when she is between the ages of five and seven,
the connection between the father and the daughter is very strong.
But Will has not the strength of Tom Brangwen, and at times
his resentment of the wife causes him to be mean to the children
—for example, when he frightens Ursula at the fair on the swingboats. Ursula more and more defines herself through her day-
dreams, through the church and spiritual longings—and then
through a number of different women who become substitutes for
the mother who is busy bearing other children.

One of the first to whom she turns is her grandmother, after
the death of the grandfather, and it is from her that she first
learns a sense of the past.

> She clung to her grandmother. Here was peace and security.
> Here, from her grandmother's peaceful room, the door opened
> on to the greater space, the past, which was so big, that all it
> contained seemed tiny, loves and births and deaths, tiny units
> and features within a vast horizon.
>
> (p. 258)

But perhaps more importantly, the grandmother teaches Ursula
that she is a person important in her own right. "Some man will
love you, child," she tells her, "because it's your nature. And I
hope it will be somebody who will love you for what you are,
and not for what he wants of you. But we have a right to what
we want" (p. 257).

As Ursula learns she must bear the responsibility for her own
life, gradually the intensity that she has felt in her commitment
to religion turns to her first love, to Skrebensky, who reminds her
of her father. In many ways, Skrebensky and Ursula duplicate the
experiences shared by father and daughter, for example, in their
ride on the swingboats, and then the experiences shared by Anna
and Tom. Ursula and Skrebensky, on the night of Fred Brangwen's
wedding, for example, repeat in their moon dance the corn dance
of her mother and father. But just as Anna could not duplicate
in her marriage what Lydia had found, so Ursula must work out a
different life. Skrebensky goes to war and she is left at school,
striving for independence.

> She was always a woman, and what she could not get because
> she was a human being, fellow to the rest of mankind, she would

get because she was a female, other than the man. In her femaleness she felt a secret riches, a reserve, she had always the price
of freedom.

(p. 333)

Although, like her mother, she believes deeply in her femaleness,
at the same time, unlike her mother, Ursula also wants to make a
conquest of the world of work and community. And this becomes
connected for Ursula with an at-first unspoken intimacy with her
class-mistress, Winifred Inger, whom Ursula admires and then
loves; Ursula's sexual awakening by Skrebensky is transferred to
her.

The two women, Lawrence tells us, become intimate, but the
attraction is not only a sexual one. Winifred enriches Ursula's
life in a number of ways, humanizing religion for her, discussing
philosophy, introducing Ursula to the women's movement. "It was
a strange world the girl was swept into, like a chaos, like the end
of the world. She was too young to understand it all. Yet the
inoculation passed into her, through her love for her mistress"
(p. 342). Then, however, the intensity of the relationship begins
to disturb Ursula; Winifred is too strong, too much in control,
both because of her age and her position, and Ursula rejects her
with as much vigour as she had earlier loved her. As always in
Lawrence, when one part of the arch becomes too strong, it
collapses. Ursula no longer sees her mistress as proud, strong,
beautiful as Diana. Instead Winifred turns into a mother figure
for Ursula, with hips "big and earthy", to be cast off like Ursula's
real mother. It is not Winifred's femaleness, however, that primarily disturbs Ursula. In part she rejects both Winifred and Ursula's
uncle, Tom, people she earlier loved, because she sees them, in
her coming maturity, as associated with the machine, mechanical.
It is the imbalance in the relationship, however, which is the
primary reason for Ursula's rejection, and Winifred is replaced
by other women, primarily Maggie Schofield, who help Ursula to
grow because they are more nearly equals.

The primary battle continues against Anna, however. Rejection
of Winifred does not lead to Ursula's return to her mother as an
alternative. After passing her matriculation exam, Ursula writes for
advice to the mistress of the High School who suggests that she
become an elementary school teacher. "I shall be proud to see one
of my girls win her own economical independence, which means

so much more than it seems. I shall be glad indeed to know that one more of my girls has provided for herself the means of freedom to choose for herself" (p. 357). For all the humiliation of Ursula's first teaching job, for all the initial sense of failure, given the impossible circumstances, Ursula nevertheless does feel free in her situation. "She was something else besides the mere daughter of William and Anna Brangwen. She was independent. She earned her own living. She was an important member of the working community" (p. 390).

It is another woman, Maggie Schofield, who then becomes her model. Ursula admires Maggie's ability to handle the difficult work situation without becoming corrupted by it. They agree about the importance of freedom, although Ursula believes that Maggie's concentration on the movement for suffrage is limited.

> She was isolated now from the life of her childhood, a foreigner in a new life, of work and mechanical consideration. She and Maggie, in their dinner-hours and their occasional teas at the little restaurant, discussed life and ideas. Maggie was a great suffragette, trusting in the vote. To Ursula the vote was never a reality. She had within her the strange, passionate knowledge of religion and living far transcending the limits of the automatic system that contained the vote. But her fundamental, organic knowledge had as yet to take form and rise to utterance. For her, as for Maggie, the liberty of woman meant something real and deep. She felt that somewhere, in something, she was not free. And she wanted to be. . . .
>
> In coming out and earning her own living she had made a strong, cruel move towards freeing herself. But having more freedom she only became more profoundly aware of the big want.
>
> (p. 406)

Although teaching is in many ways unsatisfactory for her, although she hates the bullying of the other teachers and the fact that she must sometimes be hard with the children, Ursula does become independent at the school and decides that she will continue with teaching, that she will return to school for her degree. Ursula and Maggie, although very different, sustain each other in a way far healthier than in the relationship between Winifred and Ursula, because Ursula and Maggie are not engaged in a power struggle. When Ursula leaves St Philip's, she leaves as one of the workers: "She had put in her tiny brick to the fabric man was building, she had qualified herself as co-builder" (p. 425).

Ursula returns to college with enthusiasm, although she is gradually disillusioned as she comes to know the reality of the educational system. In a moment of reflection, Ursula sees her life as a period of negative lessons.

> The last year of her college career was wheeling slowly round. She could see ahead her examination and her departure. She had the ash of disillusion gritting under her teeth. Would the next move turn out the same? Always the shining doorway ahead; and then, upon approach, always the shining doorway was a gate into another ugly yard, dirty and active and dead. Always the crest of the hill gleaming ahead under heaven: and then, from the top of the hill only another sordid valley full of amorphous squalid activity.
>
> No matter! Every hill-top was a little different, every valley was somehow new. Cossethay and her childhood with her father; the Marsh and the little Church school near the Marsh, and her grandmother and her uncles; the High School at Nottingham and Anton Skrebensky; Anton Skrebensky and the dance in the moonlight between the fires; then the time she could not think of without being blasted, Winifred Inger, and the months before becoming a school-teacher; then the horrors of Brinsley Street, lapsing into comparative peacefulness, Maggie, and Maggie's brother, whose influence she could still feel in her veins, when she conjured him up; then college, and Dorothy Russell, who was now in France, then the next move into the world again!
>
> Already it was a history. In every phase she was so different. Yet she was always Ursula Brangwen. But what did it mean, Ursula Brangwen? She did not know what she was. Only she was full of rejection, of refusal.
>
> (pp. 436–7)

Filled with the ash of disillusion, then, Ursula is ready, when Skrebensky returns to England, to accept him as the key to a new shining doorway. They become lovers, they travel, they are accepted as husband and wife. Skrebensky wants to marry, but Ursula hesitates. The affair becomes all-consuming, a passion to which Ursula gives herself completely, as Anna had given herself to Will, and she fails her exams. Uncertain, "out of fear of herself", Lawrence tells us, Ursula plans to marry Skrebensky and return with him to India. But in one frenzied week of passion, at a house party on the Lincolnshire coast, Ursula rejects Skrebensky because she knows she is stronger than he; she returns home, the engagement broken.

Then she realizes that she is pregnant, and the knowledge brings her into identification with her mother, a real first understanding of her mother's choice. Ursula decides she had been wrong in wanting freedom, "that illusory, conceited fulfilment which she had imagined she could not have with Skrebensky" (p. 484).

> Suddenly she saw her mother in a just and true light. Her mother was simple and radically true. She had taken the life that was given. She had not, in her arrogant conceit, insisted on creating life to fit herself. Her mother was right, profoundly right, and she herself had been false, trashy, conceited.
>
> (p. 484)

She gives herself to the bondage, Lawrence tells us, and she calls the bondage "peace"; she writes to Skrebensky to tell him that she is pregnant and that she wishes to marry him. "For what had a woman but to submit? What was her flesh but for childbearing, her strength for her children and her husband, the giver of life? At last she was a woman" (p. 485). But the peace that Ursula feels in choosing the life her mother chose is an unnatural peace. Ursula feels a "gathering restiveness, a tumult impending within her." And she tries to run away.

What happens, of course, is described in the last chapter, "The Rainbow", in the incredible nightmare scene of the horses. In fear Ursula faces the horses on her walk towards Willey Green, carried on by her will, reaching bottom, not giving in. She keeps on— walking, climbing, and by continuing to climb, she wins. She arrives home ill, but even in her delirium she is able to fight free of Skrebensky, of her mother and her father and her past. The knowledge of the child no longer compels her to Skrebensky; she realizes she could have the child by herself, as her own affair. And even after she knows she has aborted, she believes the child would have made no difference for the marriage. Child or not, she would not have returned to Skrebensky.

The future Ursula faces at the end of *The Rainbow* is uncertain. Her vision of the rainbow may simply be another shining doorway leading into another ugly yard. But Ursula has also made a critical change that suggests this time the future may be different, may be something more. Ursula no longer wishes to have a man of her own desires. "It was not for her to create, but to recognise a man created by God" (p. 493). Years earlier her grandmother had hoped for her that "somebody . . . will love you for what you are, and not for what he wants of you." Ursula's recognition that she will take a man for what he *is* and not for what she *wants* of him is a simultaneous recognition of her own individuality. If she is to recognize a man created by God, he will also recognize, rather than create, her. She understands now the formation of that perfect balance of two independent beings that in *The Rainbow* and later, as Birkin will tell us, in *Women in Love* is for Lawrence the ideal relationship, one in which each member stands independent and free. When conflict comes, as it surely will, it will come between two equals, neither of whom will automatically dominate. Lydia had sought shelter in a patriarchy, in which Tom was often the stronger force; Anna had established a matriarchy. Ursula sees a future in which such power relationships will no longer obtain.

Rich tells of this in *Of Woman Born*:

> Many women have been caught—have split themselves—between two mothers: one, usually the biological one, who represents the culture of domesticity, of male-centeredness, of conventional expectations, and another, perhaps a woman artist or teacher, who becomes the countervailing figure. Often this "counter-mother" is an athletics teacher who exemplifies strength and pride in her body, a freer way of being in the world; or an unmarried woman professor, alive with ideas, who represents the choice of a vigorous work life, of "living alone and liking it". This splitting may allow the young woman to fantasize alternately living as one or the other "mother", to test out two different identifications. But it can also lead to a life in which she never consciously resolves the choices, in which she alternately tries to play the hostess and please her husband as her mother did, and to write her novel or doctoral thesis. She has tried to break through the existing models, but she has not gone far enough, usually because nobody has told her how far there is to go.
> The double messages need to be disentangled.[13]

What happens to Ursula at the end of *The Rainbow* is that she does indeed disentangle the double messages. She has tried at different times to identify with first one, then the other of two mothers, Anna and Winifred Inger. At the end of *The Rainbow*, however, Ursula realizes that she cannot accept her mother's choice to devote herself to children, to become an earth-mother figure. After a lifetime of rejecting the choice, she tries to accept it, but the psychic loss is so great she is unable to sustain the decision. She also realizes that earlier attempts to break loose by leaving home for school, by working, by attaching herself to another mother figure like Winifred Inger—none of these has gone far enough either, because she was still part of someone else's plan, part of someone else's power relationship. What Ursula realizes in her delirium at the end of the novel is that while her struggle into being will always involve conflict, she must stand in that conflict not as a victim but as an independent being. She has been split between two mothers, but the choice is not between one or the other: for Ursula the choice is to be someone entirely new, part of the new creation. Ursula has learned how far there is to go, and has succeeded in taking the critical first step in getting there.

From the moment of Ursula's birth, when Anna feels a momentary regret that she has not had a son, to Ursula's own unplanned pregnancy, when she believes that she must then marry a man she does not love, Ursula moves through a series of problems that bear particularly on the relationship between mother and child. The ending of the novel is not a resolution of these problems, for they are part of a larger concern with the coming to perfection of the individual, a goal which is of necessity never completed. In the way in which Ursula redefines herself at the end of *The Rainbow*, however, the ending is also a beginning, as is true of the earlier *Sons and Lovers*, when Paul faces the hum and glow of the city. For both Ursula and Paul gain their new maturity in part through their ability to make peace with and then to break with their mothers.

In *Oedipus in Nottingham*, Daniel Weiss writes:

> The less fully resolved relationship between the father and son in [*Sons and Lovers*] is the relationship upon whose psychic residue Lawrence was to draw for the rest of his life. Indeed, his first task after *Sons and Lovers* seems to have been the conciliation, with honor, of the father, a conciliation that proceeds in a steady line of descent from father to rival, to friend, to positive identity between the father image and the son.[14]

Lawrence, however, whether he consciously recognized it or not, also owed a debt to his mother for the picture in *Sons and Lovers*, and *The Rainbow*, his next major novel, is far more clearly a working out of that. The mothers in this novel, although far from perfect, allow the daughters to both accept and reject them, and the daughters consequently are far stronger than Paul. *The Rainbow* needs to be read as a continuation of Lawrence's concern with parent, particularly mother, influence on the child, a continuation that is much richer and more interesting than the earlier *Sons and Lovers*. The way in which parents help us to define ourselves is, after all, a complex subject—one constantly in flux, one involving the most profound feelings of love and hate.

Lawrence's genius, his understanding of the constantly shifting grounds on which relationships are built, is particularly suited to probing the varied and changing ways in which parents and children influence each other, and as to be expected, he did not exhaust the subject with *The Rainbow*. The particular concern with mother-daughter relationships occurs on occasion in the poetry, for example, sometimes with humour as in "Purple Anemones" and sometimes with passion as in "Bavarian Gentians", both of which retell the great mother/daughter myth, the story of Demeter and Persephone.[15] And as in *The Rainbow*, the mother's influence on the daughter provides the central impetus to the daughter's coming to maturity in some of the shorter fiction—for example in the brilliant *St Mawr*, written in June 1924, as well as in the bitter and caustic short story, "Mother and Daughter", written shortly before Lawrence's death.[16]

The novella *St Mawr* is the story of two women, mother and daughter, who turn from the world of men to find their identity quite specifically affirmed through each other. Unlike Anna's relationship with Ursula, the mother here serves until the end of the story as a model for the daughter, helping the daughter to work out the final break with her husband, starting her on the path to a self-discovery that allows her finally to define herself, like Ursula, in the ancient meaning of "virgin", *she-who-is-unto-herself*.[17]

At the opening of the novella, both Louise and her mother, Mrs Witt, are disenchanted with men. Mrs Witt, having cut herself off from the world of men for the past fifteen years, tells Lou, "I am tired of all these men like breakfast cakes, with a teaspoonful of mind or a teaspoonful of spirit in them, for baking-powder."[18] But Lou is also in the process of learning for herself how completely unsatisfactory modern man is for the needs of modern woman. Already disenchanted with her husband Rico, she has moved into a marriage without sex; her disenchantment is reinforced when her mother arrives for a visit and turns her ironic eye on Rico and his friends. Although personable and attractive, certainly the most attractive man in the Carrington circle, Rico is innocuous—concerned with the artificial demands of society and engaged in much innocent, and not so innocent, flirting. He is representative of what both Mrs Witt and Lou see as weakness in today's male, increasingly cut off from his masculinity and willing, even eager, to castrate maleness in others.

But Lawrence also provides a number of other men for the mother and daughter to reject—the artist Cartwright, for example, who preaches the religion of the Great God Pan, "the hidden mystery—the hidden cause" (p. 54). Momentarily under Cartwright's spell, Mrs Witt muses, "Wouldn't a man be wonderful in whom Pan hadn't fallen!" But Cartwright does not see what Mrs Witt means, and in fact, tells them that he is not the Great God Pan but rather the Great Goat Pan. Both Lou and her mother agree, in later conversation, that the closest they have come to seeing the unfallen Pan is in the horse St Mawr. The horse becomes the embodiment of the spirit the two women find lacking in modern men, and when Rico determines to sell the horse, which will lead to St Mawr's castration, the mother and daughter arrive together at the decision to leave immediately with the horse, to flee to America.

Both women temporarily consider taking as lovers the grooms for their horses. But Lewis rejects Mrs Witt's proposal of marriage because he fears her strength; he wants nothing to do with a world in which women mock and even despise the men they marry. And Lou does not get very far in her consideration of Phoenix as a lover before she realizes how totally unsatisfactory in him is the "aboriginal phallic male" (p. 135).

And so the women are drawn more and more together; we see the mother-daughter relationship existing on a number of different levels. Mrs Witt "mothers" her daughter in the basic, most fundamental sense of providing for Lou's physical needs, for food and clothing, for example. Mrs Witt arranges salads, devises new ice-creams, prepares stuffings for turkey, brings her daughter ten pairs of shoes from New York. And in other ways she also protects Lou. The marital battle that we see so often in Lawrence is fought between Rico and Mrs Witt: "Rico and Mrs Witt were deadly enemies, yet neither could keep clear of the other. It might have been they who were married to one another, their duel and the duet were so relentless" (p. 31). The influence of the mother is so obvious that when Lou tells Rico to do as he wishes, his answer is "I wish to God you did as you wished, Lou dear. I'm afraid you do as Mrs Witt wishes. I've always heard that the holiest thing in the world was a mother" (pp. 115–16). The influence of the mother is so pervasive that fathers are not mentioned in the story; we hear nothing about Lou's father. Mrs Witt's husband. Only Laura Tidley speaks of hers, and her pseudo-sophistication is made momentarily poignant when she tells Lou that her father would never let her ride as a child "because we girls weren't important, in his opinion" (p. 123).

But the influence that Mrs Witt has on Lou is far deeper than physical mothering and protection. Lou both consciously and unconsciously imitates what her mother does (in the matter of taking a lover, for example, Lou tells Mrs Witt, "You see I must imitate you in all things" [p. 112]). It is through her mother that Lou sees the various rôles woman can take in a patriarchal society— virgin, Amazon, the very words Rich uses to define woman, Lawrence has Lou use to define her mother and herself.

[Mrs Witt] set her face and gazed under half-dropped lids . . . stoic, fate-like, and yet, for the first time, with a certain pure wistfulness of a young, virgin girl. This frightened Lou very much. She was so used to the matchless Amazon in her mother, that when she saw her sit there still, wistful, virginal, tender as a girl who has never taken armour, wistful at the window that only looked on graves, a serious terror took hold of the young woman. The terror of *too late*!

(p. 86)

Too late—perhaps too late, Lou realizes, for her to find herself except, like her mother, through the rôles that society has established for her in relationship to others. What has frightened Lou is her mother's reflections about life: "I never had any motherhood, except in newspaper fact. I never was a wife, except in newspaper notices. I never was a young girl, except in newspaper remarks" (p. 86).

But learning from the experiences of her mother, Lou is able to flee with St Mawr to America where she learns "the meaning of the Vestal Virgins, the Virgins of the holy fire in the old temples".

> They were symbolic of herself, of woman weary of the embrace of incompetent men, weary, weary, weary of all that, turning to the unseen gods, the unseen spirits, the hidden fire, and devoting herself to that, and that alone. Receiving thence her pacification and her fulfilment.
>
> (p. 139)

Lou's mother is able to help Lou throw off a variety of conscious and unconscious bonds. "It had long ago struck Lou how much more her mother realized and understood than ever Rico did" (p. 51). Hemmed in by a society they see as trivial and ridiculous, Lou and Mrs Witt achieve strength and reinforcement from each other, and because of that reinforcement, Lou is able to grow, so that at the end of the novel, even though her mother remains uncertain about the wisdom of buying the New Mexico ranch, Lou has found the place where she wants to be: "The time has come for me to keep to myself" (p. 158). Not long after they have arrived in New Mexico, they leave Santa Fe, passing a sign that says *Welcome, Mr Tourist*. Lou says to herself, *Welcome Also Mrs and Miss Tourist!* Their world becomes one of women who have learned together to be independent of unsatisfactory men. And while they are willing to consider the time when they might again be interested in returning to a world of men, the suggestion is very strong that this will not happen.

In *Of Woman Born*, Rich worries because there is no familiar name for a woman who chooses to define herself *through* herself, in relation neither to children nor to men. The ancient meaning of the word "virgin" (she-who-is-unto-herself) would work, Rich thinks, but that meaning no longer obtains. Lawrence, however, does use it in its ancient meaning to describe Lou as she finds herself after the pilgrimage across the ocean with St Mawr, just as it might be used to describe Ursula, although for different reasons, at the end of *The Rainbow*.

> "I am not a marrying woman," she said to herself. "I am not a lover nor a mistress nor a wife. It is no good. Love can't really

come into me from the outside, and I can never, never mate with any man, since the mystic new man will never come to me. No, no, let me know myself and my rôle. My dealings with men have only broken my stillness and messed up my doorways. It has been my own fault. I ought to stay virgin, and still, very, very still, and serve the most perfect service. I want my temple and my loneliness and my Apollo mystery of the inner fire. And with men, only the delicate, subtler, more remote relations. No coming near. A coming near only breaks the delicate veils, and broken veils, like broken flowers, only lead to rottenness."

(pp. 139–40)

Lou, in her certainty that the new man will never come to her, is a more pessimistic figure than Ursula, but in the way in which Lou is able to grow through her mother's experiences, accepting what she needs and rejecting what she does not, she is—like Ursula—a positive, healthy figure. In "Mother and Daughter", however, Lawrence shows the disastrous effects when the daughter cannot maintain a balance between the negative results of matrophobia, the fear of becoming one's mother, and the positive benefits of imitating the mother.

The story is closely derivative from St Mawr. In both St Mawr and "Mother and Daughter", a mother and daughter come back to live together after a number of years of separation. In both, the mother is wealthy, and in both she encourages the daughter to separate from the husband (or potential husband: in the short story, Virginia, for four years, "had been as good as married"). In both, the relationship between mother and daughter is very close. "They have become, in course of time, more like a married couple than mother and daughter," as Lawrence tells us in "Mother and Daughter".[19] Even in minor points, there are interesting similarities. In both stories, the mother supplies the daughter's many physical needs, with particular emphasis on shoes, for example.

However, in the short story, Lawrence sees the relationship as wholly destructive; he frequently uses the word "witch" to describe both mother and daughter, and at one point argues, "Women, very often, hypnotize one another, and then, hypnotized, they proceed gently to wring the neck of the man they think they are loving with all their hearts" (p. 806). Lawrence's most bitter attitudes about strong women emerge in his attitude towards Mrs Bodoin; Henry, the daughter's rejected lover, argues that if

Mrs Bodoin "could have had her way, everything male would have been wiped off the face of the earth, and only the female element left" (p. 810).

And unlike the relationship in *St Mawr*, the father enters into "Mother and Daughter", for one of Mrs Bodoin's realizations is that Virginia (like Gertrude Morel) is her father's daughter. Although weak and acquiescent to her mother in many ways, Virginia holds on to a hard core of strength that helps preserve her individuality. She refuses to marry the personable but ineffectual young man (very like Rico) that her mother chooses. She refuses to give up her demanding job as head of the office in a government department, even though her mother promises her a substantial income. She refuses to participate, except perfunctorily, in the decoration of their apartment. And finally, and most importantly, she makes her break with her mother, not by learning to live-unto-herself, like Lou, but by marrying a comic Armenian, a man Mrs Bodoin has viewed throughout the story with scathing contempt. When Mrs Bodoin says to her daughter, grimly and with "deep contempt" at the end of the story, "You're just the harem type, after all", Virginia agrees. "Perhaps daughters go by contraries, like dreams. All the harem was left out of you, so perhaps it all had to be put back into me."

> Mrs Bodoin flashed a look at her.
> "You have *all* my *pity!*" she said.
> "Thank you, dear. You have just a bit of mine."
>
> (p. 826)

And so the mother and daughter are left, rather than with the mutual respect of Mrs Witt and Lou, with pity for each other— torn apart by the daughter's fears of becoming her mother, fears that lead her to choose the extreme of marrying a fat, elderly, unattractive grandfather, whose interest in her stems at least in part from her mother's money. While Virginia, like Ursula and Lou, was able to break the hold of the mother, she breaks it in a way that is obviously not in her own interest. There is in Virginia's decision none of the affirmation and understanding that leave Ursula and Lou, in the end, strong daughters of strong mothers.

Those of us who are interested in mother-daughter relationships might have found Lawrence's discussion of this intense bond more satisfactory if his final work had led somewhere other than to Virginia's unhappy decision at the end of "Mother and Daughter". But Lawrence as a writer often described destructive situations, and it is just as well that we are reminded of it by this conclusion. It was part of Lawrence's great strength as an artist that he was willing to face and to give form to the most unsatisfactory consequences of relationships that failed because they became unbalanced. Part of Lawrence's genius is that he gave shape to so many varied possibilities in life, showing us the close relationship between love and hate, between life and death, reminding us that in relationships that are filled with life there will always be conflict. The risk we run in being human is that sometimes we fail.

Lawrence's seemingly inexhaustible reserves of emotional energy led him to investigate human relationships in every combination, to give form to the innumerable combinations of conflicts that shape us into being. Although his goal was always the perfection of the individual, and although he was primarily concerned with the potential in relationships between man and woman, Lawrence was also capable, particularly in his fiction, of responding sensitively to the special problems that women face together—in growing up, in working, in marriage, as mothers; one of those areas, into which his work shows particular insight, is the relationship between mother and daughter. While it is not the central concern of the Lawrence canon, Lawrence recognized that mother-daughter relationships are central in influencing women in their relationship with men. In his particular transformation of reality, Lawrence has helped fill the enormous void of Rich's great untold story, the story of mother and daughter.

The Rainbow is the most rewarding of those creations, with Lydia's influence on Anna and Anna's influence on Ursula showing how mothers and daughters interact, sometimes negatively but more often positively, in a variety of ways. If we are to share the joy of Ursula's coming to independence, we must also recognize that other daughters have broken away from their mothers in less satisfactory ways. To concentrate on the destructive relationships, however, would be as unfair to Lawrence as to pretend they are not in the canon. It is Lawrence's all-encompassing vision of the world, his ability to give form to so many possibilities, that ensures we will continue to read him—and, as Mark Kinkead-Weekes reminds us—we will continue to learn to read him.[20]

... as Demeter's pale lamps give off light,
lead me then, lead the way.

Reach me a gentian, give me a torch!
let me guide myself with the blue, forked torch of this flower
down the darker and darker stairs, where blue is darkened on
    blueness
even where Persephone goes. ...

("Bavarian Gentians", *Last Poems*)

NOTES

1   Diana Trilling, ed., *The Selected Letters of D. H. Lawrence* (New York,
    1958), p. 69.
2   Adrienne Rich, *Of Woman Born* (New York, 1976), p. 225.
3   Trilling, p. 38.
4   Rich, p. 226.
5   Trilling, p. 70.
6   *Ibid.*, p. 71.
7   Anthony Beal, ed., *D. H. Lawrence: Selected Literary Criticism* (New
    York, 1966), pp. 112–113.
8   D. H. Lawrence, *Psychoanalysis and the Unconscious* and *Fantasia
    of the Unconscious* (New York, 1960), p. 72.
9   *Ibid.*, p. 69.
10 D. H. Lawrence, *Sons and Lovers* (New York, 1972), p. 43. Subsequent
    references are in-text notes.
11 D. H. Lawrence, *The Rainbow* (New York, 1961), p. 491. Subsequent
    references are in-text notes.
12 Any analysis of *The Rainbow* must consider the wealth of birth imag-
    ery in the work, as well as Lawrence's attitudes towards matriarchy,
    both often commented upon by other critics. *The Rainbow* is filled
    with imagery of creation, of conception and gestation and birth. Nearly
    every important incident in *The Rainbow* is reported in such images,
    from the relatively straightforward description of Tom Brangwen's
    first vision of Lydia ("A swift change had taken place on the earth
    for him, as if a new creation were fulfilled, in which he had real ex-
    istence. Things had all been stark, unreal, barren, mere nullities be-
    fore" [p. 26]) to the richer imagery after Lydia agrees to marry Tom
    (he feels newly created, "as after a gestation, a new birth, in the womb
    of darkness" [pp. 40–41]). The visit Will and Anna make to Lincoln
    Cathedral is the most exhaustive: Will considers the cathedral "the
    perfect womb". Peter Balbert's fine study of *The Rainbow, D. H.
    Lawrence and the Psychology of Rhythm*, argues that the rhythm of
    birth establishes the overall form of the novel. His analysis is one

of the most recent and most thorough considerations of Lawrence's use of birth imagery in the novel; an understanding of mother-daughter relationships needs to be juxtaposed against it.

While Lawrence celebrates the creativity of birth, and the image is usually a positive one, the process also is frightening in its mystery; Lawrence's views towards matriarchy are also mixed. Anna's matriarchy, for example, is basically destructive, and it is clearly to Ursula's credit that she is able to break free from the mother's pattern. Lawrence remained characteristically ambivalent towards the larger implications of matriarchy, particularly in the travel literature where concern with matriarchal and patriarchal societies is pervasive. At times, as in Sea and Sardinia, he is drawn towards the great mother goddesses: "Why in the name of heaven should my heart stand still as I watch [Mount Eryx] which rises above the sea?" The answer is that he is in the presence of the "world mystery, the smiling Astarte". Later, however, in essays like "Matriarchy" he turns against matriarchy, particularly as evidence of the destructiveness of power relationships. Martin Green's study of Frieda, The von Richthofen Sisters: The Triumphant and the Tragic Modes of Love, is a full-scale study of the extent to which Lawrence's ideas were influenced by Frieda through her involvement in the erotic movement.

Frieda was, of course, a profound influence on Lawrence's work, affecting his understanding of women and their relationships with each other in ways that we can never exhaust. The mothers and daughters in his fiction are a reflection in part of Lawrence's understanding of Frieda and her mother; The Rainbow was written at a time when Frieda was both receiving support from her mother to stay with Lawrence and trying to cope with her guilt and anguish over leaving her own children. These biographical connections have been traced by many of Lawrence's biographers, both in basic works like Harry T. Moore's The Intelligent Heart and in more specialized books like Green's. Green writes that Lawrence seemed to have been acutely aware, in his last years, "of the way in which husbands and lovers were external to the circuit of feeling and power which united the sisters and their mother" (p. 347). George Ford in Double Measure, however, shows that Lawrence also drew on his relationship with the Burrows family for The Rainbow.

13   Rich, pp. 247–248.

14   Daniel Weiss, Oedipus in Nottingham (Seattle, 1962), p. 75.

15   George Ford, in an interesting use of the Persephone myth in his critical study Double Measure, argues that Lawrence often used the Persephone-Pluto relationship, as with Walter and Gertrude Morel, when the woman, representative of the light, marries a figure associated with the dark. In most of the works Ford analyzes, however, there is no Ceres figure to rescue the daughter of light from her union with the underworld, and so often these marriages end in disaster.

16   In February 1929, Lawrence wrote to Cynthia Asquith, thanking her for returning the proofs of "Mother and Daughter", which apparently

had been written about May 1928. I would like to express my appreciation to Professors Harry Moore and Keith Sagar for helping to date this short story.

17 The definition is the one used by Rich, p. 249.

18 D. H. Lawrence, *St Mawr* and *The Man Who Died* (New York, 1961), p. 56. Subsequent references are in-text notes.

19 D. H. Lawrence, "Mother and Daughter" in *The Complete Short Stories*, Vol. III (New York, 1967), p. 805. Subsequent references are in-text notes.

20 Mark Kinkead-Weekes, "Introduction" to *Twentieth Century Interpretations of The Rainbow* (Englewood Cliffs, N.J., 1971), p. 9.

4

Eros and Metaphor: Sexual Relationship in the Fiction of Lawrence[1]

by MARK KINKEAD-WEEKES

> Sex is the balance of male and female in the universe, the attraction, the repulsion, the transit of neutrality, the new attraction, the new repulsion, always different, always new.
>
> (*A Propos of Lady Chatterley's Lover*)

1

"Intimacy took place"—the old divorce-court formula ludicrously exposes a problem that can arise whenever anyone tries to talk about sexual relationship. For of course "intimacy" cannot "take place". Sexual intercourse and orgasm can take place in such-and-such a room at five minutes past the hour; but intimacy implies relationship, and relationship grows, extends, develops, changes, through space and time. A phrase like "sexual relationship" equally conceals a tension between two very different modes of being. To accentuate "sexual" is to emphasize the experience of the body that is an experience within the whole private being, the most "intimate" experience in that sense. The central concern is with an act, with a climax within that act, with a moment of interior being within that climax. If we accent "relationship", the emphasis moves in the opposite direction: extensive rather than intensive, concerned with continuity rather than climax, and with complex processes in space and time rather than a moment, so that the private being is involved in "intimacy" with another, with others, with the world. Yet these are only emphases, for most of us would recognize something extreme either in a sexual act that totally excluded any degree of relationship, or in a relationship which wholly excluded any consideration of sex.

Lawrence's treatment of "sexual relationship" seems, however, intent on maximizing the tension between the opposite emphases. For the degree of interest by police and magistrates in *The Rainbow*, the paintings, and *Lady Chatterley's Lover* bear witness, if witness were needed, to his insistence on direct and detailed represensation of sexual feeling and action. He is unmistakably an erotic writer even where there is no possible offence to social conventions. Yet the characteristic language of that representation also insists that sex is a way of talking about something else, so that Eros becomes Metaphor. Sexual activity and consciousness become the vehicle for exploring wider and wider relationships, within people, between them, throughout society, and the connection of man to the universe.

This tension has consequences for the method of discussion, if one is to establish the peculiar vitality of the fiction that so polarizes itself between the intensive moment and the extensive process. One will have to choose particular passages, because only in detail will the qualities of the language, both the erotic and its metaphorical extensiveness, reveal their nature. Yet because Lawrence is so uniquely exploratory a writer, concerned with the development, flux, and change of relationship, one can only see him truly by seeing his art as a continual process of discovery, not only within each novel, but from novel to novel. One cannot generalize about "Lawrence's treatment of sexual relationship" at any stage, without both superficiality and distortion. One has to try to account intensively for moments, and simultaneously for the fact that they are momentary, partial arrestings of a flowing exploration, always moving beyond.

I propose therefore to discuss four scenes from different novels, to try to establish the ways in which their different languages operate. By selecting scenes which are turning-points, I hope at least to indicate how each is merely a stage in the exploration of the novel. And I believe that by ranging them side by side, I may be able to suggest something of the tensions in the imaginative vision Lawrence brought to sexual relationship, and something, too, of the curious relationship between the author and the fictive process. For Lawrence saw in artistic creation, and in the language of fiction itself, an analogy with the sexual act. There, too, we may become aware of Eros and Metaphor.

2

I choose from *Sons and Lovers* the scene in which it becomes clear to Paul, as he reacts to the beauty of the night and the scent of flowers in his garden that he will break off his sexual relationship with Miriam[2] (pp. 358–9).

The language works directly through sense-perception to register, first, a rich beauty and vitality. Moon and sky glow gold and purple; "the air all round seemed to stir with scent, as if it were alive." The 'keen perfume" of the pinks "came sharply across the rocking, heavy scent of the lilies". But already within the first response a second has been released: a hint of something threatening, excessive. The scent of madonna lilies comes "stealthily . . . almost as if it were prowling abroad". They seem to exhaust themselves; they "flagged all loose, as if they were panting". The combined perfumes become over-rich, intoxicating; the moon grows flushed, soon it will melt down.

Cutting across the heavy seductiveness however comes a different kind of vitality: the harsh cry of the corncrake, and "like a shock . . . another perfume, something raw and coarse". The language registers now, as against the flushed moon, the darkness; as against the expended lilies leaning, the irises stiff and fleshy; as against the intoxicating perfumes, something brutal. The rhythm of sense-perception reverses the previous process. Now it begins from shock and potential repulsion, but ends by finding "at any rate, . . . something", which precipitates an inner and unthinking decision against one mode of sexuality, one relationship, and for another. The scene is erotic because the flowers are used to project and explore the sexual conflict, the different complexities of attraction and repulsion, that exist unconsciously in Paul but can be made articulate for the reader. Here the natural world becomes a metaphorical vehicle for the flow and recoil of sexual feelings.

The location of the vision is within the character. The associations are Paul's; the language cannot be made emblematic (so that different flowers would adequately "stand for" Miriam and Clara to *us*) without damaging the novel's complexity. The vocabulary is Lawrence's projection of Paul at this moment, and, as it happens, tells us nothing about the author's attitude.

Yet if we replace the scene within the continuum of exploration in the novel, reminding ourselves of other scenes which it re-orchestrates or anticipates, we see that we cannot generalize. In the opening chapter, after one of the terrible battles between Paul's parents, Mrs Morel is thrust out of doors into a garden rendered no less powerfully in terms of moonlight, flowers and perfumes (pp. 34–5). The effect however is quite different, not only because the purpose this time is to reveal at a deeper level what it is and means to be Mrs Morel, but also because the juxtaposition of character and nature involves a critical placing of this character against a dimension she has ignored. And in the scenes with Miriam that anticipate Paul's rejection, there are many kinds of tension between prsentation and analysis. If one instanced the communion over the wild rose bush (pp. 197*ff*.), the vision of the orange moon over the sandhills (pp. 220–21), and Paul's cruel attack on Miriam as she fondles the daffodil (pp. 267–8), one would find several modes of interplay between our response to what we see and feel for ourselves, the attitudes of the characters to one another, and what we are told by the narrator. Paul's criticisms become increasingly fierce, culminating in the cruel charge that Miriam's "abnormal craving is to be loved. You aren't positive, you're negative. You absorb, absorb, as if you must fill yourself up with love, because you've got a shortage somewhere." But we cannot take Paul's response as simply valid—though some critics have done so. The dramatic presentation of Miriam creates her in depth and complexity,[3] so that we often become aware that what we know of Miriam ourselves is being simplified or distorted in Paul's rationalizations of his own recoil. We have to allow for the pressure on him, towards that recoil, of the possessive love and jealousy of Mrs Morel, whose judgements he often echoes, but whose taking of him as son-and-lover is demonstrably a crippling "mischief"—though in other ways it is also a vitalizing force. We have to allow for the validity of Miriam's criticisms of Paul—"She wondered why he always claimed to be normal when he was disagreeable" (p. 270). And we are affected in various ways by the flux and reflux of the narrator's sympathies. Sometimes he is involved or even identified with Paul, seeing as he does, blind

with his blindnesses. Sometimes he is detached and critical, aware
of how Paul's relationship with his mother has made him both
victim and victimizer. The fictive life consists in complex interplay
between presentation (both dramatic and symbolic), allowing us
to see and feel for ourselves, and a *struggle* to analyse in which
both the narrator and ourselves have to be involved—involved with
Paul's deficiencies, among other things, in order to become capable
of understanding and sympathy without simplification. But "D. H.
Lawrence", because he is dramatist, symbolist and narrative
ironist,[4] as well as commentator, must never be reduced to the
narrator's commentary.

If we look back now at the scene from which we started, we
can perhaps detect something questionable about the dialectic of
Paul's sexual conflict and its momentary resolution, something
crude and overheated in its terms—without automatically refer-
ring this to Lawrence himself. For the scene is part of a continuum
which points forward as well as back. When Paul tells his mother
that he will break off with Miriam, closes his teeth unthinkingly
on the flower in his mouth, and spits the petals into the fire, there
are anticipations of the scattered petals on Clara's breast by the
river, and of the "baptism of fire" in erotic scenes like the one
in the field where the peewits cry. Yet Paul's relationship with
Clara will bring out the crudity of his sexual recoil from the over-
heavy sweetness he associates with Miriam, as well as the meaning-
fulness of his intuition of a selfhood in the irises. With Clara, in
"the immensity of passion", the key discoveries turn out to have
little to do with the coarse or brutal, and everything to do with
a vocabulary of inclusiveness, and stillness-in-the-self. Paul becomes aware of a "strong, strange, wild life, that breathed with
his in the darkness through this hour. It was all so much bigger
than themselves. . . . They had met, and included in their meeting
the thrust of the manifold grass-stems, the cry of the peewit, the
wheel of the stars. . . . There was a verification which they had
had together. Nothing could nullify it, nothing could take it away;
it was almost their belief in life" (pp. 430–31). Or again, "It was
as if he, and the stars, and the dark herbage, and Clara were
licked up in an immense tongue of flame, which tore onwards and
upwards . . . everything was still, perfect in itself, along with him.
This wonderful stillness in each thing in itself, while it was being
borne along in a very ecstasy of living, seemed the highest point

of bliss" (pp. 442–3). The erotic experience becomes a language of organic relation with the natural universe, and of new selfhood.

Yet the exploration continues, and a tentativeness—"almost", "seemed"—still accompanies the apparently big claims. For the relationship of passion, though it brings the lovers into a kind of harmony with the world of nature, does not include enough or create sufficient selfhood. In its impersonality, its immensity, the human being seems devalued. Clara becomes "only a woman", depersonalized; "She represents something, like a bubble of foam represents the sea. But what is *she*? It's not her I care for" (p. 435), "I feel", Clara says, "as if all you weren't there, and as if it weren't *me* you were taking" (p. 441). Because it proves incapable of including the full personality, and the world of conscious awareness in which Paul lives with his mother and lived with Miriam, the erotic relationship itself dwindles and becomes deathly. Paul's tragedy is that while his mother lives, he cannot offer or receive a love which includes the whole of himself; and when she dies, he has only a stubborn refusal to give in, to hold him back from the drift towards death.

I have been trying to bring out the sheer difficulty of completing a sentence that begins "Lawrence's treatment of sexual relationship in *Sons and Lovers* . . .". One cannot extrapolate scenes, because the language at any particular point is partial and temporary, giving up its significance only when it is replaced in a continuum of exploration. One cannot extrapolate authorial attitudes, because generalizations suggest a relation between author and fiction that is false to Lawrence's art. To the purist eye, the fictional process of *Sons and Lovers* is a curious blend of types, both the apparently "omniscient" analysis of complex characters and actions, and the rendering of different consciousnesses by a neutral author. But why is this? I think one glimpses an answer in the language of inclusiveness and self-definition. The certainties of omniscience may not be inclusive enough, and the uncertainties of neutrality may fail to achieve sufficient selfhood in the writer. So Lawrence's method is both a self-projection into different consciousnesses, allowed to produce themselves and expand in their own ways, in order that the vision we get at the end should be inclusive and complicated enough; *and* an insistence on involving himself and his reader in a constant struggle to understand, and

relate, and produce an analysis of what a sufficient self should be
—particularly since he is writing about his own life. And once we
grasp the form, I think we also begin to write our sentence about
the theme of sexual relationship. For here too the demand is that
there should be two opposite but equally vital processes. On the
one hand sex is seen as a mode of inclusiveness, seeking to relate
the whole self to the whole other, and both to the rhythms of the
natural universe. On the other hand, and at the same time, sex
is an opposite process, not only joining-up, but singling out
into "each thing in itself". The vocabulary is both a way of using
nature to talk about sex, and a way of seeing through the erotic
into a relation between men and women, and the universe they
inhabit. We see the centrality of sex to Lawrence in the relation of
form and theme. The subject is sexual relationship, explored as
necessarily inclusive *and* distinctive, searching for the shape of
wholeness in the story of failure. The art is both a reaching out
from the authorial self into others and the natural world, tentative,
exploratory; and an "agonized" analysis in which the author
struggles to clarify himself.

The scene we began from finally reveals its basic dialectic in the
same opposition, in rhythms of complex attraction and repulsion:
the lilies leaning, calling; the irises stiff, upright in themselves.

3

The Rainbow and *Women in Love* are, I believe, Lawrence's
finest work; and since they were originally conceived as one novel,
I propose to treat them together, using a passage from each to
bring out their connection, but also to show how qualitatively
different they became.

I choose from *The Rainbow* the coming together of Anna and
Will in the cornfield (pp. 121*ff.*), from the second of the novel's
three stories, because this scene allows one to look back at Tom
and Lydia, and forward to Ursula and Skrebensky. As the girl and
the young man carry cornsheaves under a harvest moon, and pile
them into stacks, the language embodies and explores the nature
of sexual relationship in a way that has grown out of *Sons and
Lovers*, but has a new rhythmic pulse, and a new distinctness of
opposing elements.

The two human figures move between a pull towards the darkness and an opposed pull towards the brilliant defining moon. They seem to obey forces that operate below personality, choice, or even physical passion. Will out of the darkness, Anna drenched in moonlight, set towards each other with a deep natural rhythm, the rhythm of dark tides below the moon. Gradually the beat of separate actions, the short sentences, modulate into longer cumulative swellings and turnings, until the meeting is achieved The stacking of dewy corn-tresses, hissing together like water, is rich with associations of fertility, harvest, the creative processes of nature. The human beings are at one with this, feeling its rhythms, becoming tides, gradually setting towards each other. Moreover they meet as two "others", each with its own motion; and they work together to make something out of nature beyond themselves. There is a change from being to doing, a weaving, combining, structuring. And as the two "others" come together at the end of the scene, we are made very much aware of the wonder and mystery of what one might call the marriage of opposites. "All the moonlight upon her, all the darkness within her! All the night in his arms, darkness and shine, he possessed of it all! All the night for him now, to unfold, to venture within, all the mystery to be entered, all the discovery to be made. Trembling with keen triumph, his heart was white as a star as he drove his kisses nearer." We reach a moment presented as an incandescence within a crucible of darkness, a moment when a doorway seems about to open into a mysterious dimension, beyond.

Anna and Will partly re-enact what had happened to the first generation of lovers in the book. In the betrothal scene of Tom and Lydia (pp. 42ff.), the strangers, the opposites, the man from the darkness and the woman in the lit-up room met and married in a kiss. To remind ourselves of the earlier scene is however to remember also how that marriage of opposites involved a kind of death as a condition of rebirth. The separate selves sink into oblivion, and this is "blenched agony", for it is difficult to let go of the existing self and submit to transformation at the hands of the "other". Yet the challenge is accepted, oblivion becomes the womb of new birth, and the lovers enter a new world beyond, a new freedom, a new and stronger individuality. Given to themselves more securely, but connected finally to each other, the man and woman like a pillar of cloud and a pillar of fire meet to the heavens, creating an archway to new life; and the child Anna plays in freedom between.

The corn-stacking scene partly re-enacts Tom and Lydia, but by comparison there is also a sense of anticlimax and loss. Through the coming together there has sounded a note of strain on both sides. There is a tendency in Anna to hold back, resisting the natural movement towards her lover, and its consequences. We have seen this resistance in her from her earliest childhood—the obverse of the qualities that made her a "little princess", the intelligence, self-awareness, and assurance of personality so much greater than her mother's. She is reluctant to meet Will and go through him, beyond; she insists on pulling him out of the kiss into awareness. She short-circuits the process to which Tom and Lydia were able to abandon and trust themselves. And Will's name is no accident, though this is far removed from allegory. More and more clearly we become aware of "a low, deep-sounding will in him", vibrating low at first, but beginning to drum "persistently, darkly, [till] it drowned everything else". When they meet, his voice has become "twanging and insistent". The conflict of opposites has a new tone, a struggle to withhold the self or dominate the other, which the relationship between Tom and Lydia had not. The corn-stacking, then, prepares us for a developing relationship which will partly fail to achieve the marriage of opposites, and in which the woman eventually conquers. Yet the strength of Lawrence's art is that this is far too simple a way of putting it. For Anna's rational intelligence and self-awareness, Will's religious and artistic intensities, represent a greater range of human possibility than Tom and Lydia—though this is also what makes the marriage of opposites more difficult to achieve.

Ursula, heroine of the third story, embodies all the opposites of her family at peak intensity and awareness. We watch her continually trying to resolve her contradictions by pursuing one element of herself to the exclusion of others, never finding a way of marrying them: "always the shining doorway was a gate into another ugly yard, dirty, and active, and dead". In three crises of her relationship with Anton Skrebensky, particularly, we can see further reorchestrations of the corn-stacking scene, and measure the increasing difficulty of the marriage of opposites and the destruction that can result from the assertion of a partial self. When the young lovers dance at the wedding (pp. 317*ff*.), moving between the lanterns and firelight, and the dark where corn-stacks loom under a brilliant moon, the dance becomes a destructive psychic contest in which Ursula, like her mother, is victrix. When Skrebensky returns from Africa, they achieve a physical fulfilment that is also a "superb consummation"—of a kind (pp. 445*ff*.). But the "kind" is a meeting in pure darkness, a mating of only the "dark" sides of themselves. And in the novel's most terrible scene (pp. 478*ff*.), Ursula shows that she cannot be satisfied while her infinitely aspiring, conscious, "bright" self is denied. Under an incandescent moon by the shore, beside the endless heaving of brilliant waters, Ursula tries to force the polar opposite of the "dark" consummation, a coming together in intensity of light, and succeeds only in destruction.

These are mere gestures towards the context of exploration stretching before and after the corn-stack scene; it would require far more space to do any justice to Lawrence's art in *The Rainbow*. What we ought perhaps to notice now however is a peculiarity of history. In the exploration of sexual relationship as a marriage of opposites, the aspiration towards a maximum inclusiveness, and a maximum singling-out into selfhood (which Lawrence uncovered through Paul's tragedy in *Sons and Lovers*), is investigated in different ways in three generations of lovers between 1840 and about 1910. But as it stands, the novel has a paradoxical structure. The first story is the nearest embodiment of what Lawrence then saw as a truly creative and fulfilling sexual relationship, and in one sense, after that, the novel records an increasingly terrible curve of failure. Yet the love of Tom and Lydia, beautifully as it is presented, is partial and primitive in comparison with the growing richness and complexity of the human beings in the later stories. In another sense, then, the novel records human growth, and though Ursula near the end comes close to death, the no longer wilful self that is reborn, as she recovers from miscarrying Skrebensky's child after the encounter with the horses, is one whose human potential is greater than any character Lawrence had created before. What should have followed in fiction was the story of how this daughter of man found her son of god and achieved the promise of the rainbow. What actually followed in life was the outbreak of world war, the banning of *The Rainbow*

for obscenity, and the growth in Lawrence of an apocalyptic vision
of a world heading for destruction in the year of the battle of the
Somme, a world of death-wish and pervasive hatred of life. The
second part of *The Rainbow* was never written; the novel that
developed out of its "ur"-version had a different tonality.

I can perhaps best bring out the difference by choosing what I
see as the central moment in *Women in Love*: that extraordinary
scene by the pond (pp. 277–80) which gives the chapter "Moony"
its title.[5] Because Birkin calls the moon names, as he gazes into the
dark water which reflects it, we have perhaps to ask more precisely
what moon and darkness "symbolize"; but, as always, the real
meaning of the scene comes when we respond to what the whole
rhythm of the prose enacts in us, as Birkin hurls stones to destroy
the moon's reflection. Even more starkly than in *The Rainbow*,
darkness and light are the polar opposites of *Woman in Love*. We
could say that the darkness embodies the world of the senses and
flesh, the unconscious, and the light embodies the world of conscious
knowing and definition. Ursula and Birkin have both been reacting
against the light in this sense, longing for darkness ad dissolution.
More especially, we could see the moon as Diana, the self-sufficiency
of woman repudiating man, and Ursula has been in a contemptuous
state, luminous with repudiation. The moon as Diana is obviously
hateful to Birkin. But he calls it Cybele, the "accursed" Syrian
goddess who emasculated her acolytes, woman the sexual destroyer, like the Ursula who destroyed Skrebensky on the beach.
The moon as Cybele is also Birkin's natural enemy. His odd scraps
of conversation show his quiet despair, the collapse of his faith in
salvation through sexual relationship. It is only an antiphony of
lies, an entanglement with Diana and Cybele, yet "What else is
there?" The dead flowers on the water make their comment on
the flowers he threw in the scene which marked the beginning of
his love for Ursula.

The scene that follows is an answer to the question "what else
is there?", but an answer not in terms of static symbol, but of
process, revealing imaginatively the way of salvation. It looks like
a process of destruction; it turns mysteriously into a way of heal-
ing, beauty and peace. If we trust ourselves to the fiction, we *experience* an enactment, stage by stage, first of the process of
apparent death of the old self but real birth of the new, through
the marriage of opposites—the insight of *The Rainbow*—but then

of a more sustained and violent process of disintegration, almost infinite going apart, that is central to *Women in Love*.

The moon of hard clear definition, cold fire, self-sufficiency and self-assertion, is destroyed by the flooding in of darkness and unconsciousness. This is the first stage of Lawrence's matured vision of the mystery of sex. But the whole point is then that the moon should re-form, gather itself together, refuse to be destroyed (since conflict is eternally necessary), be born again out of its death. Birkin is "satisfied of so much". But now he throws stone after stone, exploding the pool into rocking, crashing, shattering chaos and confusion, again, and again, and again. We experience, as no mere account can convey, a breaking apart, a smashing fragmentation to the very last "broken flakes" of light. But we also experience the rhythmic coming together, out of that ultimate separation, into equilibrium, polarity, peace. The moon that had looked sinister and deadly grows into a radiant rose, constellated in the dark water. We know on our pulses as we respond to the rhythms, how life separated out into either the white fire alone, or the inchoate blackness alone, would be life diminished from true fulness and beauty. Yet we are also assured in the imaginative experience, that what Lawrence called "the flux of corruption", the disintegration back to opposing elements, was *necessary*, and that when it has taken its course, a new beauty and peace are born out of the terrible conflict. What happens in the pond, happens also in the people who watch. The scene is easily explicable in emotional terms: we can see how Birkin and the watching Ursula work off bitterness, anger, repudiation, despair, the urges to death and destruction. Only, "Was it hate?", or any other "psychological" explanation of that kind? The deepest imaginative experience of the process tells us rather why they should welcome, abandon themselves to both the destruction and the reintegration, and not fasten their wills to life at one or other partial extreme. Only through both the disintegration and the tenacious coming-together of the rose-in-darkness, can they hope "to get over the disfigurement and the agitation to be whole and composed, at peace".

Lawrence had discovered his way forward by a leap of imagination, but its implication and its value lie in the ways in which it is dramatized, worked out in the complex tensions of a variety of personalities and relationships. He is able to establish what is involved for Ursula and Birkin in the way of salvation, particularly perhaps in the chapter called "Excurse", where inclusiveness and singled-out being get their most comprehensive embodiment. He is able to show also, with complex imaginative sympathy and involvement, what happens to those who fasten their wills to the extremes of partial being.

But what has happened to Lawrence's art since *Sons and Lovers?* In one direction, we can detect an enormous effort of systematic analysis: the working out in the unpublished "Foreword" to *Sons and Lovers*, the *Study of Thomas Hardy*, and *The Crown*, of a comprehensive "theory" of sexual relationship. Where *Sons and Lovers* was a painful interrogation of his own life, with no metaphysical underpinning, the insights he had gained from writing the novel, and from his marriage, were worked and reworked until they became a statement of faith in the creative and saving power of sexual relationship, that one doesn't distort by calling "religious". I mean by this that he now saw clearly in sexual relationship the operation of a universal creativity, which transcended man, but which also connected men and women with the mysterious organic life of the universe. In the reinterpreted Christian language of the *Study* and *The Rainbow*, and in the "elemental" language of *The Crown* and *Women in Love* which replaced it, he worked out a universal "metaphysic" of growth through conflict. Within every man and woman, between them, and throughout the natural world, he argued a basic conflict between opposed forces; but in sexual relationship the marriage of opposites offered a creative and continuous dialectic of growth. When the drive to unity, all-inclusiveness, and the opposed drive to singleness of being, individuation, could be exploded into each other in marriage, Lawrence believed that the full potentialities of human being could be progressively realized in new individuality, *and* in deep and vital relationship between people, *and* in organic connection between humanity and nature. As these insights developed, and as he fought to keep faith, in an increasingly terrible world, he measured the cost of growth through conflict, first by seeing sex and marriage as a kind of death in order to be born anew, and then by seeing the metaphor more grimly, in terms of disintegration of the psyche to frightening lengths, as a necessity for the achievement of reintegration, fulfilment, equilibrium.

Yet it is not Lawrence's ideas that are important, but their exploration and testing out in the fictive processes of his novels.

In one sense the new power of systematic analysis is not an un-mixed blessing. It tends to upset the balance of the mixed mode we saw as characteristic of *Sons and Lovers*, bringing with it the danger that the authorial voice will become too omniscient and overbearing. Yet this also called forth from Lawrence an opposing impulse of imagination, both poetically and dramatically. His new mode of characterization (seeking, in that famous phrase, to break down "the old *stable* ego",[6] and substitute a new more inward vision of men and women as mysteriously fluctuating and ever changing states of being), itself became a check against schematism and authorial certainty. As the more definite person-alities of *Sons and Lovers* give way to the locations of conflicting forces within the human being; and the "hard, violent style full of sensation and presentation"[7] gives way to subtler rhythms of change, there is a gain rather than a loss of complexity to be balanced against the dangers of system and insistence. The attempt, in extraordinary leaps of poetic imagination, to penetrate to un-conscious movements of the psyche, made him no less tentative and exploratory. Nevertheless, as the exploration reaches further outward and inward, and the metaphoric implications of the erotic become more extensive, the language has to take greater and greater strains. In the finest passages I think these are triumph-antly met, but there is constant danger of pretentiousness, and of nagging repetition, whenever the imagination is less than fully extended. Most important of all, however, the belief that conflict is the condition of growth encouraged Lawrence to dramatize conflicting readings of life and relationship in his characters, so that they subject one another's insights, and his, to a continuous crossfire of criticism, intenser than ever before. One of the strengths of *The Rainbow*, and especially *Women in Love*, with few excep-tions, is the way that the many-sidedness of the total vision works to prevent hardening of response and judgement, or taking sides, or neglect of the vital complexities of the fictive human beings. And in *Women in Love*, Lawrence is able to replace a represen-tative of himself in the fiction, in the person of Birkin, but in a fashion which encourages critical response. He pins down in Birkin his own tendencies to see himself as saviour of the world, to prig-gishness, to fruitiness and pretentiousness of language, to kinds of deathliness and destruction. The effect is distinctly refreshing.

4

Lady Chatterley's Lover is still in continuity with the earlier
novels, in that the vision of sexual relationship remains essentially concerned with the necessity of salvation through a process
of death and rebirth. What is new, of course, is the explicit location of that process in orgasm, and the arrangement of erotic
episodes in a specific sequence. There are eight of these, and the
central one is the fourth. (It is significant that one is driven to a
new programmatic tone.) Here the impulse to resist and the impulse
to let go, which have formed the tension of the earlier episodes,
are brought into stark relief in the two parts of the scene. In the
first part Connie is afraid, "stiffened in resistance", "her spirit
seemed to look on from the top of her head". Consequently the
sexual act seems farcical and humiliating, contemptible. But afterwards there is a storm of weeping over her separateness, and she
clings to Mellors "with uncanny force" because she desires so intensely "to be saved, from her own inward anger and resistance".
And in the second part of the scene she lets go, "with a quiver
that was like death"; and though she fears that "the potent in-
exorable entry . . . might come with the thrust of a sword in her
softly-opened body, and that would be death", she dares "to let
go everything, all herself, and be gone in the flood".

> And it seemed she was like the sea, nothing but dark waves rising
> and heaving, heaving with a great swell, so that slowly her whole
> darkness was in motion, and she was ocean rolling its dark,
> dumb mass. Oh, and far down inside her the deeps parted and
> rolled asunder, in long, far-travelling billows, and ever, at the
> quick of her, the depths parted and rolled asunder, from the
> centre of soft plunging, as the plunger went deeper and deeper,
> touching lower, and she was deeper and deeper and deeper dis-
> closed, the heavier the billows of her rolled away to some shore,
> uncovering her, and closer and closer plunged the palpable un-
> known, and further and further rolled the waves of herself away
> from herself, leaving her, till suddenly, in a soft, shuddering con-
> vulsion, the quick of all her plasm was touched, she knew herself
> touched, the consummation was upon her, and she was gone. She
> was gone, she was·not, and she was born: a woman.
>
> (p. 181)

As well as the explicit concern with orgasm, what distinguishes
this from the other passages I have discussed is the absence of

conflict and opposition. They were all rhythmic and repetitive in differing ways, but one notices about this passage both that the rhythm is mimetic of the sexual act itself, and that the process it signifies moves in one direction only, unilinearly repetitive. The key words are "parted", "asunder", "disclosed", "rolled away", "uncovered", "gone". There is no flux and reflux, the sea imagery is there only to achieve the rolling away, there is no interplay of forces. In the scenes that have led up to this one, similarly, the resistance is not in potentially creative tension with the impulse to let go; it must disappear, before Connie can become a woman. The experience is all of one kind, developing by progressive rejection of other tendencies that are seen as standing in the way. In both *Fantasia of the Unconscious*, and the concern with the Book of Revelation which began long before the first *Lady Chatterley*, and culminated after the final version in Lawrence's last book *Apocalypse*, he insists on founding his vision in the body, emphatically. I am sure that Frank Kermode[8] is right to suggest, however bizarre it may seem, that the first seven erotic episodes in *Lady Chatterley* relate to the opening of the seven seals (as Lawrence interpreted the myth of revelation) in the body. The first four episodes are concerned with rebirth out of death; the last three with a descent into the underworld. So the fifth episode discovers the separate mysterious life hidden in the genitalia; the sixth is concerned with animality and the glad acceptance of animal function; and the seventh, notoriously, with the sharp burning sensuality of anal intercourse, rendered in the imagery of the darkest underground, smelting "the heaviest ore of the body into purity". The phallic hunt burns out the last shame and fear that impede the final progress "to the very heart of the jungle of herself . . . the real bedrock of her nature". Only then, in the last encounter between the pregnant woman and her lover, can there be the release of "the bowels of compassion", the full tenderness, accepting the coming child, but proclaiming still that the sex act is "creative . . . far more than procreative".

I lack space to enlarge on the treatment of character, human relationships, society, and the natural world which stems from this central movement of the novel. Yet the characteristics immediately obvious in the progress of Connie, the location in the body (the "bowels of compassion"), can already be seen to mark a sharp discontinuity from the earlier art, which is bound to reverberate in every direction, and prove more important than any continuity in the theme of death and rebirth. Two things seem to have happened to the tension between "sexual" and "relationship" from which we started. The accent on "sexual"—always potentially momentary and interior—has become more and more pronounced, and more literally erotic, as we have moved from persons, and forces-within-persons, to the most intimate penetration of the private being in the body. At the same time, the accent on "relationship" has changed direction sharply, from inclusion to exclusion. Consequently the whole balance that characterized the earlier fiction has been upset. The earlier art aimed at being "mystically-physically satisfying"—a formula of range from *Women in Love*. The erotic moment was unquestionably sexual and interior, but the sexuality was always the way of bringing complex human potentialities in creative contact with each other and the beyond—and the emphasis fell there, in the space (as it were) *between* the word "sexual" and the word "relationship", so that the specific physical nature of the erotic action, while it would always *be* sexual and physical, had no particular importance in itself. (It could as easily be a kiss or the touch of fingers as intercourse, but Mellors will have none of that!) Now both the concept of sexuality and the concept of relationship strike one as having shrunk. *Women in Love* stands at the end of a process of greater and greater inclusiveness, based on Blakean acceptance of all human energies as divinely creative, and insistence on keeping them all in play, for "without contraries is no progression". In *Lady Chatterley* the imaginative process is founded on exclusion. "As I say it's a novel of the phallic Consciousness: or the phallic Consciousness versus the mental-spiritual Consciousness: and of course you know which side I take. The *versus* is not my fault: there should be no *versus*. The two things must be reconciled in us. But now they're daggers drawn."[9] The old Lawrence still speaks in "there should be no *versus*", but his novel turns "versus" into repudiation, of "mental-spiritual Consciousness" in the individual, of all kinds of relationship but the phallic, of a whole society. One might recognize, historically and biographically, that Lawrence's quarrel with his audience and their world, pinpointed in the aggressive Foreword to *Fantasia*, was by no means altogether his fault, but the fictive imagination of *Lady Chatterley* no longer accepts any need or possibility of reconciliation. Without repudiation is no progress, now.

The tension between *different* imaginative directions, implicit in the phrase "sexual relationship", and profoundly characteristic of "eros *and* metaphor" in Lawrence's art up to *Women in Love*, has disappeared. Both the erotic scene, and the implications which stem from it, now point in the same direction, and one level of language translates directly into the other. Instead of a language balancing tensions we have a curious cross-literalism, in which one level is no longer a field of suggestiveness pointing to another level —they have become *equivalent*. One can simply "stand for" the other, like Clifford's crippled legs, and his impotence at all levels but the mechanical. Yet the fiction still has to bear the burden of renewal of the human being, of society, or organic connection with the universe. But only for some—for the equation of potency with capacity for living raises questions about Calvinistic election that did not arise before, when Lawrence's vision at its best was a possibility for all his characters, albeit in different ways. Two quotations may serve to suggest the new strain on language imposed by the new literalness and singleness of direction—particularly if we remember how the earlier art had treated sexual relationship in men, between people, and with nature. "I believe if men could fuck with warm hearts, and the women take it warm-heartedly, everything would come all right. It's all this cold-hearted fucking that is death and idiocy" (p. 215). Or again: "My soul softly flaps in the little Pentecost flame with you, like the peace of fucking. We fucked a flame into being. Even the flowers are fucked into being between the sun and the earth" (p. 316). Mellors is of course not simply representative of Lawrence and his art, but the significant point is that such passages are only extreme examples of a tendency that lies at the heart of the novel's imaginative vision, to make "fucking" carry "everything", by repudiating complexity in both sexuality and relationship. And one can no longer draw confident distinctions between author and character, for drama has virtually disappeared, no effective opposition or cross-criticism is permitted, and author and character preach insistently and interchangeably. Process becomes programme.

In form, character, sexual situation, language, the strain is unmistakable whenever the newly insistent "X-ray" vision coincides with a "realism" more particularized than ever. In form the novel approaches fable (a coalmine, a wood, naked figures dancing in the rain); in character it approaches the morality figure (Sir Impotence, Mr Potency, and Lady Coming-to-Life). The vision cuts through complexity to reveal a basic (or a skeletal) significance. But when the fabulous coalmine and wood are historicized, to serve a serious analysis of England after the General Strike, or Connie puts on her canvas shoes to keep her feet dry, or we see in the gamekeeper or the cripple a residual complexity from the characters of the first version, there is strain. The descriptions of sex are either too fabulous, (the unfailing potency, the absence of loveplay); or they are too specific to carry the weight of significance demanded of them. The objection to the four-letter words is not to their obscenity,[10] but rather that (where erotic scene and relationship are themselves not inclusive enough) the four letters, however tenderly used, are still less adequate to carry even what the erotic has achieved. And the tenderness, about which critics have spoken movingly, while valuable and beautiful in itself, is confined to Connie and Mellors. It is damagingly absent from vision and language elsewhere. Even if one compares the novel not with the earlier fictions, but with its own first version, there is an obvious hardening of outline and shrillness of tone, an unmistakable animus directed against all but Lady Chatterley and her lover, and often quite gratuitously (as with Mellors's child)—"versus" with a vengeance.

In "life" terms, Lawrence will always be vulnerable, both to those who see his treatment of sex, even at its best, as too exclusive, and to those who see it as too inclusive. The first points to the lack of light-heartedness, of laughter, of simple pleasure in sex-in-itself, of variety of sexual experience from the ecstatic to the ordinary. The second argues that Lawrence tries to load sex with too extensive a meaning, and to insist that more of life and its significance is sexual than is actually the case. Both may object, as Lawrence himself noticed in the Foreword to *Women in Love*, to the "continual, slightly modified repetition" of the style. But the concluding word about Eros and Metaphor ought to be said in the terms of art and fictive language. Lawrence had once spoken of "Supreme" art, in the *Study of Hardy*, as analogous to the marriage of opposites, when the author does not assert his vision against "the other" to overcome it, but embraces "the other" in order to go beyond and create through conflict. He defended his style in the Foreword to *Women in Love*, as analogous to the sexual act, in which "to-and-fro" produces fulfilment: "every natural crisis in emotion or passion or understanding comes from this pulsing, frictional to-and-fro which works up to culmination." Lawrence's three major novels do, I believe, hold eros and metaphor in creative tension, but the last novel is not a culmination, it is a loss in love and language.

NOTES

1 This essay previously appeared in *Twentieth Century Studies*, No. 2, 1969.

2 All page references to the novels will be to the Penguin editions.

3 The complexity of Miriam has been persuasively argued by Louis L. Martz: "Portrait of Miriam" in Maynard Mack and Ian Gregor (eds.): *Imagined Worlds* (London, 1968), pp. 343–69.

4 No reading of Mrs Morel's quarrel with her husband (pp. 32*ff.*) for example, or of the scene between Paul and Miriam at the rose-bush (p. 197*ff.*), should fail to take into account that the accusation that Walter has got drunk on the housekeeping money happens to *be* "a lie"; and that Paul's response has as much to do with the lateness of the hour and his fear of his mother's jealousy as with the "spirituality" of Miriam—though we have to take both points for ourselves.

5 I should apologize for using again here an analysis of this scene I have already published in "The Marble and the Statue: the Exploratory Imagination of D. H. Lawrence" in *Imagined Worlds, op. cit.*, pp. 410–12. The reason for this is that the scene is so central, and the best alternative, the crucial scene in "Excurse", is far too long and complicated for the space that could be spared.

6 *The Collected Letters of D. H. Lawrence*, ed. Harry T. Moore (London, 1962), I, p. 282; *The Letters of D. H. Lawrence*, ed. Aldous Huxley (London, 1932), p. 198. (My italics.)

7 *Letters* (Moore) I, p. 259; *Letters* (Huxley) p. 172.

8 Frank Kermode, "Spenser and the Allegorists", *Proceedings of the British Academy*, Vol. XLVIII (1962), pp. 272–8; and "Lawrence and the Apocalyptic Types", *Critical Quarterly*, vol. 10 (Spring and Summer 1968), pp. 14–25.

9 Letter to the Brewsters of 1928 in Earl and Achsah Brewster, *D. H. Lawrence, Reminiscences and Correspondence* (New York, 1934), p. 166.

10 There is however a potential contradiction between Lawrence's wish to
    use the four-letter words as a shock-tactic to shake his audience's
    "mental-spiritual Consciousness" (*using* their "obscenity"), and his
    concern to rehabilitate them in a new context of tenderness (so that
    they are no longer "obscene").

5

Lawrence, Woman and the Celtic Fringe

by JULIAN MOYNAHAN

I have a great *penchant* for the Celtic races, with their melancholy and unprogressiveness.

(Matthew Arnold, to his mother from the Highlands, summer, 1864)

1

It is a truism of Lawrence studies that the novelist, in his continuing quarrel with urban-industrial civilization, especially English civilization, tends to exalt those groups—the Amerindian, the southern European peasant, Gypsies come immediately to mind—whose life is disadvantaged and marginal to that civilization. These "under-men"—the term is from *The Lost Girl*—whose fate it is to go, or remain, down in the world, are seen as living from deeper centers, as possessing a less ravaged heritage of primitive, or archaic, or instinctive virtue than do the busy, acquisitive middle and upper classes of the "advanced" nations. At the very least, their status as outsiders and losers prevents them from suffering some forms of the corruption, moral, spiritual and psychological, to which individuals inhabiting, in E. M. Forster's well-known phrase from *Howard's End*, "the world of telegrams and anger", are constantly exposed. Yet Lawrence's view of these pariah groups falls well below idolatry. Given the right circumstances an under-man (or -woman) may misbehave as flagrantly as a stockbroker from Connecticut or a titled owner of lands and mines from Nottinghamshire. These circumstances, however, do not so often arise. The pariah groups remain fortunate in their misfortunes: lacking the fire power, mobility and world-wide communications networks of the civilization which excludes them or forces them under, they remain less damaged at the central core, less capable of doing great mischief, more in hope of saving their souls.

The notion of pariah groups transvaluated gives us one fix on Lawrence's cult of the Celt, on the considerable, continuing attraction he shows in his artistic productions and in life to characters, themes and scenes drawn from the "Celtic fringe" of Scotland, Wales, Cornwall and Ireland. It is, of course, arguable that Lawrence was wrong in seeing anything marginal or disadvantaged about the Celtic peoples in relation to modern times and specifically in relation to England. We can claim, if we like, that England, well before Lawrence's time, had settled or made accommodation with the Celts whom she had previously dominated even to the point of heavily eroding or actually suppressing their native languages, cultures and polities. Had she not entered into Acts of Union with Scotland and Ireland by the opening of the nineteenth century? Had not the Welsh in particular shown unbroken loyalty as British subjects during several centuries? If Ireland had gained partial independence from the United Kingdom through armed conflict with Britain between 1916 and 1921, had not this independence been ratified in 1922 by a legal treaty passed by parliamentary bodies from both islands? Certainly from the early eighteenth century onwards there had been numerous politicians, soldiers, businessmen, scientists and artists from the Celtic regions who made brilliant careers among the English. The English could claim, with some show of reason, to have been fair to their Celtic brethren in modern times, if not in all times, and might properly resent the aspersion that their attitude towards the fringe of "nations" half-encircling them from Scotland on the north to Cornwall in the southwest has remained superior and disparaging. And besides, have we not learned in this century that so-called Celts and Saxons are not even racially distinct, both comprising mixtures of Germanic, Scandinavian, Celtic and even more exotic strains?

All very true, but we are dealing with attitudes and their history, not with objective facts. Certain illusions about ethnic and racial differences do persist even in these enlightened times, and these illusions were much more rooted and diffused fifty to seventy years ago when Lawrence wrote. Lawrence, whose usual tactic in dealing with the racial or ethnic varieties was to stand English ethnocentrism on its head, perceived the Celt as profoundly other and was drawn to the Celtic character and characteristics, as he understood them, for that very reason.

In interpreting Celtic traits he was not operating in a vacuum, however. Consciously or not he was drawing on a view of the Celt widely disseminated in the English-speaking world by the end of the nineteenth century, but originating somewhat earlier in two immensely influential essays by the mid-nineteenth century savants, Matthew Arnold and Ernest Renan. We shall need to look into their work a little in order to understand Lawrence's perception of the Celtic character and to make out a connection between that and his presentation of women in some of his most important works.

2

Arnold's long essay, "On the Study of Celtic Literature" (1867), was shaped from two sets of lectures he delivered at Oxford earlier in the 1860s and it incorporates a number of points from Renan's essay, *Poésie des races celtiques* (1859), which was not available in English translation until 1896. By the 1890s, in the era of the Celtic Literary Revival, interest in and sympathy with Celtic subjects and sensibility were widespread among English readers. But this was scarcely the case before 1860, when the poet Tennyson talked in "In Memoriam" of "the blind hysterics of the Celt" and remarked of Ireland to his distressed Anglo-Irish admirer, William Allingham, "Couldn't they blow up that horrible island with dynamite and carry it off in pieces—a long way off?"[1]

In statecraft there was Lord Lyndhurst, whose dictum, supposedly uttered in Parliamentary debate during 1836, to the effect that the Irish — Acts of Union not withstanding — are "aliens in speech, in religion, in blood", became the popular wisdom of mid-Victorian society. And in pedagogy there was Arnold's own father, Thomas Arnold of Rugby, who was an inveterate Celt-hater, harping constantly on the utter difference between the "races":

> I remember when I was young, I was taught to think of Celt as separated by an impassable gulf from Teuton; my father in particular, was never weary of contrasting them; he insisted much oftener on the separation between us and them than on the separation between us and any other race in the world.[2]

"Teuton" here of course means Anglo-Saxon, or English, and Dr Arnold's strenuously reiterated views gain an added dimension of brutality when the information is supplied that Mrs Arnold, Matthew's mother, was a Cornishwoman.

The son's *Study*, more than any other single factor, was to change this harsh, racialist mid-Victorian climate of opinion, and it is fascinating that his interest in Celtic civilization developed in large part from a desire to explore that part of his heritage which came to him from his mother. In the late 1850s Arnold travelled to Britanny and wrote her excited letters mentioning how much he felt at home in this out-of-the-way region of misty skies, grey rock and pounding seas, and of how he kept detecting the facial features of his maternal uncles among Bretons encountered along the way. An interest in the problem of the origins of the romantic or chivalric elevation of women in medieval European literature led him to Renan, who had written on the subject, and he was delighted to discover that the great Breton historian of ancient cultures and religions held the view that the romantic cult of woman was of Celtic derivation. In carrying through the lectures and the resulting *Study* Arnold reviewed a good deal of the current ethnographic, literary and linguistic scholarship on the origins and development of early Celtic civilizations. He also broadened his knowledge of Celtic territories by several long visits to Wales and Scotland. A point frequently made about the *Study* is that it is persuasive even where the knowledge is limited, the scholarship faulty. That partly stems from Arnold's infectious enthusiasm for his subject, in part from the fundamental tactic of his argument, which is to convince the English reader that the Celtic heritage is a positive resource to draw upon, not merely an alien element to be despised and repressed.

In essence, Arnold makes three points. He shows that Celts and Saxons ("Teutons") have a common descent from Indo-European roots and that because of frequent migration and intermingling of stocks within the British Isles most of the English will possess a Celtic component in their racial makeup. This cuts the ground from under Lord Lyndhurst's "alien" aspersions but still leaves open the question of the Celtic component and what English people are to make of it. Second, he draws a profile of the Celtic temperament or character as this may be revealed in the records of early Celtic civilizations where the type may still be exhibited in some purity and isolation. Stress is laid upon the extreme emotionalism and imaginativeness of the Celt, upon the strong and close Celtic feeling for nature, and upon an abiding irrationalism. This irrationalism leads to resistance to what he calls "the tyranny of fact" and to an incapacity for self-government. It also helps to explain Celtic divisiveness and the Celts' long history of defeat and successful invasion by their enemies—the motto of the *Study* is Ossian's, "They went forth to the war, but they always fell." One other trait, melancholy, may be the result of this disastrous history, or attributable to excess of imaginativeness. Or it even may owe something to the misty, shape-changing, sea-invaded climate characteristic of the Celtic territories.

Arnold's account of these traits constantly reassures the English reader by stressing the complementary "Teutonic" traits of steadiness, gravity, respect for fact, and self-control. The dullness of the pure Saxon temperament is to be lightened and brightened by the brilliant imaginative instabilities of the Celtic temperament, but of course the Saxon element will remain the dominant and controlling one; just as, in the political sphere, the government of the Celtic territories must be conducted in perpetuity by the Westminster Parliament, expressing the sober genius of the British Constitution, with its roots in Teutonic, not Celtic tribalism.

The final point made is the one most familiar to modern readers. Here Arnold attempts to identify those qualities in English literature which are contributed by the Celtic genius and comes up with the triad of a turn for style, a turn for melancholy, and a turn for "natural magic". In answer to the query of an imaginary English reader, "Why should I put up with Celtic irrationalism?" he is answering, "Look what you get, have already gotten, along with it." Indeed, the entire argument of the *Study* is a compromise with English prejudices, yet with the hidden aim of reducing the harshness of these prejudices towards zero point. No doubt Arnold is himself prejudiced, never granting that the Celt could stand on his own base and govern himself. Drawn as he is to the magic of his mother's tradition, he continues to believe that his father's magic is stronger, more commanding. Or is it that he is, once again, "wandering between two worlds"?

3

I have been hinting, rather broadly, that there is a confusion in the mid-Victorian mind, even in a mind as liberal as Arnold's, and certainly in Tennyson's mind, between ideas of Celtic nature and of woman's nature. The English however, have no monoply on this confusion. It is already spelled out in so many words in Ernest Renan's *Poésie des races celtiques*:

> S'il était permis d'assigner un sexe aux nations commes au individus, il faudrait dire sans hésiter que la race celtique . . . est une race essentiellement féminine. Aucune famille humaine, je crois, n'a porté dans l'amour autant de mystère. Nulle autre n'a conçu avec plus de délicatesse, l'idéal de la femme et n'en été plus dominee.[3]

This comes after paragraphs devoted to the sadness and defeats of the Celts and just before remarks about their imaginative power and inwardness.

The equivalent passage in Arnold, after attributing the origin of the chivalric glorification of the feminine to "the Celtic sensibility", says:

> But putting all this question of chivalry and its origin on one side, no doubt the sensibility of the Celtic nature, its nervous exaltation, have something feminine in them, and the Celt is thus peculiarly disposed to feel the spell of the feminine idiosyncrasy; he has an affinity to it; he is not far from its secret.[4]

This is immediately followed by a description of the intimate "feeling of nature" of the Celtic temperament and of the tendency of this temperament towards the "undisciplinable, anarchical, and turbulent". It would appear, on this view, that not only is the Celt a woman but a wild woman, a Rochester's wife rather than a Jane Eyre, a hoyden rather than a lady.

We may amuse ourselves over the shortcomings of these nineteenth-century men as anthropologists and ethnologists, but the fact is that the Celt-woman equation or ratio does persist into more modern times. As late as 1927, we find Havelock Ellis writing as follows in the revised edition of his *A Study of British Genius*:[5] "Quick sensibility, again, or rapid feminine response in harmony with, or in reaction against, external stimuli, is *of all qualities* that which we most readily attribute to the Celt." He is obviously following the Renan–Arnold line but specifically takes issue with Arnold's ascription of a deep emotionalism to the Celtic nature, claiming that it shows a mere "nervous texture", an "intelligent quality of quick sensation and response". Evidently, near the end of his career the great sexologist had surrendered his belief in woman's deep emotional nature, which is so evident in the essays he wrote on Hardy's fiction in the 1880s and 1890s. Or perhaps woman is being sacrificed here in order to make a somewhat debunking point about Celtic shallowness.

Ellis's attempt to correlate woman's nature and the Celtic nature is itself shallow and stereotyped, just as the general argument of his book, about a correlation between various aspects of British "genius" and various ethnic and even regional factors, is pseudo-scientific and obscurantist. In the field of the sciences and social sciences arguments by loose analogy invalidate the very propositions they are meant to support. However, in imaginative literature the tracing of resemblances, affinities and hidden connections has an altogether different status and may lead to discoveries that have validity in their own sphere. Let us turn now to D. H. Lawrence and see how he worked the equation of woman and Celt, if it was an equation, in his work and life.

4

The treatment of Celtic themes in one part of E. M. Forster's *Howard's End* (1910)[6] will provide a way into Lawrence's fuller and more radical treatment of similar materials. So often Forster can be seen as a precursor—sometimes a faint hearted one—of Lawrentian insights and emphases. In Chapters XXV–XXVI Margaret Schlegel, now engaged to Mr Henry Wilcox, accompanies Evie Wilcox's wedding party to Oniton Grange, which the Wilcoxes own, in Shropshire on the Welsh border, where Evie plans to be married in the local church. When Margaret draws near to the Celtic regions she is described as experiencing a deep rapport with the mysterious, ever-retreating west, which is the "holder of a secret . . . no practical man will ever discover" (p. 211), and within a few more paragraphs she has revolted against the domineering Charles Wilcox's orders by leaping from a moving motor car after the vehicle has run over a cat in the road: "Charles had never been in such a position before. It was a woman in revolt who was hobbling away from him" (p. 213). Subsequently, Margaret's attraction to Oniton, a border village where "Saxon" and "Kelt" confront each other, grows apace and she plans to make her home there after being married to Henry. The Welsh West is represented in fairly standard Celtic Revival terms as the crepuscular abode of faery, and of Druidic mysteries, while the English side is all motor cars, money, and cosmopolitan chatter. Unfortunately, after the unsettling, ill-timed arrival on the scene of her sister Helen, accompanied by the dishevelled Bast couple, Margaret loses her nerve and decides that the hectoring, bossy Saxon men, such as the Wilcoxes, father and son, know best and should rule. She abandons her enthusiasm for Oniton with the following, somewhat self-deprecating reflections:

> Oniton, like herself, was imperfect. Its apple-trees were stunted, its castle ruinous. It, too, had suffered in the border warfare between the Anglo-Saxon and the Kelt, between things as they are and as they ought to be. Once more the west was retreating, once again the orderly stars were dotting the eastern sky.
>
> (p. 231)

The orderly Saxon stars appear to have been borrowed from a famous sonnet by the half-Welsh George Meredith, who had his own problems in sorting out the ethnic components and influences in his makeup and left his last novel, *Celt or Saxon*, unfinished, but the defeatism is pure Forster. He brings his character to a boundary beyond which lies an immense, mysterious promise, but since that promise entails self-assertive revolt and is associated with a potential for suffering and ruin, the signal is given to go back, the order of the day becoming, "Let the men take charge."

Lawrence is characteristically bolder and more extreme. When his woman characters turn west, they go farther and deeper, and there is no turning back. Consider the ending of *The Fox*. After Banford's death, March marries Cornish Henry and "they went to Cornwall, to his own village, on the sea" (p. 211).[7] There, facing west, March submits to a curious, sinister, rather pitiful breaking down and emptying out process. It is called "the realisation of emptiness" (p. 222) and we are reminded that in Lawrence's correspondence, from Cornwall in 1916 and in a single letter from Inverness in Scotland in 1926, Lawrence consistently stresses and glories in the emptiness, barrenness and archaism of Celtic places, their remoteness from what he calls "the made world", the special opportunities they provide for new starts. The following, written to Katherine Mansfield on 7 January 1916, is typical and is echoed in several other letters of that time written to correspondents as diverse as J. D. Beresford, Ottoline Morrell and Middleton Murry:

> I love being here in Cornwall—so peaceful, so far off from the world. But the world has disappeared forever—there is no more world anymore: only here, and a fine, thin air which nobody and nothing pollutes . . . The world is gone, extinguished like the lights of last night's Café Royal—gone forever. There is a new world with a new thin unsullied air and no people in it but new-born people: *moi-même et* Frieda.[8]

Many readers object to Henry Grenfel's apparent dominance over March at the end of *The Fox* but I think a more adequate reading would be to see Henry as a piece of embodied Celtic nature, essential to March but not really in control of her as she searches down to the bedrock of her nature, becoming "deanglicized" and "empty" in the process. In a global world there are wests beyond wests, beginnings beyond endings, a new, self-liberating movement beyond the stilled "under-sea" experience of the early weeks of the marriage:

> yet there, sitting in a niche of the high wild cliffs of West Cornwall, looking over the westward sea, she stretched her eyes wider and wider. Away to the West, Canada, America . . .
>
> (p. 223)

At certain points Lawrence's treatment of the Celt-woman link may seem somewhat self-contradictory, but on closer inspection these contradictions tend to resolve themselves. For instance, in his reflective and critical writing he invariably has high praise for the Scottish poet, Robert Burns, remarking that with the Elizabethans a rupture in human consciousness was initiated, "the mental consciousness recoiling in violence away from the physical, instinctive, intuitive", and that this "physical consciousness", on which Lawrence evidently places the highest value, gives "a last song in Burns" before dying out.[9] On the other hand, Lawrence has little use for Jane Austen, whom he consistently interprets as a novelist operating exclusively on the basis of the "mental consciousness" which is so dominant in modern civilization, and which is making us all sick and miserable. However, in this account the fact that Jane Austen is a woman is incidental, not essential. The more important thing is that Burns, inhabiting a pastoral Celtic remoteness, was able to keep "physical consciousness", which probably means an unbroken connection or circuit between the conceiving mind and the deep life instincts, alive for a little longer than any English writer, male or female. The mysterious promise of the Celtic territories, a promise to which the women characters in Lawrence are particularly alive, continues to beckon.

Other difficulties may arise when we consider that two women characters in important Lawrence narratives—Captain Hepburn's Irish wife in *The Captain's Doll* and the Scottish Dolly Urquhart in *The Princess*—are simultaneously Celtic in background and yet represented as sick unto death of the diseases bred in the soul by civilization and its dominant mode of consciousness. But there is really no problem. Both these characters exhibit feyness, that unfortunate airy-fairy pseudo-Celtic trait invented and publicized by Celtic Revival writers of the third and fourth rank, and deserve the fates they come to. In *The Captain's Doll* it is Hepburn himself, who is in profound revolt against contemporary civilization, especially against its habit of analytical thought and language, who carries the deep Celtic values, and with whom young Hannele must come to terms if she is to escape the staleness and stasis of the fag-end Hapsburg tradition of Central Europe epitomized by her elderly fiancé, the Herr Regierungsrat.

It appears that whenever we examine the Celt-woman link in Lawrence we find associated with it the notion of rebellion and of removal from the European and industrialized world, for even Captain Hepburn plans to remove from Austria and refocus his moon telescope from the vantage point of an African astronomical observatory. In these terms, Kate Leslie in *The Plumed Serpent* must represent a culmination, since she is Irish, has been married to an Irish revolutionary and departs Europe to become a co-conspirator in a subversive native Mexican movement of revolt which intends to topple the European-style Mexican democracy and to replace the European-introduced worship of Christ and his mother with a restored pantheon of the old Aztec gods and goddesses. That is true, only *The Plumed Serpent* is scarcely a culmination in terms of Lawrence's art. Let us conclude this essay with some consideration of *St Mawr*, a work wholly satisfying as art as well as deeply implicated with Lawrence's theme of woman and the Celt.

5

St Mawr[10] (1925) is probably the stoutest blow Lawrence ever struck for woman's liberation, and it is interesting that the women in the case, the south-western American, Mrs Witt, and her daughter, Lou Carrington, are prepared for liberation—schooled as it were—mainly by the influence of a killer stallion from the Welsh borders and a small, black-bearded Welsh groom who attends him. The essence of the lesson learned is refusal. St Mawr refuses to be a steady, reliable riding horse, suitable for outings in Hyde Park's Rotten Row, refuses to service mares at stud, and precipitates the crisis of the story by refusing to pass by a viper in the path. Lewis the groom is also skilled in negation, refusing to take much notice of the fashionable London world into which he has been displaced, along with the horse, and even refusing an impulsive offer of marriage from the widowed Mrs Witt during the enchanting ride they take together, off the roads and across England from Shropshire near Wales to a place near Oxford.

The lesson is remarkably well learned, the women eventually outstripping their mentors at the art of refusal. First English society and Lou's social-climbing, anglicized Australian husband, Rico, are given the go-by. Then, after Lewis and St Mawr are dropped off at Mrs Witt's Texas ranch, left behind to cut a figure among the cowboys and quarter horses, mother and daughter go farther west into the mountains of northern New Mexico. All contact with men is left behind after Lou repudiates her Indian-Mexican servant Phoenix's unspoken but pressing sexual overtures. This turn towards feminine celibacy may be something of a relief for Mrs Witt, who has had quite a sexual run, in and out of marriage, but it entails a real sacrifice for Lou Carrington, who is young and beautiful and not used to being alone. Yet she will remain alone on the little goat ranch in the high mountains, facing west, gone all the way west in her attitudes, a new kind of Vestal, tending a flame which was lighted when she first saw St Mawr's head—

> looming like some god out of the darkness, with the wide, terrible, questioning eyes. And she felt it forbade her to be her

ordinary, commonplace self. It forbade her to be just Rico's wife, young Lady Carrington.

(p.14)

She will remain celibate until a man appears "in whom Pan hadn't fallen" (p. 47), who isn't to her "third eye . . . a sort of pancake" (p. 47). If no such man appears she will make do with "the unseen Gods . . . the hidden fire" (p. 128) immanent in the high American wilderness.

St Mawr and Lewis between them express that root concept of "physical consciousness" which Lawrence celebrated in his praise of the poet Burns. He is thorough in his scheme of transvaluation, for what is, at bottom, a principle of spiritual authority operates in heavy disguise, wearing the masks of a servile groom and an impotent horse of panic habit. We may be reminded a little of ancient epic, where gods and goddesses speak in the guise of old serving women, or take the shape of animals and other natural phenomena when they wish to exert force upon human affairs.

Should we want to rate the stallion for his Celtic attributes we might cite in addition to his name and place of origin his red-gold color, which seems somehow ur-Celtic, his temperament, which fits rather closely Arnold's "undisciplinable, anarchical, and turbulent", and Lady Carrington's puzzlement—so often a feature in the history of Anglo-Saxon dealings with Celts—over whether St Mawr's episodes of violence proceed from the meanness of a slave or from "the natural wild thing in him" (p. 69). But where St Mawr really comes into his Celtic own is at the scene of Rico's accident.

Recalling the Oniton chapter of *Howard's End* it is staged in Shropshire, within a few miles of the Welsh border, at a spot where "the spirit of aboriginal England still lingers, the old savage England, whose last blood flows still in a few Englishmen, Welshmen, Cornishmen" (p. 59). The stallion rears when Rico attempts to spur him past a snake which his own instinct tells him to be dangerous. Rico's modern "English" mind set, his will to dominate, his inability to surrender or loosen the reins of his control cause the horse to topple backwards upon the rider, and Rico is considerably injured. The event takes its place in the long long history of English–Celtic border incidents. Even the aftermath has somehow a familiar ring to it: St Mawr is to be gelded, as compensation for the injuries received by Rico and another young

Englishman who was kicked in the face while reaching for the reins. Only the horse escapes this fate, through the connivance of Mrs Witt and her daughter, who feel a deep complicity with St Mawr's nature and behavior.

Lewis the groom is not unlike St Mawr in that initially he is viewed, by Mrs Witt in particular, as mindless and servile, an under-man and not a real man, at best to be paired with Phoenix as victims of racial dispossession:

> both enemies in the great white camp, disguised as servants, waiting the incalculable opportunity. What the opportunity might be, none knew.
>
> (p. 82)

But on the long ride he emerges as Mrs Witt's match, with his cool self-possession and entertaining nonsense about Druidic tree spirits and moon creatures. Perhaps he is more than her match when he refuses to marry her. He has, however, no intention of vaunting over her, for his reasons in refusing are both self-respecting and respectful.

Is there any conclusion to be drawn from the foregoing? Just an obvious one: over a substantial period of historical time Celts and women had in common, along with many other groups in the world, particularly the poor everywhere, the sharing of a servile and inferior condition. Abolish this condition, create full equality for all, and the connection ends. It does not seem paradoxical to claim that Lawrence, in perceiving and working with the Celt-woman link, was working for women's liberation and the liberation of all from the fettered past.

NOTES

1 Quoted in *William Allingham*, by Alan Warner (London, 1975), p. 68. Allingham also heard Tennyson splutter at the dinner table, on an unspecified date, "The Kelts are so utterly unreasonable! . . . The Kelt rages and shrieks and tears everything to pieces!" Also on p. 68.
2 "On the Study of Celtic Literature", *The Complete Prose Works of Matthew Arnold*, ed. R. H. Super (1962), III, 299–300.
3 The same, p. 508. Quoted in the "Critical and Explanatory Notes".
4 The same, p. 347.

5   London: Constable. All quotations are from p. 214.

6   All quotations are from the New York: Vintage Books Edition, which is undated.

7   All quotations for *The Fox* are from the first American edition: *The Captain's Doll, The Fox, The Ladybird* (New York, 1923).

8   *The Collected Letters of D. H. Lawrence*, ed. Harry T. Moore (New York, 1962), I, 410.

9   From "Introduction to These Paintings", *Phoenix: the Posthumous Papers of D. H. Lawrence*, ed. E. D. McDonald (New York, 1936), p. 552. See also the treatment of Burns in "Pornography and Obscenity", *Phoenix*, p. 181.

10 All quotations for *St Mawr* are from the Heinemann edition, London, 1930.

6

Eros and Death (Lawrence, Freud and Women)

by PHILIPPA TRISTRAM

When Anna and Will are married in *The Rainbow*, Tom Brangwen, Anna's stepfather, "wanted to make a speech":

> For the first time in his life, he must spread himself wordily.
>
> "Marriage," he began, his eyes twinkling and yet quite profound, for he was deeply serious and hugely amused at the same time, "Marriage," he said, speaking in the slow, full-mouthed way of the Brangwens, "is what we're made for—"
>
> "Let him talk," said Alfred Brangwen, slowly and inscrutably, "let him talk." Mrs Alfred darted indignant eyes at her husband.
>
> "A man," continued Tom Brangwen, "enjoys being a man: for what purpose was he made a man, if not to enjoy it?"
>
> "That's a true word," said Frank, floridly.
>
> "And likewise," continued Tom Brangwen, "a woman enjoys being a woman: at least we surmise she does—"
>
> "Oh, don't you bother—" called a farmer's wife.
>
> "You may back your life they'd be summisin'," said Frank's wife.
>
> "Now," continued Tom Brangwen, "for a man to be a man, it takes a woman—"
>
> "It does that," said a woman grimly.
>
> "And for a woman to be a woman, it takes a *man*—" continued Tom Brangwen.
>
> "All speak up, men," chimed in a feminine voice.
>
> "Therefore we have marriage," continued Tom Brangwen.
>
> (p. 127)

On similar occasions every reader must have sat uneasily through such wordy paternal spreadings and wished them well over. Al-

though Lawrence despised "the old stable *ego* of the character",
few novelists can capture with more precision the essence of the
everyday. But the scene does not rest at observation merely:
Lawrence, as Hueffer remarked, is an "investigator into the bases
of the normal".[1] That episode engenders much more than an all-
too-familiar discomfort: it is a drama in little of the tensions, the
uneasy compacts, between the sexes. The assurance of the men,
so firmly rooted in their masculinity, is evident; a man clearly
enjoys being a man. But do the women equally enjoy being women,
as Tom "surmises"? Their comments are oblique and barbed,
answering not to their own sense of themselves, but to men's view
of them.

In writing on Lawrence's treatment of women, I do not, like
Kate Millett, want to attack him as "a counter-revolutionary sexual
politician"; equally, I do not want to affirm with Mailer that he
"understood women as they had never been understood before".[2]
One could adopt either position, at different times and on different
levels of his work; that scene could itself be engaged in both
causes. My own feelings about Lawrence are divided, both admir-
tion and anger finding their focus in his attitude—or rather attitudes—to women. I admire deeply the observer's insight in the
first two generations of *The Rainbow*, which penetrates beneath
the "stable *ego*" of Lydia and Anna to the instabilities, the flux
and the profound continuities of life. I grow uneasy with the
Ursula of the third generation, and positively angry with the two
sisters in *Women in Love*—though that novel has often been
acclaimed as his greatest work. There the observer's distance is
abandoned: "I don't so much care about what the woman *feels*—"
Lawrence writes to Garnett in 1914, "I only care about what the
woman *is*—what she IS—inhumanly, physiologically, materially."
This anatomizer, vivisectionist, is a kind of Frankenstein, who
creates in that novel the woman he does not find in life; and then,
understandably recoiling from his creature, seeks to destroy it.
"Your hatred of me," he writes to Cecil Gray in 1917–18, "like
Frieda's hatred of me, is your cleavage to a world of knowledge
and being which you ought to forsake." His women (those of the
novels) "though in a cringing, bad fashion . . . represent none the
less the threshold of a new world, or underworld, of knowledge
and being . . . like Magdalene at her feet-washing." It may be no
exaggeration to say that the "bad fashion" of those Magdalenes

ultimately sickened Lawrence. I admire, more than most readers appear to have done, the power and scope of his subsequent novel, *Aaron's Rod*, where the "surmising" is at an end, the woman and the marriage both abandoned, and Aaron goes out to wrestle with the singleness of his own nature.

From his first novel to his last, Lawrence is of course deeply concerned, in varying modes and degrees, with sexual relationships. But that sequence of three novels—*The Rainbow, Women in Love, Aaron's Rod*—seems a central focus.[3] *The Rainbow* is first drafted March–June 1913; *Women in Love* April–June 1916; *Aaron's Rod* is begun in December 1917, but the first draft is not completed until September 1919. *The Rainbow* is therefore substantially a pre-war novel, *Women in Love* a war experience; whilst *Aaron's Rod* is an aftermath of war. These years also coincide with Lawrence's interest in Freud, though they are not quite co-extensive with it. Lawrence was first introduced to Freud's ideas by Frieda in 1912, in time for those ideas to influence the final version of *Sons and Lovers*. His knowledge of Freud was largely at second-hand, though in 1914 he became acquainted with some professional Freudians. Between December 1919 and July 1921 he made his peace with psycho-analysis—by declaring war upon it in the two tracts, *Psychoanalysis and the Unconscious, Fantasia of the Unconscious*.[4]

Lawrence resented Freud's "adventure into the hinterland of the human consciousness" more, perhaps, because an explorer does not like to feel that his journey has been anticipated, than because, as Frieda alleged, their maps were different. The overt argument was, however, based upon that difference. "In attributing a sexual motive to all human experience," psychoananlysis, Lawrence contended, was "out, under a therapeutic disguise, to do away entirely with the moral faculty in man." In the later *Fantasia*, Lawrence modified his position slightly:

> We are thankful that Freud pulled us somewhat to earth, out of all our clouds of superfineness. What Freud says is always partly true. And half a loaf is better than no bread.
> But really, there is the other half of the loaf. All is *not* sex.
>
> (p. 11)

It is possibly an impatience to get on with that search for the other half of the loaf which leads Lawrence to assail his female characters in *Women in Love*; it is clearly Aaron's goal in the subsequent novel. Lawrence died in 1930; Freud's *Future of an Illusion* and *Civilization and its Discontents*, published in 1927 and 1930 respectively, came too late to modify his opinions. Had he lived longer, he might well have felt that Freud, in the aftermath of one war and the approaching shadow of another, was mapping a territory more extensive and familiar than he had at first supposed. But quite likely Lawrence would have continued to resent that coincidence. Where Freud sought to know, Lawrence sought to be. Where Freud felt that men needed to bring the forms which moved in darkness into the light of consciousness, Lawrence was convinced that they must "forsake that world of knowledge", and discover their true being in "pristine unconsciousness":

> Long ago we watched in frightened anticipation when Freud set out on his adventure into the hinterland of human consciousness. He was seeking for the unknown sources of the mysterious stream of consciousness. Immortal phrase of the immortal James! Oh stream of hell which undermined my adolescence! I felt it streaming through my brain, in at one ear and out at the other. . . . Horrid stream!
>
> (*Psych. & Unc.*, p. 199)

Where Lawrence fought the cerebration of psychoanalysis as the enemy, Freud always allowed that the experience of literature had anticipated him, and more fully. He concluded his tentative lecture on "Femininity" by observing: "If you want to know more about femininity, enquire from your own experiences of life, or turn to the poets."[5] Since criticism, at least, is cerebral, it seems not unfair to redress the balance a little by allowing Freud's own observations to illuminate Lawrence's novels on occasion.

It is doubtful, however, that Freud can throw much light upon the early *Rainbow*; which is to say that Lawrence, in the first two generations of Brangwens, needs no expositor. The delightful early work of Freud's, *The Psychopathology of Everyday Life*, might offer some clues to *The Rainbow*, but their use would be limited. Where Freud speculates, say, on the breaking of an inkstand, Lawrence's insight into such insignificant everyday events has an unstated significance. During Anna's childhood, for example, it emerges that on market days Tom Brangwen "loved buying things, odd things that he thought would be useful". On Anna's betrothal to Will, Tom "suffered agony . . . Oh, he was ashamed. He trampled himself to extinguish himself." He makes his peace with "odd things", abetting Anna's nesting:

> With more particular thought [than Will he] spied out what he called handy little things for her. He appeared with a set of new-fangled cooking-pans, with a special sort of hanging-lamp, though the rooms were so low, with canny little machines for grinding meat or mashing potatoes or whisking eggs. . . . On market days there was always a long thrill of anticipation.
>
> (pp. 120–21)

This is the Lawrence of a letter of 1913:

> I got the blues thinking of the future, so I left off and made some marmalade. It's amazing how it cheers one up to shred oranges or scrub the floor.

At another extreme, Tom's gifts of "odd things" express, without stating, much that Freud perceived of the relations between daughters, fathers and husbands.

At this period in his writing, Lawrence made actual women his study. He would ask the women he knew to write down what they felt in certain situations, and he would use their accounts as source material for his novels.[6] "The great living experience for every man is his adventure into the woman," Lawrence wrote to Russell in 1915. "The man embraces in the woman all that is not himself." That experience of sexual otherness is finely captured in *The Rainbow*, when Tom observes Lydia, unaware with her child, through the bright kitchen window at the vicarage:

> The wind boomed strongly. Mother and child sat motionless, silent, the child staring with vacant dark eyes into the fire, the mother looking into space. The little girl was almost asleep. It was her will which kept her eyes so wide.
>
> (pp. 35–6)

Lawrence marvellously understood the distinct nature of maternal love. Its "visceral" characteristics are finely delineated in *Psychoanalysis and the Unconscious*:

> Child and mother have, in the first place, no objective consciousness of each other, and certainly no *idea* of each other. Each is a blind desideratum to the other. The strong love between them is effectual in the great abdominal centres, where all love, real love, is primarily based.
>
> (p. 227)

Freud might have agreed. Certainly he asserts the sexual nature of maternal love, as against " 'pure' love" ("ideal behaviour", "love in the head" as Lawrence would say), and defends the former as Lawrence does: the mother "is only fulfilling her task in teaching the child to love".[7]

In the Foreword to *Fantasia*, Lawrence writes: "I do not believe in evolution, but in the strangeness and rainbow-change of ever-renewed creative civilizations." For the early *Rainbow* itself, one might substitute the word "relationships" for "civilizations". No theory, or need, or willed conclusion imposes itself on the relationships of Tom and Lydia, Will and Anna:

> All things about her had become intimate, she had known them near and lovely, like presences hovering upon her. What if they should all go hard and separate again, standing back from her terrible and distinct, and she, having known them, should be at their mercy?
>
> (p. 158)

Intimate, separate; complements, opposites; now lovers, now enemies—the relationships of men and women answer to a rhythm beyond their comprehension. If Freud and Lawrence both asked the question—was femininity created in nature, or made in culture —then the early *Rainbow* seems to answer: created in nature.

Ursula's story, in the later *Rainbow*, is, however, a different matter. Throughout the novel Lawrence writes at a level other than that of the conscious mind; yet in the earlier, stable world of the first two generations, the movement between cerebral and "visceral" convictions, between articulacy and the inarticulable, is scarcely perceptible, save as a recurrent rhythm. In *Psychoanalysis and the Unconscious*, Lawrence writes:

> The term *unconscious* is only another word for life. But life is a general force, whereas the unconscious is essentially single and unique in each individual organism; it is the active, self-evolving soul bringing forth its own incarnation and self-manifestation. . . . And consciousness is like a web woven finally in the mind from the various silken strands spun forth from the primal centre of the unconscious.
>
> (p. 241)

These sentences finely express the process of the early *Rainbow*. Things "may go hard and separate" in Anna's environment, but they may equally return to intimacy, "near and lovely"; in the worlds of Cossethay and the Marsh Farm, the soul is enabled to evolve, to incarnate and manifest itself. But Anna's daughter enters upon that wider world which her forebears only glimpsed distantly, and the abrasive environment of the "man's world" of Brinsley Street School leaves her at the mercy of things incurably hard and separate. Bereft of a context that nurtures personal life, neither Ursula nor Lawrence can achieve that finely woven, silken web of consciousness. The final sequence in which Ursula encounters the horses calls for the kind of exposition and comment which Freud offers in his case history of little Hans.

This process, both in the writing and in the heroine, is continued in *Women in Love*, for, where *The Rainbow* is rooted in nature, its successor is deracinated in culture. It is not only that the generations of Brangwens move out from the inarticulate, instinctual life of the Marsh Farm, into the over-articulate, moribund culture of London and Europe: one must not forget that *Women in Love* is a war book. If *The Rainbow* was banned as pornography because of Lawrence's attitude to war rather than to sex, as has been claimed, one might also suspect that his engagement in its successor was with war rather than women. In the Foreword to *Women in Love* Lawrence himself asserts:

> It is a novel which took its final shape in the midst of a period of war, though it does not concern the war itself. I should wish the time to remain unfixed, so that the bitterness of the war may be taken for granted in the characters.

The reminder is timely. Freud's words in *Civilization and its Discontents*, written at a later date but in recoil from the same experience, might form an epigraph for *Women in Love*:

> The meaning of the evolution of civilization is no longer obscure to us. It must present the struggle between Eros and Death, between the instinct of life and the instinct of destruction, as it works itself out in the human species.[8]

He glosses this statement in 1932, in his open letter to Einstein, "Why War?":

> Neither of these instincts is any less essential than the other; the phenomena of life arise from the concurrent or mutually opposing action of both.[9]

These statements will be taken into the novel shortly; at the moment it is only necessary to observe that Eros, in *Women in*

Love, is strictly male, and Death female. Even the novel's most fervent admirers, like Dr Leavis, have demurred at the phallic insistence of its prose:

> With perfect fine finger-tips of reality she would touch the reality in him, the suave, pure, untranslatable reality of his loins of darkness. To touch, mindlessly in darkness to come in pure touching upon the living reality of him, his suave perfect loins and thighs of darkness, this was her sustaining anticipation.
>
> (p. 311)

Leavis's comment on a related passage formulates this characteristic weakness:

> In these places Lawrence betrays by an insistent and overemphatic explicitness, running at times to something one can only call jargon, that he is uncertain—uncertain of the value of what he offers; uncertain whether he really holds it—whether a valid communication has really been defined and conveyed in terms of his creative art.[10]

But one might also observe that the loins, which figure so insistently in the prose, are always male. His women do not have them. They have stockings.

Such stockings—and in all colours! On the second page Gudrun's are "emerald-green", and they cause comment amongst the "common people" at the church door: " 'What price the stockings!' " Gudrun "would have liked them all annihilated, cleared away, so that the world was left clear for her." Hermione wisely sticks to "brownish-grey" on the same occasion, and Gudrun, perhaps in response, confines herself to "dark green" when she visits Breadalby. But in the "coal dust" of home, the sisters flame out again:

> Ursula had an orange coloured knitted coat, Gudrun a pale yellow. Ursula wore canary yellow stockings, Gudrun bright rose.

A young miner assesses " 'her with the red stockings' " as worth a " 'week's wages for five minutes' ", and on this occasion Gudrun merely "loathes" these "sinister creatures". But even her father feels her garments call for comment when she dons "pink silk stockings" for the water-party, to set off her black, pink and yellow clothing: " 'Don't you think you might as well get yourself up for a Christmas cracker, an' ha' done with it?' " It seems significant that at the Pompadour, when Gudrun makes her gesture on Lawrence's behalf, her stockings should be merely "silver-grey", whereas scarlet and royal blue, each time in contrast with her skirt, become a positive uniform for her confrontations with Gerald, which lead ultimately to his destruction.[11] It also seems significant that, before the sisters part, Gudrun, with sacramental intensity, confers stockings on Ursula:

> Gudrun came to Ursula's bedroom with three pairs of the coloured stockings for which she was notorious, and she threw them on the bed. But these were thick silk stockings, vermilion, cornflower blue, and grey, bought in Paris. The grey ones were knitted, seamless and heavy. Ursula was in raptures. She knew Gudrun must be feeling *very* loving, to give away such treasures.
>
> "I can't take them from you, Prune," she cried. "I can't possibly deprive you of them—the jewels."
>
> "*Aren't* they jewels!" cried Gudrun, eyeing her gifts with an envious eye. "*Aren't* they real lambs!"
>
> "Yes, you *must* keep them," said Ursula.
>
> "I don't *want* them, I've got three more pairs. I *want* you to keep them—I want you to have them. They're yours, there—"
>
> And with trembling, excited hands she put the coveted stockings under Ursula's pillow.
>
> "One does get the greatest joy of all out of really lovely stockings," said Ursula.
>
> "One does," replied Gudrun; "the greatest joy of all."
>
> (pp. 427–8)

" 'Jewels?' " " 'Lambs?' " " 'The greatest joy of all?' " One cannot help feeling that stockings, like loins, are receiving undue emphasis. The "over-explicitness" which Leavis notes seems produced by a need to assert a significance which Lawrence cannot fully account for. One might suggest, in Freud's terms, that, where male loins emphasize the neglected Eros, female stockings repudiate carnality and the instinct for life; they allure men to an embrace which will destroy them. That assured movement in the early *Rainbow* between the self and the world which encompasses it, enables the expression of unconscious states without their rationalization. But in *Women in Love* that expressiveness has gone, because the realities of the external world have simply collapsed; in "the bitterness of war" everyday objects assume a distorted significance.

One has only to recall Anna's nesting with Tom's "odd things" in *The Rainbow*, and then to consider the corresponding chapter, "A Chair", in *Women in Love*, where Ursula and Birkin determine that they will *not* nest. The chair itself recalls a past which can no longer exist, as Birkin remarks:

> "When I see that clear, beautiful chair, and I think of England, even Jane Austen's England—it had living thoughts to unfold even then, and pure happiness in unfolding them. And now, we can only fish among the rubbish-heaps for the remnants of their old expression. There is no production in us now, only sordid and foul mechanicalness."
>
> (p. 347)

Ursula protests against Birkin's nostalgia for the past, but wishes that the chair " 'had been smashed up when its day was over' ". She is " 'sick of the beloved past' ", but, as Birkin retorts, " 'not so sick as I am of the accursed present' ". The egg whisks, potato mashers and meat grinders of *The Rainbow* were still, one may remember, "canny little machines", not " 'foul mechanicalness' ". They can be humanized as offerings by the inarticulate Tom to the daughter he once loved and was ashamed, in her marriage, to hate. The chair is a symbol, which Ursula wants to destroy, and Birkin to decline. In the end they give it away to a "common" couple, forcibly betrothed in the old mode because the woman is pregnant. " '*I* won't aid and abet them in it,' " Birkin demurs. " 'Oh yes,' cried Ursula. 'It's right for them—there's nothing else for them.' "

" 'There's nothing else for them.' " The phrase should be allowed to reverberate a little. From its first page, *Women in Love* presents the desolation after the cataclysm, the battlefield strewn with the wreckage of a former order. The old containing continuities and securities of *The Rainbow* are gone: neither sister wishes to marry or bear children, regarding a domestic destiny as " ' the end of experience' ". The unenlightened may continue to mate and breed because there is nothing else for them; but is there, in this desolate world, any more for the enlightened? *Women in Love* pursues that question down a cul-de-sac, and predictably arrives at no conclusion.

For Lawrence, the "front line" existed in art. "After all," he writes to Garnett in 1914, "this is the real fighting line, not where soldiers pull triggers." If he claimed at that time to Harriet Monroe, "I am much too valuable a creature to offer myself to a Ger-

man bullet gratis and for fun", he was willing to expose himself
to the bullets of public opinion in his writing:

> It is the business of the artist to follow the war to the heart of
> the individual fighters—not to talk in armies and nations and
> numbers—but to track it home—home—their war—and it's at
> the bottom of every Englishman's heart—the war—the desire
> for war—the *will* to war—and at the bottom of every German
> heart.

As his letter to Einstein shows, Freud would have agreed: if life
were produced by an incessant struggle between Eros and Death,
then no League of Nations could put an end to conflict. The
malaise of a civilization is continuous with the malaise of a relationship, or, as Lawrence was later to think, of an individual. But
in *Women in Love* the battle between Eros and Death is polarized
into male and female. Men possess the instinct for life; women the
instinct for destruction.

It is not difficult to glimpse this paradigm in Gerald and Gudrun, or to foresee its outcome in Gerald's death. From the moment
of their meeting, the Eros in Gerald's "fair sun-tanned type" is
prospectively frozen. "In his clear northern flesh and his fair hair
was a glisten like sunshine refracted through crystals of ice." He is
"pure as an arctic thing." " 'Is there really some pale gold, arctic
light that envelopes only us two?' " Gudrun speculates. Gerald has
traded his instinct for life for "foul mechanicalness"; he is the
murderee who, in Birkin's view, invites his murderer. When Gudrun flashes her stockings at him, he reacts—the cliché is unvoid-
able—like a bull to a red rag:

> Her fingers had him under their power. The fathomless, fathomless
> desire they could evoke in him was deeper than death, where he
> had no choice.
>
> (p. 324)

In this kinship of the corrupt there is little to choose, except that
Gerald has a chance and Gudrun doesn't.

Ursula, though another modern woman "nerve-worn with consciousness", has other possibilities. She is not entirely a creature
of destruction: after an impulse to destroy it, she gives the
chair away; she wishes that Gerald would spare his mare, when
Gudrun cries "in a strange, high voice, like a gull, or like a witch
screaming out from the side of the road: 'I should think you're

proud.' " But if Ursula is not to be a destroyer, the woman in her must be mastered, as Birkin warns her:

> "And woman is the same as horses: two wills act in opposition inside her. With one will, she wants to subject herself utterly. With the other she wants to bolt, and pitch her rider to perdition."
>
> (p. 132)

Undeterred by Birkin's assurance that subjection is " 'the last, perhaps highest, love-impulse: resign your will to the higher being' ", Ursula, at this stage, elects to bolt. But later, despite occasional spurts of resistance, she allows Birkin to school her in his image of womanhood. His programme is graphically outlined in *Fantasia*:

> Let her learn the domestic arts in their perfection. Let us even artificially set her to spin and weave. Anything to keep her busy, to prevent her reading and becoming self-conscious.
>
> (p. 83)

> Make her yield to her own real unconscious self, and absolutely stamp on the self she's got in her head. Drive her forcibly back, back into her own true unconsciousness.
>
> (p. 188)

> When once she . . . knows that the loneliness of waiting and following is inevitable, that it must be so; ah, then how wonderful it is! How wonderful it is to come back to her, at evening, as she sits half in fear and waits! How good it is when the night falls! How richly the evening passes!
>
> (p. 190)

Those statements have an all-too-familiar ring.

"The chief clue to *Women in Love*," John Murry wrote, is "the endeavour to force upon the woman a sexual or sensual homage to the man." It is *a* clue certainly, but Murry's explanation of this "endeavour" seems rather less certain: Lawrence, he claims, is a covert homosexual, whose "loathing for women only grew with the years". In consequence he argues that "*The Rainbow* is, radically, the history of Lawrence's final sexual failure."[12] I certainly do not share that suspicion of *The Rainbow*, nor do I think his view of *Women in Love* more than partially true. One might recall Freud at this point: "In all of us, throughout life, the libido normally oscillates between male and female objects."[13] It is true that Lawrence will not permit that oscillation in women: Ursula's relationship with Winifred Inger in *The Rainbow* is clearly debased in "foul mechanicalness"; where the chapter "Man to Man" in *Women in Love*, is centred upon the true affections of Gerald and Birkin, "Woman to Woman" focuses the animosities of Ursula and Hermione. It is rather *because* the women in the novel come to personify the instinct of destruction, that Birkin's need for Gerald, and Gerald's for him, is only the instinct of life in another guise. " 'He should have loved me,' " Birkin says of the dead Gerald, looking at Ursula "with dark, almost vengeful eyes." Ursula, the destroyer, retorts:

> "What difference would it have made!"
> "It would!" he said. "It would."

It is also clear that, for the moment at least, that search for the other half of the loaf which is *not* sex, has failed. The novel ends with Ursula disputing:

> "You can't have two kinds of love. Why should you!"
> "It seems as if I can't," he said. "Yet I wanted it."
> "You can't have it, because it's false, impossible," she said.
> "I don't believe that," he answered.

It is not necessary, however, to believe that this other impulse is simply another kind of love, for a man. That is not centrally what Birkin needs to draw him from a dead world into life again. The emphasis is not upon alternative relationships; it is upon singleness. Thus Birkin rebukes Ursula:

> "I don't want love, . . . I don't want to know you. I want to be gone out of myself, and you to be lost to yourself, so we are found different."
>
> (p. 179)

To Gerald he makes a similar proposal: " 'An impersonal union that leaves one free.' " (p. 199). Between these two proposals, he reflects:

> Sex is subordinate, but perfectly polarized. Each has a single, separate being, with its own laws.
>
> (p. 193)

When he wrote *Women in Love*, woman, or indeed man, was for Lawrence the way back from "knowing" into "being" oneself, a ground for complaint in Ursula's view of Birkin:

He said the individual was *more* than love, or than any relationship. For him, the bright, single soul accepted love as one of its
conditions, a condition of its own equilibrium.

(p. 258)

Woman is thus no more than the way back from consciousness, as
she was the way into it: "She is the door for our in-going and
our out-coming. In her we go back to the Father . . . blind and
unconscious."

It is not surprising that the door should so often seem to slam
in Birkin's face, or that he, and Lawrence too, should have become impatient with their uncooperative creations. If women will
not facilitate the search, they necessarily impede it. It is true that
Birkin wishes Ursula to achieve "a single, separate being" as well;
but a return to *Fantasia* suggests she had grounds for hesitation:

> Once man vacates his camp of sincere, passionate positivity in
> disinterested being, his supreme responsibility to fulfil his own
> profoundest impulses, with reference to none but God or his own
> soul, not taking woman into count at all, in this primary respon-
> sibility of his own deepest soul; once man vacates this strong
> citadel of his own genuine, not spurious, divinity, then in comes
> woman, picks up the sceptre and begins to conduct a rag-time
> band. . . .
> Of course there should be a great balance between the sexes.
> Man, in the daytime, must follow his own soul's greatest impulse,
> and give himself to life-work and risk himself to death. It is not
> woman who claims the highest in man. It is man's own religious
> soul that drives him on beyond woman, to his supreme activity.
> For his highest, man is responsible to God alone. He may not
> pause to remember that he has a life to lose, or a wife and chil-
> dren to leave. He must carry forward the banner of life, though
> seven worlds perish, with all the wives and mothers and children
> in them.
>
> (pp. 97–8)

In one mood that can sound very much like Milton: "He for God
only, she for God in him." In another, one may notice that, if
Lawrence had left women out of it altogether, and had used
"man", in the generic sense of "mankind", the impulse (if not
its conditions) could give no cause for quarrel. That endeavour to
rise out of destruction, "to give oneself to life-work and risk
oneself to death", is surely admirable. No doubt Lawrence was
right to draw the "fighting line" in the self. He was mistaken to

identify the enemy with women, not with the enemy within. It impeded his search.

It is for this reason that *Aaron's Rod* seems to me a more satisfying novel. Aaron does "not pause to remember that he has a life to lose, or a wife or children to leave": in order "to give himself to life-work and risk himself to death" he simply walks out on them. In consequence the instinct to life and the instinct to destruction are no longer polarized into male and female; their struggle is both more inward and more outward, dramatized on the one hand in Aaron's single self, on the other in a wider social context. For Italy, in the aftermath of war, possesses, "in spite of everything":

> The one manly quality, undying, acrid fearlessness. The eternal challenge of the unquenched human soul. Perhaps too acrid and challenging today, when there is nothing left to challenge. But men—who existed without apology and without justification. Men who would neither justify themselves nor apologize for themselves. Just men, the rarest thing left in our sweet Christendom.
> (p. 209)

But Italy also possesses the mob who destroy Aaron's rod, anarchists who kindle the instinct to destruction in Aaron himself:

> He didn't care whether he were hit by a bomb, or whether he himself threw the next bomb, and hit somebody. He just didn't care about anything any more in life or death. It was as if the reins of his life slipped from his hands, and he would let everything run where it would, so long as it did run.
> (p. 275)

This break with relationships is as significant for Lawrence the writer, as for Aaron the man; he too is freed to pursue the other half of the loaf which is not sex. As a result, he recovers the observer's distance, and with it the validity of an external world. At Christmas, for example, Aaron's daughter asks him for candles:

> "Shall you buy us some, father? Shall you?"
> "Candles!" he repeated, putting the piccolo to his mouth and blowing a few piercing, preparatory notes.
> "Yes, little Christmas-tree candles—blue ones and red ones, in boxes—shall you, father?"
> "We'll see—if I see any—"
> "But *shall* you?" she insisted desperately. She wisely mistrusted his vagueness.
> (p. 9–10)

As he puts on his coat, his wife enjoins:

> "Bring the children some candles for their tree, and don't be
> so selfish . . ."
> "All right," he said, going out.
> "Don't say *All right* if you never mean to do it," she cried,
> with sudden anger.

Aaron:

> Did not intend to trouble himself. And yet, when he glanced in
> passing into the sweet-shop window, and saw it bare as a board,
> the very fact that he probably *could not* buy the things made him
> hesitate, and try.
>
> (pp. 11–12)

He succeeds, but decides to leave home, and spends the night at
a stranger's house:

> When Jim woke in the morning Aaron had gone. Only on the
> floor were two packets of Christmas-tree candles, fallen from the
> stranger's pockets.
>
> (p. 34)

The child's mistrust, the wife's resentment, the husband's reluctance—as in *The Rainbow*, Lawrence captures the profound validity of the familiar. But in the aftermath of war the significance
of the everyday is negative; it destroys those relationships that it
once confirmed. Tom wants to give Anna those unsolicited "odd
things"; Aaron is reluctant to trouble himself with the tiny gift
his wife and child have demanded. The novel seems neither to condemn nor condone Aaron's desertion: it is neither right nor wrong,
but necessary. Those two fallen packets are poignant; Aaron continues to think of "his wife and children at home". Equally, he remains "glad not to have a cosy hearth, and his own arm-chair."
It is necessary for him to possess his soul in singleness, and because domesticity impedes this singleness, it remains matter for
discussion in the novel; but it is discussion only, amongst men removed from a context of domestic discord.

Compared with *The Rainbow*, *Aaron's Rod* is an exhausted
novel; Aaron's eyes look out upon the ruins of that earlier world
in which the soul was once able to incarnate itself. Nonetheless,
having possessed his soul in singleness once more, he *does* look
out. That intercourse between the soul and its context, which was

disrupted in the later *Rainbow* and in *Women in Love*, is recovered in *Aaron's Rod* in a different kind:

> [Aaron] sat for long hours among the cypress trees of Tuscany. And never had any trees seemed so like ghosts, like soft, strange, pregnant presences. He lay and watched tall cypresses breathing and communicating, faintly moving and as it were walking in the small wind. And his soul seemed to leave him and to go far away, far back, perhaps, to where life was all different and time passed otherwise than time passes now. As in clairvoyance he perceived it: that our life is only a fragment of the shell of life. That there has been and will be life, human life such as we do not begin to conceive. Much that is life has passed away from men, leaving us all mere bits. In the dark, mindful silence and inflection of the cypress trees, lost races, lost languages, lost human ways of feeling and knowing. Men have known as we can no more know, have felt as we can no more feel. Great life-realities gone into the darkness. But the cypresses commemorate.
>
> (p. 257)

This passage has none of the confident power of those sequences in *The Rainbow*, where a cow-shed at night, or Christmas Eve seem a consummation of individual existence. There is a sense of loss and of distance, but none of the confusion one feels in Ursula's encounter with the horses, or the strident emphasis that characterizes so much of the prose of *Women in Love*. One might look to Freud again, but not for exposition:

> I have never doubted that religious phenomena are only to be understood . . . as the return of long since forgotten, important events in the primaeval history of the human family—and that they have to thank precisely this origin for their compulsive character and that, accordingly, they are effective on human beings by force of the historical truth of their content.[14]

One might also notice that, although the cypresses emphasize chiefly a sense of what is past and lost, one finds in Lawrence, rather than Freud, the assurance that there "will be life, human life such as we do not begin to conceive".

Where then does the quest for singleness lead Aaron, and indeed Lawrence? Into homosexuality, Murry claims; into Fascism, Mailer asserts:

> There is a stretch in the middle of his work, out in such unread tracts as *Aaron's Rod* and *Kangaroo*, when the uneasy feeling

arrives that perhaps it was just as well Lawrence died when he did, for he could have been the literary adviser to Oswald Mosely about the time Hitler came in.[15]

Those two viewpoints have their connection, and together do much to explain the neglect of this novel. The need to be oneself necessitates a context in which the self will be enabled to flower. On a personal level, beyond the failure of the marriage, this can look very much like homosexuality, as in Aaron's relationship with Lilly. On a social level, as in *Fantasia*, it can look very like Fascism:

> It is the business of very few to understand, and for the mass, it is their business to believe and not to bother, but to be honourable and humanly to fulfil their human responsibilities. To give active obedience to their leaders, and to possess their own souls in natural pride.
>
> (p. 91)

A few pages later, Lawrence writes of "the working man", much as he writes of women:

> I would like him to give me back the responsibility for general affairs, a responsibility which he can't acquit, and which saps his life. I would like him to give me back the responsibility for the future. I would like him to give me back the responsibility for thought, for direction. . . .
>
> I would like him to give me back books and newspapers and theories. And I would give him back, in return, his old insouciance, and rich, original spontaneity and fullness of lfe.
>
> (p. 113)

One may, or may not, agree that this is the context to promote individuality; but that urgent wish that each man should possess his own soul in singleness has, in itself, little to do with Fascism or homosexuality. In the aftermath of war, Aaron visits the station at Novara, "where soldiers were camped in every corner":

> For the first time he saw the cock-feathers of the Bersaglieri. There seemed a new life-quality everywhere. Many worlds, not one world. But alas, the one world triumphing more and more over the many worlds, the big oneness swallowing up the many small diversities in its insatiable gnawing appetite, leaving a dreary sameness throughout the world, that means at last complete sterility.
>
> (p. 148)

That problem is increasingly with us, and the wish to fight one's way back to an individual quality of life remains as urgent as it is difficult. There is, however, a connection between a variety of worlds, individuality of being, and a capacity to notice "the cock-feathers of the Bersaglieri". The conditions that foster art are those that foster life, in individuals and in societies. A man needs to be at peace with himself, in order to promote individuality outside the self. A reawakened sensitivity to the external world in *Aaron's Rod* is at least an indication that the journey was not in vain.

For most writers, the connection between art and life is intimate; for Lawrence it was particularly so. "My motto is 'Art for my sake'," he writes in the letters. "One sheds one's sickness in books —repeats and presents again one's emotions to be master of them." In the novel, Aaron does exactly this when he writes to Sir William:

> Well, here was a letter for a poor old man to receive. But, in the dryness of his withered mind, Aaron got it out of himself. When a man writes a letter to himself, it is a pity to post it to somebody else. Perhaps the same is true of a book.
>
> His letter written, however, he stamped it and sealed it and put it in the box. That made it final.
>
> (p. 256)

I am glad that Lawrence too posted his "letters", even *Women in Love*. One's sense that a novel is a wrestle with life does not invalidate it. Gudrun's statement—" 'life doesn't *really* matter—it is one's art which is central' "—has far less validity; it results in her fastidiously tiny images of a creation alternative to man. Aaron's rod, on the other hand, is at once an image of Lawrence's pen, a religious symbol, and a phallic one. The breaking of the lute may itself be a sign that the journey is completed:

> "It'll grow again. It's a reed, a water-plant. You can't kill it," said Lilly. . . . "You'll have to live without a rod, meanwhile."
>
> (p. 276)

The sublimation of neuroses is, Freud writes, "one of the origins of artistic activity".[16] But such an account, as he says elsewhere, cannot "explain an author's genius"; it can merely "show what motive forces aroused it".[17] The three novels that have been discussed are, on one level, the account of personal crisis—the lapse from a secure state of being in *The Rainbow*, into the total disorientation of *Women in Love*; the painful quickening into "a new life-quality" in *Aaron's Rod*. On the other level, that of an author's genius, the three stories form an account of Europe itself in that traumatic period; and if I consider that *Women in Love* has mistaken the enemy, so too perhaps did the colliding forces in the First World War. It was a battle that no one could win.

NOTES

1 Quoted by Sagar, *The Art of D. H. Lawrence* (1966), p. 19.
2 Norman Mailer, "The Prisoner of Sex", *Harper's Magazine*, March 1971, pp. 70, 78.
3 *The Lost Girl* seems to have been begun early in 1913, under the title *The Insurrection of Miss Houghton*. It was set aside when Lawrence began work the following year upon *The Sisters*, which later developed into *The Rainbow* and *Women in Love*. The final version of *The Lost Girl* was not completed until 1920, after the first draft of *Aaron's Rod* had been written in 1919. It is, in other words, displaced by the other three novels. Dates are based upon Sagar's chronology, *op. cit.*
4 *Cf.* Harry T. Moore, *The Intelligent Heart* (1954), pp. 131–2, 165.
5 Standard Edition, Vol. XXII, p. 135.
6 Moore. *op. cit.*, pp. 41*ff*.
7 Standard Edition, Vol. X.
8 Standard Edition, Vol. XXI, p. 122.
9 Standard Edition, Vol. XXII, p. 209.
10 *D. H. Lawrence: Novelist* (1956), p. 179.
11 *Cf.* pp. 272, 388, 410.
12 *Son of Woman* (1931), pp. 95, 28, 71.
13 Standard Edition, Vol. XVII, p. 215.
14 *Moses and Monotheism*, Standard Edition, Vol. XXIII, p. 58.
15 *Op. cit.*, pp. 70–71.
16 *Three Essays on Sexuality*, Standard Edition, Vol. VII, p. 238.
17 Standard Edition, Vol. XXII, p. 254.

7

Let's Hear What the Male Chauvinist is Saying: *The Plumed Serpent*

by T. E. APTER

It is a precept of the current women's movements that prevalent concepts of masculine and feminine have distorted and limited personal development, and that the unsatisfactory, restricting aspects of these concepts are symptoms of deeply rooted and wide-spread flaws in the culture that produced them. This, too, is the starting point of *The Plumed Serpent*[1]: Kate Leslie's revulsion from life is based upon her disdain for what men are and for what they think they ought to be; also it stems from her bewilderment as to what it means to be a woman, now that the more "obvious" rôles of wife and mother can no longer occupy her—for Kate is now a widow, her children are grown and, as she approaches her fortieth birthday, she is no longer interested in love as a typically youthful phenomenon. Her disgust with the world is based upon the lack of substance in the notions "male" and "female", and this lack of sub-stance is the focus of criticism of the cultures which have degraded these concepts. Lawrence's diagnosis and proposed treatment are quite apart from the spirit of the modern women's movements, but the differences are not always to his disadvantage and it is worth-while disentangling his prejudices from his honest explorations of a very difficult subject; for, despite the apparent justification of the charge "male chauvinism" to some of his attitudes, his approach involves a sanity and depth which those of the women's movements often lack. Lawrence's purpose is to preserve the substance of these concepts; sensibility and vitality must re-forge them and renew their vitality, and such processes depend upon criticism of current conceptions; but unlike those offered by the women's movements, Lawrence's criticisms treat the traditional concepts with respect; they are geared towards a discovery of powerful and elemental differences and conflicts whose meeting and resolution provide, as he sees it, the richest source of meaning.

The success of the novel rests upon his study of a woman's needs. Though Lawrence's vision is biased towards sex he here avoids the limiting simplicity of *Lady Chatterley's Lover*, for Kate Leslie's sexually based dissatisfaction is not defined as a straightforward case of sexual frustration, nor is it remedied by sexual satisfaction. The opening chapters present Kate's need to respect some purpose and activity alongside the world's inability to provide cause for such respect. Her sense of poverty and insufficiency as she attends the bull-fight is based upon her disgust with what is meant to be bold and grand. The pathetic bull gouges out the stomachs of old, blindfolded horses, and the sexless matador underlines the impossibility of her finding here a resolution of her depression:

> She had always been afraid of bulls, fear tempered with reverence for the great Mithraic beast. And now she saw how stupid he was, in spite of his long horns and his massive maleness. Blindly and stupidly he ran at the rag, each time, and the toreadors skipped like fat-hipped girls showing off. Probably it needed skill and courage, but it *looked* silly.
>
> ("Beginnings of a Bull-fight", p. 14)

The bull and the pathetic blood game of course cast her depression in a sexual light, but the bull-fight is not a simple analogy of her sexual attitudes. Her compulsion to mock nearly everything is a symptom of a disease from which the world, not Kate, suffers. Despite the bitch-like tone of her thoughts it is clear that her scorn registers objective faults. First, there is her American companions' sham solicitude for the woman who leaves the bull-fight without their protection: "Oh, how did you get on [Owen] cried the moment he saw her, afraid almost like a boy of his own sin of omission." The assumption that it was his job to look after her is obviously ridiculous to both of them, but he is nonetheless ashamed of not performing that task; and this useless, pseudo-protectiveness is not surprisingly combined with a distorted notion of bravery:

> After all, one must be able to look on blood and bursten bowels calmly: even with a certain thrill. The young hero! But there were dark rings round his eyes, like a debauch.
>
> ("Tea-Party in Tlacolula", p. 25)

Kate's pride sets her above this petty conception of maleness, but her pride is not enough to give her life meaning. Her conviction that she would be better at fulfilling the male rôle than are the males she actually sees, does not liberate her from her need for the realization of the male principle, but only aggravates her tormenting anger:

> Dirty little boys maiming flies—that's what they are. Oh, I wish I could be a bull, just for five minutes. Bastard, that's what I call it!
>
> (Ibid., p. 24)

There is comedy in the distinctly feminine quality of her scorn, yet Lawrence treats it seriously, too, for the feminine thoroughness and conviction of her anger stem from the degradation involved in feeling superior to everything round her. At the bull-fight she feels "utterly humiliated, crushed by a sense of human indecency, cowardice of two-legged humanity", and it is his characteristically creative insight into this agony of disgust that justifies Lawrence's postulation of a need for a masculine element. Her ennui is real despair, and the page of her future seems "black, black and empty". The sensibility that is satisfied by this blood and guts game defines her sense of a lack of substance in the universe, which seems intent upon destroying mystery:

> 'Oh, it was GREAT!' [Villiers] said, lounging on one hip.
> 'GREAT! They killed seven BULLS.'
>
> (Ibid., p. 25)

There is a sense—a small one—that Lawrence is being unfair to Owen and Villiers. After all, they are so ordinary. It is easy to imagine people just like them—tourists especially—whose indiscriminate enthusiasm about foreign spectacles does not reveal an essential shallowness but simply indicates a confusion about what one is supposed to do in a strange country and how one is supposed to respond and what "having a good holiday" means. Lawrence describes the Americans as people who are grubbing for sensations, as though this holiday anxiety indicated, without reference to further behaviour, a way of life. The swiftness with which Lawrence condemns the American pair, however, is in accord with Kate's anger, which uses every annoyance as an occasion for brooding over the world's limitations.

The initial presentation of themes, with empty, ordinary life placed amid the threatening, dragon-like aspects of Mexico, bears the outlines of a typically romantic theme; and *The Plumed Serpent* is a story about a woman who is isolated from commonplace existence by a longing which she cannot understand, and who is subsequently thrust, in a challenging, even threatening manner, into a dark, enchanted atmosphere by a lover. There are further similarities, also, between Kate's story and that of, for example, the Flying Dutchman's Senta or Tristan's Isolde: sex for these women is a spiritual as well as sensuous ecstasy; the union between man and woman is, in each work, a mystical union with the universe and demands a dissolution of individuality—which in Wagner's operas is portrayed by death as spiritual transfiguration. Romantic longing and fulfilment, however, though frequently presented in the emotions of a highly feminine, even ideal woman, do not deal with a specifically female psychology, nor do they investigate the tension between a woman's need to be balanced by the male principle and her need to realize both her self and her womanhood. Lawrence shows that these latter two aspects of a woman do not coincide, and that, therefore, the need for a union with a man goes beyond or, as in Kate's case, is totally different from, the need for tenderness and sympathy and companionship—those safeguards of the self. Lawrence here defies even the notion of companionship as an important aspect of union; love is directed towards womanhood alone, and leaves the self out of account, not because it is unimportant but because it is not pertinent to the realization of womanhood. In contrast, the typically romantic tale seems open to the charge of sentimentality for the way it simply assumes, so easily, that the fulfilment of one's need for love will overcome one's need for a self. It is Lawrence's exploration of this division that makes this work so modern, so pertinent to current re-considerations of womanhood and a woman's independence.

Lawrence is not, however, greatly impressed by a woman's achievement of independence. He begins his story with a woman who has already perfected her independence, her self, and then asks "Where can she go from here?" For independence is not an end in itself. One has to discover some good as the result of independence. It is, indeed, an end to various demands and commitments, but that end cannot be seen as fulfilment. Individuality and independence are for Kate a dead end. The secure command she has upon her self and her solitude limits the world and diminishes her respect for it: if each person is as limited by his respective self as she is by hers, he becomes a monkey in her eyes, when he believes in his own importance. Her disdain for the world, then, stems not only from her culture, which provides no cause for respect, but also from her singleness, which prevents her from looking beyond that culture to something larger than her self. Lawrence shows her independence, ultimately, to aggravate her ennui: his story is that she discovers true maleness—the absence of which made the bull and the toreadors so nauseous—in the men of Quetzalcoatl, yet her willful singleness prevents her from submitting to it and thus from realizing her womanhood.

It is easy, when casting off an indeterminate set of beliefs, as the women's movements are trying to do, to combine criticism of commonplace beliefs and expectations with the discovery that such criticism does not always protect oneself from those beliefs and expectations. Habitual reactions (e.g. a woman's impatience with her male companion for not being able to attract a waiter's attention could indicate that, despite her feminist convictions, she believes that the man should take the aggressive part) and common uses of language (a woman might ask her husband to help her prepare the dinner, thus acknowledging that it is her special job to prepare the dinner and that anything her husband does towards the dinner—though presumably he will eat it, too—is a favour to his wife) contain many pitfalls for the revised or revolutionary precepts, and the feminist sees that guards and reminders are continally necessary. The tension of such constant criticism gives rise to the cry of "Sexist!" or "Male chauvinist!" whenever an invidious attitude seems at all probable; the critical reaction becomes a platitude, and the suspicious area is not given a fair investigation. Lawrence does bring together the terms "womanhood" and "submission" in a most suspicious manner, but a hasty dismissal would only cloud the novel's theme. The submission recommended as a cure for Kate's depression is not to a specific male will; in fact, her obligations, as a result of this submission, remain a completely open question; submission and dissolution of her own individuality does not involve subjection to someone else's individuality. The submission which Lawrence sees as a good is submission to the mystery of the universe; this submission then allows the woman to achieve that "vivid blood-relation between man and woman" that forms "the clue to all present living and future possibility". The submission of which Lawrence speaks involves not domination but reverence:

> Men and women alike danced with faces lowered and expressionless, abstract, gone in the deep absorption of men into the greater manhood, women into the greater womanhood. It was sex, but the greater, not the lesser sex. The waters over the earth wheeling upon the waters under the earth, like an eagle silently wheeling above its own shadow.
>
> [Kate] felt her sex and her womanhood caught up and identified in the slowly revolving ocean of nascent life, the dark sky of the men lowering and wheeling above. She was not herself, she was gone, and her own desires were gone in the ocean of great desire . . .
>
> She did not know the face of the man whose fingers she held. Her personal eyes had gone blind, his face was the face of dark heaven, only the touch of his fingers a star that was both hers and his.
>
> ("The Plaza", p. 143)

This first participation on Kate's part in the world of Quetzalcoatl points to the good of the dissolution of the individual will, and shows the meeting of man and woman, as both submit to something beyond their individuality, to be a complementary rather than a hierarchical conjunction; but the way in which Lawrence presents the difficulties of maintaining such a state of profound impersonality and participation in the "slowly revolving ocean of nascent life" involves a bias against women that cannot be ignored. It is the women, always, who try to destroy submission to the greater mystery with a desire for possession and knowledge of the individual male, and their desire is shown to be not merely misguided but actually vindictive. Carlota's desperation stems from a sense that she owns so little of her husband, and her quarrel with his beliefs does not involve religious matters as much as the separation of his interests from hers. Accordingly, her proclaimed concern for his soul is merely a cloak for her wish to keep his soul for herself, to tame him, to murder that part of him which is independent of her. Though Kate lacks Carlota's specific purpose, her desire to know Ramón as an individual is an attack upon him; her gaze, as she studies the man, is like a knife in his back, and Lawrence says that she is subsequently ashamed of her prying. This theme of knowledge and concern as vindictiveness and possessiveness is more fully developed in Lawrence's earlier works. In *Women in Love* such challenges form part of the fabric of love, for both the women and the men; Birkin pontificates about singleness, but Ursula's mockery is seen to have its point, and the man's theories become entangled and stretched with the growth of his love. In *The Plumed Serpent*, however, such desires are shown not only to be peculiar to women but to be without justification, motivated only by greed and the desire to diminish the man's freedom.

The realization of the greater manhood is said to be complemented by the greater womanhood: Kate is told by the men of Quetzalcoatl that a woman who is joined to a man who has perfected his manhood will find her way to perfect womanhood. Despite the substance Lawrence gives this claim in his explicit depiction of the mingling of a person's sensuous appreciation of herself or himself with a person's attraction to another, not as a matter of vanity or silliness (as in *Madame Bovary*) but as one of the self-realizing aspects of sexual attraction, his vision is limited by its emphasis on male sexuality; womanhood, it seems, is not merely realized by union with and appreciation of manhood, but consists in an appreciation of and respect for manhood. The woman's access to the greater mystery, too, seems to stem from her power to enhance the man's sexuality. This is no longer in accord with Birkin's recommendation of a man/woman relationship as two individual stars balancing one another's orbit, nor does it recommend a dissolution of personality for the sake of mystical awareness and particiption; this is a picture of womanhood as defined by manhood alone, whose sole purpose is to advance manhood. Ramón's second wife Teresa appears as the most successful woman—as woman—in the novel, and Kate muses over her peculiar qualities:

> What a curious will the little dark woman had! What a subtle female power inside her rather skinny body! She had the power to make him into a big, golden, full glory of a man. Whilst she

herself became almost inconspicuous, save for her big black eyes
lit with a tigerish power.

("Teresa", p. 435)

In *Women in Love* Gudrun felt subjected by Gerald's beauty, and
often her will wishes to merge with his, so that his greatness as
an industrial magnate would be partly hers. In that richer, more
complex novel such self-annihilation for the purpose of identifying
with another's will power was shown to be destructive; the other
face of this wilful submission was seen to be a desire to inflict
one's will upon the other, and to destroy the other to accomplish
this. Moreover, this desire to syphon off one's will into another's
was shown as part of a particular relationship, and as stemming
from the characters' particular psychologies, but in *The Plumed
Serpent* Teresa's reaction to Ramón is seen as an objective, and
healthy response to his manhood. The static insistence of "a big,
golden, full glory of a man" reveals not only the stifling idolatry in Teresa's reaction, but also Lawrence's limited vision of a
woman's fulfilling appreciation of manhood. Kate dislikes Teresa's
adoration; to her Teresa seems somewhat of a slave, with a harem-
like mentality, but Lawrence makes it clear that envy motivates
her judgement and, furthermore, that she sees Ramón—as did
Carlota—in precisely the same way and that she would like to be
in a position to annihilate herself on his behalf, to realize her
womanhood through admiration for him—for though a woman's
self and womanhood are not identical, the kind of womanhood
Teresa realizes does diminish her self, and Kate's refusal to allow
her self to be diminished by her union with a man does indicate
a failure in the realization of her womanhood; for this reason she
can never integrate her various emotions and attitudes, for this
reason she continues to suffer the peculiar irritable ennui of a
person with eternally divided interests.

   In his essay on Thomas Hardy, Lawrence presents his definition
of Male and Female: the male exists in doing, the female in being;
the male lives in the satisfaction of some purpose achieved, the
female in the satisfaction of some purpose contained (ch. VII);
the woman grows downwards, like a root, towards the centre and
darkness and origin, whereas the man grows upwards, like a stalk,
towards discovery and light and utterance (ch. X). This kind of
definition is currently a signal for rage and disdain, but distinctions
should be made among types and purposes of such definitions.

First, Lawrence is discussing concepts, not describing either what men and women are or what they want to be; he says that "every man comprises male and female in his being, the male always struggling for predominance. A woman likewise consists in male and female, with female predominant" (ch. VII). He is making use of old, old conceptual divisions which cannot be denied without absurdly severe psychic surgery. Lawrence's use of these definitions in *The Plumed Serpent*, however, is more explicit than in his earlier works, and there is often a sense that his conceptions of male and female have become didactic; he is not only throwing light on concepts but is also pressing his characters into a conceptual mould, and the mingling of sex elements within one person, which he admits in the Hardy essay, is criticized in the novel. The woman is a source of energy, but the energy she supplies is a man's energy; and the only way, it seems, that she can keep energy for herself is to covet the man's energy as both Kate and Carlota covet Ramón's. The passivity Lawrence recommends for the woman is, he insists, a positive passivity, and this insistence is sufficiently convincing to waylay a straightforward rejection of his recommendation. Of Kate's union with Cipriano Lawrence says:

> It was strange to be married to him. He made her go all vague and quiet, as if she sank away heavy and still, away from the surface of life, and lay deep in the underlife.
> The strange, heavy, *positive* passivity. For the first time in her life she felt absolutely at rest. And talk, and thought, had become trivial, superficial to her: as the ripples on the surface of the lake are as nothing to the creatures that live away below in the unwavering deeps.
>
> ("Kate is a Wife", p. 462)

And this mystic stupor is an answer—her answer, not one simply forced upon her by a man's belief as to her place in life—to that humiliating despair which Lawrence presented in the opening chapters. Nevertheless, the way in which the woman is seen as she emerges from this positive passivity into a more active, appetitive being, does indicate that Lawrence believes she is taking the wrong path when she uses her will as her own. In Lawrence's works the will is that small sphere of consciousness that controls one's energies and sensibilities with the result that those energies and sensibilities become cruel and shallow, and as they fight to become free, control becomes an obsession; the result is that one believes one's survival depends upon one's will, for one identifies oneself with one's conscious, manipulative self, and this does depend upon one's ability to control oneself and one's world. The will, then, creates its own sense of necessity, and thus aggravates its faults with the ensuing desperation lest the will be impaired. In *Women in Love*, where this notion is most fully developed, the self aggravating viciousness of the will is not a peculiarly female phenomenon. Gerald and his father, as well as Hermione and Gudrun, become both murderous and self destructive through their anxiety to impale all their impulses upon their conscious knowledge and to tame other people's emotions and energies by the force of their own wills. In the earlier novel the notion of will covers a broad area of social and personal behaviour, and though the sexual arena is a place where it is often clearly on display, the problem of the will is not specifically a sexual or a sexist problem. In *The Plumed Serpent*, however, the will is not a general problem but a woman's problem and infects particularly her relationship with men. Despite Ramón's and Cipriano's revolutionary and didactic purposes, Lawrence finds them untainted by will to an extent that seems thoroughly naïve. Do they see their mission only as a noble necessity? Do they not enjoy the fight? Is their anger towards their enemies actually nothing more than an objective weighing of their enemies' faults, is it completely lacking in the irrational fire of an angry will? Is their desire to see the woman relinquish her possession of them not more than an appreciation of the merging necessary for a religious consciousness? Is it not a desire to have their own way, without being hindered and without being judged? But Lawrence finds no cause for criticism, whereas the woman's purposes are seen to be motivated not only by her petty desire to maintain her individuality but also by her desire to possess and to diminish the man. Indeed, Lawrence confuses these two aspects of the will, so that Kate's inability to submit totally to the greater mystery of sex becomes aggression towards Ramón and Cipriano; her refusal to submit to their purpose is too simply correlated with her inability to retain her mystic sensibility, and her ennui then becomes distinctly feminine not simply in the sense that it is vividly portrayed in a distinctly female character but in that it stems from a pettiness and reluctance which Lawrence presents as characteristics of women. The portrait of Carlota, the analysis of her religiousness as self-pity and sadism, might have been acceptable had it been balanced by other, less stark portrayals of a woman's will, but as it is Carlota remains an image of the vindictive, grasping woman and Lawrence's dislike of her is seen as a dislike of something peculiarly feminine, and this dislike leads to the distortion whereby the woman's will is totally evil and petty and the man's purpose is refined to perfect objectivity.

Dislike, however, does not always lead a novelist astray, and when Lawrence's attitude towards the female will takes the form of revulsion for aspects of female sexuality, the understanding of the part revulsion plays in his criticism does not constitute a dismissal of his criticism. This revulsion for the wilful aspects of a woman's pleasure is very strong in *Lady Chatterley*. Despite the emphasis Lawrence places upon Connie's satisfaction, her ecstasies are a measure of Mellor's manhood. I find it impossible to see Lawrence's portrayal of her sexual orgies as good in themselves or as leading to any good other than her subjection to the gamekeeper. The vindictiveness I find in Lawrence's description of Connie's ecstasies is more explicit in *The Plumed Serpent*, yet as he explains his revulsion for Kate's sexual appetites he also reveals his capacity for making fine, original distinctions among types of sexual response:

> Curious as it may seem [Cipriano] made her aware of her own old desire for frictional, irritant sensation. She realised how all her old love had been frictional, charged with the fire of irritation and the spasms of frictional voluptuousness . . . She had loved Joachim for this, that again, and again, and again he could give her this orgiastic 'satisfaction,' in spasms that made her cry aloud.
>
> But Cipriano would not. By a dark and powerful instinct he drew away from her as soon as this desire rose again in her, for the white Aphrodite of the foam. She could see that to him, it was repulsive. He just removed himself, dark and unchangeable, away from her.
>
> And she, as she lay, would realise the worthlessness of this foam-effervescence, its strange externality to her. It seemed to come upon her from without, not from within. And succeeding the first moment of disappointment, when this sort of 'satisfaction' was denied her, came the knowledge that she did not really want it, that it was really nauseous to her.
>
> And he, in his dark, hot silence, would bring her back to the new, soft, heavy hot flow, when she was like a fountain gushing noiseless and with urgent softness from the volcanic deeps. Then

she was open to him, soft and hot, yet gushing with a noiseless soft power. And there was no such thing as conscious 'satisfaction'. What happened was dark and untellable, so different from the beak-like friction of Aphrodite of the foam, the friction which flares out in circles of phosphorescent ecstasy, to the last wild spasm which utters the involuntary cry, like a death-cry, the final love-cry.

("Kate is a Wife", pp. 462–3)

This passage is usually taken to mean that Kate relinquishes orgasm for some more passive and more profound fulfilment. This common reading is not exactly a mis-reading, but it misses the point of Lawrence's criticism, which must be disentangled from a variety of elements. Indeed, Cipriano's behaviour seems infuriating, and Kate's acceptance of it—after the first moment!—is surprising to the extent that one cannot quite believe that what is being shown is what is actually taking place. Enforcing this disbelief is the fact that Cipriano's revulsion is presented as a straightforward judgement, fully endorsed by Lawrence, whereas the Lawrence of *Women in Love* saw every revulsion as imbedded in a complex psychology and value system. Revulsion involves a sensitivity—and a vulnerability through one's sensitivity—to the object that repels; that object is seen to dominate through one's own possible response to it, and therefore revulsion does not register a totally negative reaction. In *The Plumed Serpent*, however, Lawrence lacks this depth of vision. He misses this opportunity to give Cipriano's sexuality a further and perhaps a somewhat comic dimension by connecting this revulsion to his need to idealize the white woman,[2] or to his fear of being on intimate terms with a woman who can judge him, and for whose judgement he has respect. The absence of any psychological context for Cipriano's revulsion gives it a bullying character, as though his aspersion were enough to condemn; nonetheless Lawrence succeeds here in criticizing a seldom questioned aspect of sexual satisfaction, one which is protected by the present culture's assumptions as to the point and good of sex. Successful sex is considered equivalent to pleasurable sex. One must do one's best, it is supposed, to make sex as pleasurable as possible for one's self and for one's partner. One is given a number of techniques to help one with the job of increasing pleasure; one is even given behavioural therapy to overcome those inhibitions which impede pleasure. Anything which interferes with pleasure is seen as unnatural, a fault, a personal limitation. Such assumptions dismiss the possibility that problematic aspects of sex and pleasure are natural—natural, that is, in the human world, in which straightforward judgements as to what is natural or perverted or conditioned are impossible. However blatant the naïveté of such clichéed thinking, it is impervious to criticism since its terms are so satisfyingly simple, and any criticism that would destroy that simplicity would demand a new language.

I am not denying that sex and pleasure are inextricably connected: sex stems from desire, and the fulfilment of that desire may be peculiarly, intensely pleasurable, but it is not pleasure alone that makes sex so deeply-rooted in our lives, nor is it the substance nor explanation of a sexual bond to another person. Moreover—and this is Lawrence's point—the assumption that pleasure of the sort he describes—and which very well describes the aims of the sex therapists—is the substance of good sex, does thwart a more profound response, and is superficial in contrast to the more elemental and untamable aspects of sex, which are ignored in obsession with the height and frequency of orgasm. Kate rightly connects her criticism of this notion of sexual fulfilment to a much broader area of consciousness, so that her sexual purpose and character are thoroughly re-evaluated:

> Suddenly, she saw herself as men often saw her: the great cat, with its spasms of voluptuousness and its lifelong lustful enjoyment of its own isolated individuality. Voluptuously to enjoy contact. Then with a lustful feline gratification, to break the contact, and roam alone in a sense of power. Each time, to seize a sort of power, purring upon her own isolated individuality.
>
> ("Here!", p. 480)

It is surprising, and certainly incorrect, to be shown this selfish hoarding of voluptuous satisfaction as a peculiarly female trait, but it is nonetheless a fine description of a human phenomenon, in which a shallow notion of sex gives rise to the belief that the pleasure of sex is one's own concern (and why not, if that is the purpose of sex?) and a measure of one's own achievement; thus, sex isolates rather than connects one with anything beyond oneself, and this isolation, this mere individuality makes impossible, in Lawrence's view, any continuing sense of meaning.

The point and good of sex, for Lawrence, is an abiding connection with the deepest mystery of the universe, and an awareness of the world as vital and profound. This end justifies and explains a dissolution of individuality and the submission to something beyond and greater than oneself; but though in his earlier works Lawrence has shown his greatness to be his capacity for rendering such mystery vivid and immediate, the focus of mystery here is extremely limited and, ultimately, cannot convince Kate to relinquish her hold upon her insouciant pride of individuality. Part of the difficulty is that Lawrence does not here, as he does in *The Rainbow*, describe the mystery of the living cosmos as part of a way of life; here he is trying to salvage and to re-define a mystery that has been degraded by ordinary life and thus seems to be at odds with ordinary life. His thesis is that the white man's consciousness is now a total loss and that the dark races have easier access to the essential elements of life. This thesis is not interestingly controversial in itself: if Lawrence's imagination had been stimulated by this belief to realize a re-vitalization of mystery that was in accord with the more general thesis, then that thesis would be justified within the novel, but in fact Lawrence has been unable to present a satisfactory image of mystic or religious depth. The portrayal of the Queztalcoatl prayers and rites does not begin to express the commitment and ecstasy upon which Lawrence's themes depend:

> He took off his clothes, and in the darkness thrust his clenched fist upwards above his head, in a terrible tension of stretched, upright prayer. In his eyes was only darkness, and slowly the darkness revolved in his brain, too, till he was mindless. Only a powerful will stretched itself and quivered from his spine in an immense tension of prayer. Stretched the invisible bow of his body in the darkness with inhuman tension, erect, till the arrows of his soul, mindless, shot to the mark, and the prayer reached its goal.
>
> ("Lords of the Day and Night", p. 186)

The grotestque, strained simplicity of this metaphor is characteristic of the men's solemnity, which is infected with unacknowledged will and narcissism. Kate's sensitivity to the religion is more convincing than either the men's hymns or their prayers, but her sensitivity is more to an evocative, vaguely allusive mood than to a life-directing vision:

Then one of the men in the circle lifted his voice, and began to sing a hymn. He sang in the fashion of the Old Red Indians, with intensity and restraint, singing inwardly, singing to his own soul, not outwardly to the world, nor yet even upward to God, as the Christians sing. But with a sort of suppressed, tranced intensity, singing to the inner mystery, singing not into space, but into the other dimension of man's existence, where he finds himself in the infinite room that lies inside the axis of our wheeling space. Space, like the world, cannot but move. And like the world, there is an axis. And the axis of our worldly space, when you enter it, is a vastness where even trees come and go, and the soul is at home in its own dream, noble and unquestioned.

. . . There was no recognisable rhythm, no recognisable emotion, it was hardly music. Rather a far-off, perfect crying in the night. But it went straight to the soul, the most ancient and everlasting soul of all men, where alone can the human family assemble in immediate contact.

Kate knew it at once, like a sort of fate. It was no good resisting. There was neither urge nor effort, nor any speciality. The sound sounded in the innermost far-off place of the human core, the ever-present, where there is neither hope nor emotion, but passion sits with folded wings on the nest, and faith is a tree of shadow.

("The Plaza", pp. 137–8)

There is in this, certainly, a mystical caress which offers the reassurance of a place in the living universe, but this protective evocation cannot contain the entire story of the universe's mystery nor can it satisfy, by this soothing denial, the impulses and strivings of the individual self. The Quetzalcoatl religion is meant to answer the question initially raised by the presentation of Kate's ennui: what is worth more than her independence and individuality? Ideally, it would resolve those broken desires and values which aggravate her depression into some larger, finer frame. And, initially, Lawrence seems to accept the need for this resolution. Kate's fascination with Mexico is based upon the country's violence and primitive glamour; she despises the ordinary world for its insipid and distorted notion of potency; her woman's pride is outraged by the enveloping weakness and crudeness of the bull-fight, and she searches for a deeper, more daemonic vision in Mexico and in Cipriano, who shares the heavy, black fatality of his country. It is surprising, in this novel of extremely uneven quality, to find the Mexican theme consistently excellent. In his descriptions of the landscape Lawrence evokes a mingling of primitive evil with vitality, and balances the country's compelling splendour against its vacuity, inertia and cruelty. Characters such as Juana, whose unabashed vulgarity reveals the limiting, pedestrian aspects of the place, and the boatman, whose assurance, both secretive and exultant, first introduces her to the people's vision of Quetzalcoatl, appear as easily recognizable types, yet they are so fully adapted to Lawrence's spiritual purpose that *his* Mexico becomes inevitable and convincing. The fascination of this country, with its cruel, down-dragging, destructive spirit, and the eternity of its burning wilderness, arises from its naked and elemental force; it is this fascination that insists upon the more profound aspects of reality being acknowledged, so that England appears insignificant and false in Kate's eyes,[3] and she feels, without qualification, that real life is contained here, and that here alone resides a force and mystery to which she is tempted to submit.

The religion of Quetzalcoatl is meant to be a re-forming of these primitive vital elements Kate senses in Mexico; it is an attempt to release energies more profound than practical or conscious energies, of which the Mexicans make a hash, anyway, and which thwart the natural flow of their blood. Lawrence understands that such a release is not a simple, good thing; his argument, after all, has been against a distorted desire to tame fierce, elemental energies whose profundity goes hand in hand with their bitter, destructive spirit. But though Mexico itself remains a harsh, arid landscape of instinct and blood, the men of Quetzalcoatl, Lawrence insists, while returning to archaic feelings, are able to choose only the finer aspects of primitivism. Kate quotes her husband as having said that evil is "the lapsing back to old life-modes that have been surpassed in us". This brings murder and lust, but Cipriano assures her that his and Ramón's religion is "not a helpless, panic reversal. It is conscious, carefully chosen." This complacency, however, is extremely disappointing in face of the pains Lawrence has taken to sharpen one's sense of the reality of evil and bitterness; Cipriano's complacency becomes a denial of Lawrence's art. Indeed, this inability to cope with the darker side of impulse, this refusal to acknowledge the cruelty which is part of that universal mystery, destroys the credibility of the Quetzalcoatl's leaders' belief in themselves and makes their teachings ultimately insipid. The obvious falseness of Lawrence's position on these matters emerges

in the most repulsive scene in the novel—the execution of Ramón's
would-be assassins and the young woman who aided them. Critics
have been repelled by this scene because of its cruelty: it is an
execution without trial, they complain; it is a barbaric and tyran-
nical approach to justice. What I find most repelling in this scene,
however, is not the cruelty but the pretence that there is no
cruelty. The evil and violence which Lawrence acknowledges in his
description of the countryside bandits is a refreshing contrast to this
hypocrisy of control and morality. The bandits' behaviour indicates
a dynamic psychology (which is nearly always lacking in the behaviour of the men of Quetzalcoatl) within the evil, a national
and class character which explains the evil and which commands
a startling sympathy without denying the horror:

> Uncreated, half-created, such a people was at the mercy of old black
> influences that lay in a sediment at the bottom of them. While
> they were quiet, they were gentle and kindly, with a sort of limp
> naïveté. But when anything shook them at the depths, the black
> clouds would arise, and they were gone again in the old grisly
> passions of death, blood-lust, incarnate hate. A people incomplete
> and at the mercy of old, upstarting lusts.
>
> Somewhere at the bottom of their souls, she felt, was a fathom-
> less resentment, like a raw wound. The heavy, blood-eyed resent-
> ment of men who have never been able to win a soul for
> themselves, never been able to win themselves a nucleus, an
> individual integrity out of the chaos of passions and potencies
> and death . . .[4]
>
> So these men, unable to overcome the elements, men held down
> by the serpent tangle of sun and electricity and volcanic emission,
> they are subject to an ever-recurring, fathomless lust of resent-
> ment, a demonish hatred of life itself. Then, the instriking thud of
> a heavy knife, stabbing into a living body, this is the best. No
> lust of women can equal that lust. The clutching throb of grati-
> fication as the knife strikes in and blood spurts out!
>
> ("Night in the House", pp. 147–8)

Lawrence might have done something like this in the execution
scene; he could have pointed to an outrage and terror which made
the people of Quetzalcoatl see justice in their absurd rites. Yet
Lawrence does not look beyond their own belief that the darker
side of their nature is fully controlled. This diminished vision cuts
through Lawrence's entire treatment of the Quetzalcoatl religion

and defeats his own achievement in presenting the truly problematic aspects of impulse and energy. He *tries* to integrate his deeper vision with his religious proposals: Cipriano explains to Kate that the horror she feels inherent in Mexico does not constitute a reason for avoiding the country; "The bit of horror is like the sesame seed in the nougat, it gives the sharp wild flavour. It is good to have it there." But here, even as Cipriano pretends to give horror its due, he denies its reality; to accept the reality of horror is not to appreciate its tang but to fear and loathe it while seeing its in-evitable—and inevitably uncontrolled—place in our lives.

The new religion's view of the soul is accordingly pale and un-satisfactory. Repeatedly, the soul is referred to as a flower, and the flower's potency of sleep and stillness is presented as its final realization. This is not one aspect of the soul's good, but its total good, and therefore Lawrence's insistence upon the positive, par-ticipating aspect of mystical passivity remains only half developed. Essentially it is an escapist religion, at odds with daily life: "It was hard to have to bear the contact of commonplace things," Lawrence says of Ramón, "when his soul and body were naked to the cosmos." But how can a religious view which does not help Kate find mean-ing in her actual, lived life, satisfy her? Lawrence portrays her daily activities in Mexico after her conversion to Quetzalcoatl as a kind of sleep-walk: her participation in the greater mystery of the universe—which Lawrence calls "the greater sex", thus limiting the range of vitality he has actually succeeded in presenting—is a submersion within it, and a disintegration of identity. Not only does she escape the limitations of her self as she achieves this new mystic awareness but, in accord with the predominantly passive aspect of this mysticism, she relinquishes the pride of having a self more valuable in character than that of other creatures. There-fore, as Kate muses over the reptile she rejects her pity for its lowly place in the scale of creation: perhaps, she reflects, there is no reason to regret such a limitation, for fulfilment lies in partici-pation in the living cosmos, and that participation involves a denial of individuality, a denial of difference. Lawrence is here showing her to be true to the Quetzalcoatl religion, but Kate's momentary acceptance does not show her as being true to her needs. A woman who is naturally a "soldier among women" and whose sensibility is keenly critical of the values embodied round her and aware of grades of value, cannot be content with a submerged, undifferen-

tiated consciousness, however rich the accompanying passivity.
Her scorn for her American companions' and the peons' enthrall-
ment with the bull-fight underlines her need for real strength, real
drive, real assertion—all of which are as much a part of the universe
in which she believes as its evocative, hypnotic pulse. Kate's refusal
to submit entirely to the men is a symptom of her deeper knowledge, and however fascinating she finds them, she is forced to
acknowledge their limitations:

> For a pure moment, she wished for men who were not handsome
> as these dark natives were. Even their beauty was suddenly re-
> pulsive to her; the dark beauty of half-created, half-evolved
> things, left in the old reptile-like smoothness. It made her shudder.
> The soul! If only the soul in man, in woman, would speak to
> her, not always in this strange, perverse materialism, or a dis-
> torted animalism. If only people were souls, and their bodies were
> gestures from the soul! If one could but forget both bodies and
> facts, and be present with strong, living souls!
>
> ("The Attack on Jamiltepec", pp. 333–4)

Indeed, Kate's need for meaning is a need for a meaning that is
enacted, and enactment demands integration with daily life. Neither
the ritual isolated from ordinary life, nor the attitude that ordinary life is little more than a tedious necessity when it demands
effort and little more than a comfortable back-cloth to mystic
submersion when it does not involve effort—rituals and attitudes
such as the men of Quetzalcoatl exhibit[5]—provides that realization of soul Kate seeks. Quetzalcoatl is, according to Lawrence's
definitions in the Hardy essay, a highly feminine religion, a religion
that sees being as separate from doing and striving and asserting.
It is, however, to Lawrence's credit as a novelist that despite his
obvious idolatry of the men of Quetzalcoatl, his vision of Kate's
needs is sufficiently clear to prevent him from portraying her
acceptance of a more passive and limited rôle than her Male/
Female nature demands. The compromise Kate eventually accepts
is not an ignoble one, nor is it clearly a mistake. Kate is not an
all-or-nothing romanticist, but a woman who is trying to establish a way of life in the worlds available to her. A limited sense of
meaning is preferable to the emptiness that lies behind her cynicism in the opening chapters, and though her cynicism registers
objective faults in the two cultures—Mexican and Anglo-American
—of her ambience, it is a personal impasse, and she wants to be

protected from it. While she is still bound to her European culture, Lawrence says that she watches other people as one reads the pages of a novel, "with a certain disinterested amusement". She has never, it is clear, been committed to a person in a way that renders the grotesque or absurd aspects of humanity irrelevant and secures, generally, an attitude in which terms such as "respect" and "disrespect" have any point. She admits, shame-facedly, but with the conviction of irritation, that even her children could easily appear as no more than monkeys to her. Lawrence uses her attitude to focus upon the shallowness of self-importance and its prominence in worldly ambition and purpose, but however justified Kate's view, she suffers from it and must try to overcome it. Only her fascination with Mexico puts a halt to her soul-destructive mockery, and therefore she must grapple with the drawbacks of this fascination. As well as the limitation to the Male aspect of her development, the drawbacks are emotional; for, despite Kate's belief that, at forty, her need for human companionship and tenderness is at an end, she reveals a distinctly feminine vulnerability in her need for reassurance and confirmation of importance. In the final chapter Lawrence presents the combination and conflict of her various needs in regard to her attachment to Mexico. Her plans to leave the country are partly an assertion of the distorted aggressiveness of her nature, which can only emerge as a deadly rejection, and partly an expression of her need to be wanted and to be protected from her own self, which is at a loss as to how to make good use of its intelligence and drive:

> "You are going already?" [Cipriano] said in Spanish.
> And then she knew, at last, that he was offended . . . She could almost feel the waves of successive shadow and coldness go through his blood, his mind hardly aware at all. And again a fear of losing his contact melted her heart.
> It was somehow, to her, beautiful, to feel shadows, and cold gleams, and a hardness like stone, then the strange heavy inertia of the tropical mid-day, the stupor of the sun, moving upon him while he stood motionless, watching her. In the end it was that weird, sultry, tropical stupor of the hot hours, a heat-swoon of sheer indifference . . .
> And she knew he had already released her, in the dark, sultry stupor of his blood. He would make no further effort after her. This also was the doom of his race . . .

> She was alone, as usual . . . She always had to recoil upon her
> own individuality, as a cat does.
>
> ("Here!", pp. 479–80)

Kate's choice is between her British culture, which preserves her self but channels its energies into a limiting selfishness, resulting in a deadly disdain, and the disconcerting fascination of Mexico, which stimulates her senses but becalms her mental energy, thus relieving her of her aggressive ennui but also preventing a positive realization of her energy. Her desperation in the opening chapters makes her choice plausible, and, of course, being what she is, she continues to resist the limitations a total acceptance of her lot would involve. Her submission is not to the men's will, but to her fascination, and her compromise is not due to reverence of the men, but to a need for human connection. Her choice is based upon a precarious balance of her complex and somewhat incompatible needs, but it is her needs, always, which guide her. It is this that makes the novel not primarily a tale of men's glory and a woman's admiration, but a tale of a woman who could not realize the positive, striving aspect of her nature and who finds a rare if limited meaning through a passive but richly mystic awareness that obliterates the irritation and pettiness of the self. Kate's success is only moderate, but the cultures in which she seeks fulfilment are uncongenial to the realization of a woman's deepest needs— and that is the point of the novel.

NOTES

1 References throughout are to the Penguin editions.
2 For the theme of Kate as goddess is absurd. The best thing in the novel on this subject is the discussion between Kate and Teresa about who will wear the green dress of Malintzi. In this discussion Kate displays a crude pettiness that is not characteristic of her, yet her behaviour is made plausible through her combined envy and disdain for Teresa, which suddenly erupts in a common, competitive spirit.
3 Her image of England, however, consists of little more than buses passing through the mud in Piccadilly and fruitiers' stalls in Hampstead decorated with mistletoe for Christmas and a scornful view of her women friends chatting in a drawing room. In short, Kate's England does not provide a real foil for her Mexico.
4 Lawrence's language is not perfectly consistent, for he cites a lack of

individuality as a reason for being half created and, consequently, primitively cruel, while he cites Kate's individuality as a reason for her being shut off from any meaningful connection with the universe. Presumably, it is a matter of degree: complete absence of individuality destroys one's capacity for making good use of archaic energies, and too much prevents one from making any use of them at all; but Lawrence does not develop these differences, and when he speaks about the good of the Quetzalcoatl religion and the need for submission he seems to be speaking for the complete dissolution of individuality.

5   The men are active as Quetzalcoatl missionaries, but the activity is only a tedious means to an end and offers no enjoyment in itself; and though Cipriano is referred to as 'a fighting male' he simply *feels* very hostile, he does not act upon the hostility; much more prominent is his passive stupor, the doom of his race.

8

Bert Lawrence and Lady Jane

by HARRY T. MOORE

Like most members of our civilization, D. H. Lawrence was brought up in the tradition of male dominance. Unlike most others, however, he was aware of this situation and, although he often accepted it, if only unconsciously, he often fought against it—something for which he has not usually been credited.

His experiences with women, notably his mother, when he was young, could have left him psychologically crippled for life, but he was inwardly too strong for that. Those who have tried to fit Lawrence into a pathological straitjacket have, themselves, usually been caught too tightly in theoretical rigidities. Most commentators bring up the Oedipus Complex, and certainly in Lawrence's childhood and youth his mother's ferocious love damaged him. Her intentions, as a Victorian–puritan mother who wanted to do "the right thing", were what we can think of as "good", though the staunchness with which she carried them out was frequently harmful, to her husband and her children, particularly the frail young Bert, whom she smothered with intense love. Almost two years after she died, Lawrence in November 1912 completed the final version of *Sons and Lovers*, having written it out of an agony that was a catharsis.

Such a procedure is in keeping with the Church's confession box and the psychoanalyst's couch, where the participant can often banish his troubles by acutely reliving the experiences that brought them about; and this sometimes happens in the case of writers who, however painfully, dramatize their traumata. Goethe is a prime example of this, and he recognized the process in himself, saying that he was like a snake: "I slough my skin and start afresh." He also noted, in this connection, that "people continue to shoot at me even after I am miles out of range." Other authors have made similar statements, and Lawrence once noted that "one sheds one's sicknesses in books."

In one of the finest studies of this author, Father Martin Jarrett-Kerr ("Father William Tiverton"), in *D. H. Lawrence and Human Existence*, said that some Lawrence critics and biographers "have . . . much exaggerated his Oedipus Complex", for, after the purgation of *Sons and Lovers*, he grew, "into a separate existence which cannot be interpreted in terms of Mrs Lawrence".[1] He dealt only once more with the strong mother-son relationship, in one of his last stories, the feeble little melodramatic comedy, "The Lovely Lady", which is essentially satiric, really a parody of *Sons and Lovers*. The liberating influence of the creation of *Sons and Lovers* attracted the attention of F. R. Leavis in *D. H. Lawrence: Novelist*, who finds that Lawrence's severest emotional troubles were overcome by an intelligence realizing itself through artistic creation: "He is now freed for the work of the greatest kind of artist." In a later paragraph, Dr Leavis qualifies this statement somewhat when he says that, "For all the emancipating triumph of intelligence represented by *Sons and Lovers*, the disastrous relationship established with him by his mother had its permanent consequences." Somewhat further on, Dr Leavis states, in discussing *The Rainbow*, a somewhat different idea, as when he says that the catharsis brought about by *Sons and Lovers* "was complete and final; and those who talk as if Lawrence had been warped for life or in some way disabled by the strain set up in babyhood would be hard put to it to assemble any weight of critical evidence from the writings."[2] Such statements, however, have not dissuaded later examiners from interpreting Lawrence almost entirely from a psychoanalytic angle; Margaret Beede Howe's *The Art of the Self in D. H. Lawrence*, as recently as 1977, is an example.[3]

But Dr Howe does not go to the lengths of Kate Millett, whose *Sexual Politics* was a feminist attack on Lawrence as well as Henry Miller, Jean Genet, and Norman Mailer. Dr Howe quotes Kate Millett only once, in a note indicating that she disagrees with her on the subject of Lawrence's social thinking. Norman Mailer, mentioned earlier as one of the victims of *Sexual Politics*, answers her in *The Prisoner of Sex*, in which he defends not only Lawrence, Miller, and Genet, but also himself.[4] He mentions that she ends her discussion of Lawrence with a violent attack on his story,

"The Woman Who Rode Away", in which the American wife of a Dutch owner of silver mines in Mexico rides away from her home and lets the descendants of pre-Columbian tribes kill her in a sacrificial rite. Dr Millett finds this "sadistic pornography", a surrender of the female at once sexual and political: "Probably it is the perversion of sexuality into slaughter, indeed, the story's very travesty and denial of sexuality, which accounts for its monstrous, even demented air."[5] These mistaken oversimplifications are typical of her approach to Lawrence, at its fiercest extreme in relation to this symbolic story whose true symbolism she completely misses.

Norman Mailer cites the sentence quoted above and suggests that at least some women will realize that after Lawrence "purged his blood of murder", he would write Lady Chatterley's Lover— this helps but little, though he approves of that book, for with it "Lawrence has closed the circle, the man and women are joined, separate and joined."[6] In discussing "The Woman Who Rode Away", Norman Mailer states, as he does several other times in his book, the case against Kate Millett's distortions, pointing out that she "is not interested in the dialectic by which writers deliver their themes to themselves; she is more interested in hiding the process, and so her second way of concealing how much Lawrence has still to tell us about men and women is simply to distort the complexity of his brain into snarling maxims, take him at his worst and make him even worse, take him at his best and bring pinking shears to his context."[7]

It is evident that, although Norman Mailer is willing to defend Lawrence against Millett in many instances, he finds that she has a certain amount of believable evidence, in connection with Lawrence's poorest books (like most commentators, Mailer likes the "leadership" novels, Aaron's Rod, Kangaroo, and The Plumed Serpent, least of all; to him they are somewhat fascist books in which Lawrence "flirts" with homosexuality). Mailer believes that Lawrence may have been "a great writer", though his work is "certainly flawed". In most cases, however, Mailer finds Kate Millet a "malignant prosecutor" who twists evidence; he says that Lawrence wrote "more intimately about woman" than other novelists, and although he loved them greatly he was ready to see them "murdered"; true as this may be in "The Woman Who Rode Away"—that symbolic death—he had purged his blood of such "murders" and would then write Lady Chatterley's Lover. He had become "the sacramental poet of a sacramental act",[8] Mailer states; the present writer had noted a dozen years earlier (*New York Times Book Review,* 3 May 1959) that *Lady Chatterley's Lover* was "our century's most astonishing romance", which dealt "with love as a serious, major, and sacred theme".[9] This had been apparent from *The Rainbow* on.

One outstanding example of Dr Millett's misreading of Lawrence is in seeing Ursula, Lawrence's version of the "new woman" who had appeared previously in the early-century work of H. G. Wells and Bernard Shaw, as a vixen. She is anything but that, for she is a highly idealized young woman with whom Lawrence often identifies, particularly when he gives her his own experiences as a teacher in mining-country schools. In the publisher's blurb for *The Rainbow,* which Lawrence either wrote or approved of, Ursula is described as "the leading-shoot of the restless, fearless family", who "stands waiting at the advanced post of our time to blaze a path into the future". But, in Kate Millett's words, "Anton [Skrebensky] must be sacrificed as an object lesson in how monstrous the new woman can be."[10]

Certainly Lawrence wanted to "destroy" Skrebensky, as the blindly obedient soldier and lover of empire, but it is just as certain that Lawrence did not attempt to make Ursula "monstrous". She might at times be "difficult", yes, but she was finding her way towards truth. There is a new woman in the book whom Lawrence does present unfavourably—Winifred Inger, whom Ursula tires of and passes on to her uncle, an industrialized decadent. But Kate Millett misses this, as she misses the central philosophy of *Women in Love*—that a married couple should be "two single equal stars balanced in conjunction".[11] This condition is a difficult one to bring about, and since Lawrence is not a stickily popular author with contrived happy endings, he does not give us what is called a pat ending. But Birkin, who uses the balanced-stars phrase more than a dozen times in the novel, at least hopes to bring the condition about. And, even in the rather truncated ending of the novel, it seems as if Birkin and Ursula will become balanced stars, just as at the end of *Lady Chatterley's Lover,* the reader may assume that Mellors and Connie will be reunited. In the world's literature, except sometimes in the case of the greatest tragedies, unresolved situations occur fairly often. To take one example, there is the ending of Dostoevsky's *Crime and Punish-*

ment: Raskolnikov has not yet purged himself of his crime; he is only beginning to understand that he must; but that, as the author explains, would take a whole new book to show in a convincing way, for the conversion would take a long while, and the present story had drawn to its conclusion. And Dostoevsky never wrote along those particular lines again.

Neither did Lawrence, though some readers feel that Lilly in *Aaron's Rod* and Somers in *Kangaroo* are continuations of Birkin. Actually, they are more Lawrence himself than Birkin ever was, for Birkin was only Lawrence in part, a figure in a novel who represented some of Lawrence's beliefs, but was in many ways different. Lawrence rather simply and literally put himself into Lilly and Somers, but those books are more statements than novels; as this writer has pointed out elsewhere, *Kangaroo* is no more a novel than *Also Sprach Zarathustra* and *Sartor Resartus* are novels. In any event, *Aaron's Rod* and *Kangaroo* tell us plenty about Lawrence himself: in the former book, Aaron Sisson tells us some things about Lawrence: the argument with Sir William Frank at Novara is taken from one Lawrence engaged in at Turin in 1919 with his host there, Sir Walter Becker.

Aaron's abandonment of his wife and children was not taken from Lawrence's own experience, and although no one has yet been able to show that Aaron's brief affairs with Josephine Ford in London and the Marchesa Del Torre in Florence were an actual part of that experience, they have an authentic ring. And they do present the reader with Aaron's views of three different types of women. Kate Millett blames him for leaving his wife Lottie, but fails to point out that, on the three occasions when she is present, she is portrayed as a bully and a scold. Josephine Ford has told Lilly, who in turn tells Aaron, that there is no such thing as love; its attempted manifestations occur because men are afraid of being alone. As for women, they indulged in love merely to avoid boredom: "A woman is like a violinist: any fiddle, any instrument rather than empty hands and no tune going." But Aaron has already fled from Josephine; the American-born Marchesa with whom he has the affair in Florence seems equally menacing, if only in the way she clings to him. Chapter 19 is significantly named "Cleopatra, but not Antony".

What Lawrence and some of his male characters dreaded most of all in women was implementation of pure will, less applicable to the last two of Aaron's three women than to Hermione Roddice in *Women in Love*, or some of his later bullying mothers, including those who were defeated in "Mother and Daughter" and "The Lovely Lady". In *Aaron's Rod*, Lottie seems to be will driven, though we catch only glimpses of her, at times when she is outraged at Aaron's rejection; but Josephine Ford and the Marchesa seem less culpable, though Aaron gives them little opportunity to show themselves in any degree of fulness; they nevertheless come through as brightly living, because of Lawrence's magic touch with even the least of characters. At another level, the book is a superb travel volume, with prose pictures of Italy which could be equalled by no one else.

The ending of *Aaron's Rod* is a regrettable one, often severely criticized. In May 1921 Lawrence wrote to his friend Mrs Achsah Brewster that he was finishing *Aaron's Rod* and he knew she wouldn't "like it *at all*", for instead of bringing Aaron "nearer to heaven, in leaps and bounds, he's misbehaving and putting ten fingers to his nose at everything"—and Lawrence proceeded to damn heaven, holiness, and Nirvana. In discussing the book with the Brewsters, on Capri in 1921, he told them the story of the novel and said after showing Aaron's departure from his wife, he did not really know what to do with him after that firm breaking with his past. The Brewsters said that Aaron should either go to Monte Cassino or "through the whole cycle of experience". Lawrence said with a chuckle that he had been considering those possibilities, "that first he had intended sending him to Monte Cassino, but found instead that Aaron had to go to destruction and find his way through from the lowest depths."[12]

The ending, in any event, is not really precise, though critics have read much into it, interpreting Aaron's possible complete acceptance of Lilly's "leadership" as being both homosexual and fascist; the latter notion, however, is implausible, and those who attempt to put the same labels on *Kangaroo*, are definitely wrong. Somer's interest in Kangaroo and his personality does not in any way seem sexual, and his rejection of fascism, as well as socialism, is clear. What Lawrence's spokesman Somers *does* fail to perceive is that he can make this choice because he is a free man living in a democracy. It must be said in Lawrence's behalf that he had become disillusioned with the democratic process during the 1914–18 war, as the *Kangaroo* chapter "The Nightmare" shows, in its

vital picture of a nonconformist Englishman and his German wife
during their enforced stay in Great Britain. This chapter is the
finest twentieth-century account of the mass bullying, both by
authorities and busybody self-designated authorities at such times,
and perhaps Lawrence cannot altogether be blamed if his personal
sufferings (pointedly accurate in the book) somewhat blurred his
vision of democracy. A few years after *Kangaroo,* he rather fool-
ishly celebrated the imagined resurrection of pre-Columbian Indian
rites in Mexico, the leaders of which have absolute power over life
and death. The woman in the story, Kate Leslie, a forty-year-old
Irish widow, is a projection of Frieda Lawrence, seen with enough
objectivity to make her skeptical of the Mexican nonsense and,
though submitting to some of it, reluctant to make a complete commitment and suggesting that her attachment is not permanent. In
John Middleton Murry's *Son of Woman* the author suggests that
Lawrence, at the time he wrote *The Plumed Serpent,* had given up
living and so portrayed Kate as a widow; actually, Lawrence put
himself imaginatively into both Cipriano and Don Ramón, with
their silly utterances.

Lawrence again became a spokesman for his philosophy when
he put himself into the framework of Mellors in *Lady Chatterley's
Lover,* mentioned earlier as a book which Norman Mailer approves
of and which seems to be beyond the understanding of Kate
Millett. The point is that Mellors brings Connie alive. And in his
next (and really last) important fiction, the short novel *The
Escaped Cock,* known also as *The Man Who Died,* it is the priestess
of Isis (the seeker after Osiris) who takes the initiative in the love
scene which, like so many in Lawrence, is sexual-mystical, a revelation to the man who had been crucified and who had died and
come alive again, wandering after giving up prophecy itself; and
the priestess of Isis in Search insists on calling him Osiris. Their
relationship must end, however, for he might be captured by the
Roman soldiers—Lawrence hated the iron rule of the Romans and
lets his resurrected prophet escape after his resurrection is completed by his initiation into love. The man who had been crucified
and the woman who was the Priestess of Osiris may not meet
again, but each of them has realized what perfection can be.

We now need a conclusion, which will be a fairly long one, in
regard to Lawrence's attitudes to woman and love.

The Millett accusations are made at great length and could be answered in full in larger space; but perhaps the indication in the foregoing of her oversimple approach to Lawrence has shown how wrong she can be; and Norman Mailer, although not always sympathetic to Lawrence, has rather effectively answered some of her principal criticisms. But what actually was Lawrence's experience with women and what did he say about them?

The previously mentioned relationship with his mother could have been crippling. The other important woman in his youth was Jessie Chambers, called Miriam Leivers in *Sons and Lovers*. There was probably more of physical attraction in his association with Louisa Burrows and Alice Dax, whom he perhaps combined in the character of Clara Dawes in that novel; the friendship with Helen Corke, the Helena of *The Trespasser*, was apparently what we call platonic. His life was greatly changed, and his writing bloomed, after he met Frieda Weekley-Richthofen in 1912 and lured her away from her husband and with her made his first visits to Germany and Italy.

Jessie Chambers, whom he knew from their adolescence until well into their maturity, would probably have become his wife— for she was intelligent, pretty, and talented—except for the fact that she shared one outstanding characteristic with his mother; she was will driven. Louisa Burrows apparently was not, though she was educated and, like Jessie, intelligent; judging by the surviving photographs, she was more magnetizing physically than Jessie. It was perhaps this last element that attracted Lawrence most of all. But eventually he felt that they could not have a continued relationship, and as he was recovering from his severe illness of 1911–12, he wrote to tell her that doctors in the London suburb where he was living, and at Bournemouth, where he had gone to recuperate, had advised him not to marry, at that time or perhaps at any time. His illness, he told Louisa, had changed him greatly and broken many of the bonds that had once held him. In a letter three days later, he was more blunt: "I don't think now I have the proper love to marry on. Have you not felt it so?" She apparently felt no resentment, a few years later, over being part of the character (along with Frieda) of Ursula in *The Rainbow*, but Jessie Chambers was embittered at being put into *Sons and Lovers* as Miriam. She makes out a pathetic case for herself in *D. H. Lawrence: A Personal Record* (1935), published five years after Lawrence's death, under the disguising initials E.T.; Lawrence had treated her badly, but after all he was writing a novel. Many of his friends throughout his life would suffer from his tendency to include people he knew in his fiction, often as caricatures. He did this with men as well as women.

His friends Lady Ottoline Morrell and Mabel Dodge Luhan each appeared as rather monstrous creatures, Lady Ottoline as Hermione in *Women in Love* and Mrs Luhan in several of his stories. Lady Ottoline was deeply hurt and broke off her friendship with Lawrence for a number of years; Mrs Luhan, whom Lawrence pointedly evaded during his last visits to New Mexico, wrote to him after he had left for Europe for the last time, and he answered her politely enough. But she and Lady Ottoline stand out among women Lawrence knew in later life whom he saw as will-propelled dangers; they had not attracted him erotically, but had drawn him into their literary-social circles, and he grew weary of their tendencies to dominate.

A letter from Lawrence to Lady Ottoline in 1915 prefigures his fictional portrait of her as Hermione: at the Morrells' estate, a young Belgian refugee, Maria Nys (later Mrs Aldous Huxley), had tried to kill herself, and Lawrence scolded Lady Ottoline for having dominated the girl with her will, asking why she must always be using her will, and adding that she is "always grasping and trying to know and to dominate". He then ruefully admits, "I'm too much like this myself."[13]

And this was true enough, until he and Frieda eventually worked out their "equal-stars-in-conjunction" accord. Lawrence had early recognized the dangers in assertions of will, though he had known it only unconsciously in the case of his mother, at least until after he had completed *Sons and Lovers*. Nearly ten years later, in Ceylon, he told his American friends, Earl and Achsah Brewster, that he "felt like rewriting it" because the book "had not done justice to his father". And he went on to give the Brewsters an unpleasant verbal picture of his mother exercising her will over the family. As for Mrs Luhan, her memoir of Lawrence is full of his comments on her will, and in one letter she prints he tells her, "I do assert that, primarily, I *don't* exert my own will to predominate;" rather he wants his own will to be only "a servant of the 'flow', the lion that attends Una, the virgin; or the angel with the bright sword, at the gate". And this is all, in 1924, that he wanted his will to be, above all "not a rampaging Lucifer. But in you, even your affection is a subordinate part of your everlasting will." And there is much else.

Kate Millett quotes an appalling letter from Frieda to John Middleton Murry, in 1951, in which Frieda tells Murry of an occasion when Lawrence put his hands on her throat, pressed her against the wall, and insisted he was the master. Frieda said that she replied, "Is that all? You can be master as much as you like, I don't care." And, she went on, "His hands dropped away, he looked at me in astonishment and was all right."[14] (Dr Millett failed to note a paragraph in Frieda's memoir of Lawrence, in which she described what he once did when she stunned herself somewhat by bumping her head against a shutter; she was astonished when Lawrence was put into "an agony of sympathy and tenderness. . . . When I had bumped my head before, nobody seemed to bother, but Lawrence was different: To be so enveloped in tenderness was a miracle in itself for me."[15]) The "I-am-master" incident possibly occurred during the 1922 visit to Australia, when Lawrence was writing *Kangaroo*, for the episode sounds like something out of that book. The point is, Frieda knew how to put up with Lawrence's sometimes extreme assertions, as he did with hers, so things remained "all right". In *Kangaroo* the rather slangily written chapter, "Harriett and Lovatt at Sea in Marriage", amusingly discusses the lord-and-master idea, along with that of the perfect lover, and the friend and companion, most of it seen in terms of a man and woman aboard a marriage bark that runs into heavy seas. In many ways the chapter is unsatisfactory because at the end it plunges into a kind of mysticism which is difficult to understand and would certainly be difficult to follow in any actual sense. Yet it is also satisfactory because Richard Lovatt Somers sees that Harriett would never accept him until he admits the dark god Lawrence tended to worship, who would be the true Lord and master.

Lawrence uses a nautical metaphor-symbol again, in the second of the three versions of *Lady Chatterley's Lover*, the one published as *John Thomas and Lady Jane*, often the finest of the triad. And its marriage-bark passages are extremely satisfactory, with Constance Chatterley seeing herself and the gamekeeper as "two sailing vessels crossing a sea to the same port", each captain handling his vessel differently, "and the ships stay apart, for their own safety." But they go on to the same destination:

So it must be: a voyage apart, in the same direction. Grapple the two vessels together, lash them side by side, and the first storm will smash them to pieces. That is marriage, in the bad weather of civilisation. But leave the two vessels apart, to make their voyage to the same port, each according to its own skill and power, and an unseen life connects them, a magnetism which cannot be forced. And that is marriage as it will be, when this is broken down.[16]

This is a variant of the "equal-stars" theme, a seasoned development of it.

We must recognize that Lawrence began life under handicaps —social, physical and psychological—and that he overcame all except that of health, for this frail man died, at forty-four, of the disease that strikes down so many miners, lung disease. Despite this he wrote some magnificent books, "written" more brilliantly than most of their competitors. In his relationships with women, he was sometimes "wrong", but he tried to be right; and he learned, as his picture of Connie Chatterley and her gamekeeper shows, and as his resurrected man who died also shows. Essentially, Lawrence regarded love—and women—in a way that can only be called religious.

NOTES

1   *D. H. Lawrence and Human Existence* (1951), p. 25.
2   *D. H. Lawrence: Novelist* (1955), *passim.*
3   Howe, *passim.*
4   Mailer, 1971, *passim.*
5   Millett, *Sexual Politics* (1971), p. 293.
6   Mailer, pp. 141–42.
7   *Ibid.*, pp. 141–42.
8   *Ibid.*
9   Reprinted in *Age of the Modern* (1971).
10 Millett, *ibid.*, p. 262.
11 Birkin says this throughout *Women in Love.*
12 E. and A. Brewster, *D. H. Lawrence: Reminiscences and Correspondence* (1934), p. 243.
13 *D. H. Lawrence, The Collected Letters* (ed. Moore), p. 355.
14 *Frieda Lawrence: The Memoirs and Correspondence* (ed. Tedlock, 1964).
15 Frieda Lawrence, *"Not I, but the Wind . . ."* (1974), p. 78.
16 *John Thomas and Lady Jane* (1972), p. 297.

9

On Lawrence's Hostility to Wilful Women: The Chatterley Solution

by MARK SPILKA

In his recent book, *Man and Woman: A Study of Love and the Novel, 1740–1940*, A. O. J. Cockshut speaks of the difficulty of placing Lawrence fairly "in any tradition in his idea of the will".[1] Where previous novelists follow the pagan and Christian view that man's will is weak "so that he often prefers the evil he does not desire to the good he does", Lawrence seems to say "that if you are too weak to do what you intended, it only proves that you didn't really intend it at all." And where modern progressives like Havelock Ellis come near to equating will with impulse, so that their sacred gospel is "Doing as One Likes", Lawrence usually emphasizes responsibility for creating that third thing between two people which is love. He seems to be saying, then, that will is neither weak nor equatable with impulse, "that it must press on to its true goal; and that when it appears to be weak, this is only because of concealed insincerity". Cockshut is accordingly puzzled by

> . . . the strange failure to distinguish in the plot of *Women in Love* between what the characters intend and what happens to them. Did Gerald intend to kill his brother? Is his death in the snow his destiny or his intention? Perhaps Lawrence fails to answer clearly because he does not admit the validity of the question.[2]

Perhaps. It seems more likely, however, that Lawrence implies some fusion between destiny and intention by which characters are held responsible for their fates; and that he assigns unconscious as well as conscious dimensions to volition to account for its apparent weaknesses. He is like Freud in this last respect, and like him too in his insistence on that "passionate struggle into conscious being" by which true intentions become manifest. Thus Gerald did "intend" to kill his brother when they were boys, if we are to take Ursula's outburst at face value:

> Perhaps there *was* an unconscious will behind it. . . . This playing at killing has some primitive *desire* for killing in it, don't you think? . . . I couldn't pull the trigger of the emptiest gun in the world, not if someone were looking down the barrel. One instinctively doesn't do it—one can't.[3]

And Gerald's death in the snow is his "intended" destiny, if we are to credit Birkin's speculations on how he might have saved himself; or his passionate cry that Gerald should have loved him, for then "death would not have mattered"; or his comparison in this light of the dead Gerald's repugnant "mass of maleness" with the beautiful dead face of one whom Birkin had loved, "who died still having the faith to yield to the mystery", so that "no one could call [her face] cold, mute, material", nor remember it "without gaining faith in the mystery, without the soul's warming with new, deep life trust" (p. 471). With Lawrence, it seems, we are as responsible for the quality of our deaths as for the quality and direction of our lives and loves.[4] It is this strenuous burden of "life-responsibility", much more than his radical sexual views, which makes him such a troubling writer for many readers, and which lends some credence to Cockshut's notion that Lawrence's sexual initiates are few because, like a band of ascetic monks, "they are asking more of themselves than ordinary human nature can be expected to give."

If Lawrence is saying thereby that we choose to be the kind of people we finally are, and so choose our destinies, then—strength of will aside—he does derive from a blend of monkish traditions. He is like Dante and the medieval theologians, for whom mind and will are instrumental and of no value in themselves, their function being to discover the true modes of love and to choose them over false ones—which is how mind and will are used by Lawrence's questing characters as they realize themselves through love. Of course these characters prefer sensual to spiritual modes of love and find the latter false, inadequate, or outworn: but their monk-like striving, as Cockshut notes, is otherwise appropriate. Dr Leavis would invoke the Puritan tradition here, and insist on the individualistic vigor of such striving: but the instrumental function of mind and will is shared by both traditions. The Faustian uses of mind and will as terminal powers, dominating and exploiting emotional life, would be Lawrence's version then of the anti-Christ, and he was not above putting Christ himself in that position in *The Man Who Died*. The men and women who adopt this terminal mode in *Women in Love*—Hermione, Gerald, Gudrun, Loerke—are as strenuous in pursuing it as the questing characters, and I believe we must finally say they choose their own destruction.

It is in this special context—the instrumental and terminal uses of the will by monklike or Faustian strivers—that Lawrence's hostility to women has to be considered. Though he creates credible social contexts and plausible characters, he seldom deals with ordinary people in an ordinary world; his primary concern, in fact, is with states of being in a cosmic field—with the "dark gods" within us and around us. As Cockshut points out, moreover, his "dark gods were powerless to improve society" and were more obviously opposed to it, more interested in its destruction than its reform. Thus, Cockshut refuses the oversimplifications of "the Lawrence cult", by which Lawrence is connected with Havelock Ellis and his friends as "reformers, pioneers", exploring new territory "which would one day be within the reach of all". Within the reach of some, he might concede, and perhaps he might consider also Lawrence's obvious influence on the counter-culture movements of the 1960s, many of which absorbed his more predictive views. Whatever the case, his private solutions for public conditions, and his representations of phases and tendencies of modern culture, have their bearing on public and private life today and are fair game for re-examination in the light of current criticisms from feminist and other quarters. It is only necessary to separate them from irrelevant issues—careers for women when neither his men nor his women questers endorse careers, sisterhood as well as brotherhood when none of his brotherly compacts take hold— and to attend fairly to the marriage compacts which do take hold and to the attempt to imagine a more viable basis for modern marriage.

1

As I have elsewhere observed, Lawrence was about as hostile in his treatment of women as Doris Lessing in her treatment of men.[5] He also liked women, as she likes men, and his treatment of women characters has in this respect attracted as many admiring women readers as her work has attracted male admirers. Yet both saw the opposite sex as essentially threatening to personal integrity. To put them together is, in a way, to see where we are now in the ongoing battle of the sexes (namely, at an impasse). But our question is, where was Lawrence in the earlier decades of the century? Were his fears about women personal, representative, or predictive? Something of all three, surely, and therefore humanly interesting and instructive. Paul Morel's fear of his mother's ego-usurping love is the obvious starting-point. Threaded through an otherwise sympathetic portrait of a vital, long-suffering, intelligent, decidedly attractive woman, it helps to explain his unconscious stake in hastening her death.[6] Lawrence would be still harder on usurping mothers as his career progressed, and softer on irresponsible fathers, whose more attractive qualities would gradually emerge. The pattern is unmistakable and lends much credence to the view that Lawrence spent a lifetime trying to set his parents' marriage straight. But it was his own marriage which essentially preoccupied him from *The Rainbow* onward, and his struggles with Frieda may be taken as the source and pattern for his fictive conflicts, his paradigm for the exigencies of modern love. Her will to power, her yieldings and unyieldings, yeasted his conflictual tales. How to make that proud unfaithful insufferably romantic lady acquiesce of her own indomitably free will? How indeed to *break* a woman's will? The very statement signals hostility, and yet it is love, true love, which seems to demand such dreadful yielding!

There is a marvellous scene in *Women in Love*, from the chapter called "Carpetting", which will serve as our *exemplum*. In it Birkin objects harshly to Hermione's belief that "The will can cure anything, and put anything right." "It is fatal to use the will like that," Birkin cries, "disgusting. Such a will is an obscenity." Then, watching her maddeningly slow response to his attack, he oddly concludes that "he would never, never dare to break her will, and let loose the maelstrom of her subconsciousness, and see her in her ultimate madness. Yet he was always striking at her" (pp. 131–2). The statement is odd because, save for a few verbal sallies, he has bottled up his own rage throughout this chapter, obeyed her almost meekly, allowed her to supervise the decoration of his rooms, accepted from her the gift of a rug he doesn't want—and all this *after* the head-bashing incident at Breadalby which supposedly ended their affair. Apparently he is not much of a will-breaker himself, more of a pond-stoner, a provoker of women like Hermione and Ursula whose wills seem stronger, if anything, than his own.

What does he want from such women? That bash on the head from Hermione which he in fact prescribed for *her* in an early chapter ("If one cracked your skull perhaps one might get a spontaneously passionate woman out of you, with real sensuality" [p. 36])? That dressing-down from Ursula which dissolves the "tight knot of consciousness" in his own cracked skull, and which accordingly breaks Hermione's hold on him, and frees *him* for real sensuality? Is Birkin then a man who needs the defiance of stronger-willed women to realize himself? Is he a tester of superior wills, in search of someone willing *not* to break his own? One thing seems certain: he knows that terminal uses of the will are "fatal" and "obscene", and since he wants to live himself, the challenge which he now provokes from Ursula is respectfully provoked.

I refer to the ongoing discussion about horse-breaking to which our first exchange belongs. Ursula has been reproving Gerald for his mare-beating tactics at the railroad crossing in the chapter called "Coal-Dust". Responding to Gerald's defense that "A horse has got a will like a man", and accordingly must be mastered, Birkin holds that "Every horse, strictly, has two wills." With one "it wants to put itself in the human power completely—and with the other, it wants to be free, wild. The two wills sometimes lock," he continues; "you know that, if you've ever felt a horse bolt." Gerald refuses the last point, Hermione ceases to listen, but Ursula, sensing the implications for herself, pushes them into the open:

> "Why should a horse want to put itself in the human power?" asked Ursula "That is quite incomprehensible to me. I don't believe it ever wanted it."

"Yes it did. It's the last, perhaps highest, love-impulse: resign your will to the higher being," said Birkin.

"What curious notions you have of love," jeered Ursula.

"And woman is the same as horses: two wills act in opposition inside her. With one will, she wants to subject herself utterly. With the other she wants to bolt, and pitch her rider to perdition."

"Then I'm a bolter," said Ursula, with a burst of laughter.

"It's a dangerous thing to domesticate even horses, let alone women," said Birkin. "The dominant principle has some rare antagonists."

(pp. 130–2)

In *Sexual Politics* Kate Millett argues that Birkin finds Gerald's mastery of the mare "agreeable" and that he equates it with the mastery of women, in obvious contradiction of his own marital doctrine of polarity between equals.[7] It would be fairer to say, however, that Birkin is on both sides of the question and can be identified with neither: he is telling Gerald that there is no mastery unless horse or woman wants to be mastered, telling Ursula that the horse or woman is free to bolt, and finding something admirable—wildness, devotion—in either choice. Considering Lawrence's high opinion of "wild life", moreover, the horse/woman equation is probably a compliment, though provoker Birkin no doubt goads with spurs in speaking of higher beings. His playful awareness of the dangers of domestication, his admiring bow to rare antagonists, show further that he has picked up and relishes Ursula's response. For surely he *perceives* the dangers of the dominance game, the will-breaking game, the deadly compact he has known with Hermione and may fall into again with Ursula as she challenges him now, and, "consciously or unconsciously", he accepts. "It was a fight to the death between them—or to new life, though in what the conflict lay, no one could say," writes Lawrence as the chapter ends.

A fight to the death—or to new life: these are the odds, this is how Lawrence sees courtship and marriage. The compact is necessarily conflictual and the stakes and risks are extremely high. It is in the area of deadly risks that Lawrence's hostility problems lie, in his flirtations with dominance and with bending, if not breaking, a woman's will. In the early fiction, interestingly, it is the men whose wills are bent or broken. Thus, in *Sons and Lovers*, Walter Morel's manhood is broken in the struggle with his wife, and Paul is supine before Miriam, derelict after his mother's death, saved only by a last-ditch exertion of will. In *The Rainbow*, though Tom Brangwen finally holds his own against his foreign wife's friability and independent strength, Will Brangwen is defeated by her wilful daughter Anna, and Skrebensky is broken under the moon's aegis in Ursula's fierce embrace. Like many of his male contemporaries—Joyce, Hemingway, Thomas Wolfe—Lawrence felt that women were the stronger sex, the likely dominators, in emotional relations. They could be and sometimes were beneficent initiators, as in early tales like "Daughters of the Vicar"; but plainly they were indomitable.

Thus the balances arrived at in mid-career, in novels and tales like *Women in Love* and *The Captain's Doll*, reflect an emerging and rather shortlived *equivalence* in male strength, an equivalence easily confused with the urge to dominate because that issue is, for the first time, stridently posed. One might more feasibly argue, however, that Ursula's strength is constant throughout the novel and that Birkin has all he can do to fight through his own weaknesses and her justified resistances to the point where she will bring him an affirming flower; and that Hepburn too has all he can do to overcome his abjectness with his estranged wife, and the threat of dollhood with his mistress Hannele, before he can win that stronger woman's assent and respect in marriage. The talk of dominance and obedience is there, but these are arguably more "surface assertion" —Millett's term for the polarity pronouncements in *Women in Love*—than dramatically realized relations. Whereas the balances of this period—the polarities which Millett denies—seem to me genuinely achieved, the assent and respect freely given and fairly won, the strength and memorability of Ursula and Hannele among the finest testimonies we have of Lawrence's liking for—and profound respect for—women.[8] Can anyone really believe—beyond point-scoring argument—that such women will be effaced into nonentities by their fictive marriages?

The Fox, written and rewritten in the same period, had a longer tail tacked onto it in its final stage which indicates the next phase in will-breaking; and here the animus toward women becomes truly problematic. A powerful tale, in many ways one of Lawrence's finest novellas, *The Fox* deals head on with the clashing of wills between men and women, and with the sexual differences defined by it. The intrusion of a pernicious fox into the farm life of two land girls of the postwar period, Banford and March, is Lawrence's dramatic device for defining the masculine and feminine principles. A young soldier, Henry Grenfel, returned from the war, looking for his grandfather, the former owner, joins the farm girls, hunts game for them and so becomes associated with the fox, which has fascinated March, the ostensibly masculine member of this muted lesbian pair. She agrees to marry him, and when he wills the fox's death and secures its power and place in her imagination, she dreams in turn of Banford's death, discards her manly land uniform and begins to wear dresses. At this point the strong-willed Banford pulls her back, and the story takes a vicious turn when Grenfel rallies to meet her challenge: for he now wills Banford's death by warning her to stand clear of a tree he is about to fell and so enlisting her defiant cooperation in self-murder. With Banford so effaced he marries March and tries to get her to relinquish responsibility for the world's happiness; he wants her to become passive, acquiescent, to sleep in the shelter of his own responsible arms; he wants to "put her independent spirit to sleep". Then "She would not be a man any more, an independent woman with a man's responsibility. Nay, even the responsibility for her own soul she would have to commit to him."[9] March understandably resists such soul-absorption—resists it "like a child that . . . fights against sleep as if sleep were death"; and the story ends with the strain between them unresolved. The wished-for sleep is only Henry's dream.

If Lawrence were describing an impasse, rather than prescribing pernicious doctrines, such honest touches would be more commendable. It is one thing to assign death-wishes to spiteful lesbians, quite another to sanction murder in the name of life; and still quite another to assume responsibility for accessible, hence vulnerable women, while denying them independent spirit and responsibility for their own souls. As such a parent-child relation suggests, Lawrence has begun to impose on his heroines the ego-usurping pressures of Paul Morel's mother, and to visit upon their wilful spirits, or wilful alter-egos, her merciful demise. Thus, in *The Captain's Doll*, Mrs Hepburn falls to her death from a third-floor bedroom window, the ostensible victim of vertigo, and so frees her husband to marry Hannele. It is a comic death in what Lawrence rightly considered a "very funny" novella; but, after *The Fox*, we may wonder if the Captain really shaved on innocently

in his dressing-room during the tumble, or lent a helping shove.
There can be no such doubts about the phantasmagoric ending of
"The Woman Who Rode Away", wherein the heroine lies on a
sacrificial slab of stone in a drugged state of acquiescence before
Chilchui Indians whose aged naked priest will "strike home" his
flint knife when the sun's rays reach the shaft of ice at the mouth
of the cave. "Strike home" indeed. Kate Millett's word for it is
"sexual cannibalism": "substitute the knife for the penis and penetration, the cave for a womb, and for a bed, a place of execution—
and you provide a murder whereby one acquires one's victim's
power. . . . Lawrence himself seems envious, afraid—murderous."[10]
The charges stick for this phase of his life and fiction, if not for
his whole career. And even here the knife never falls, the women
never wholly acquiesce. Thus, in *The Plumed Serpent*, the heroine,
Kate Leslie, resists the offer of a place in the new pantheon of
Mexican gods and remains undecided, strongly doubtful, at the
end. As well she might be in a mythic land where women are
denied sexual satisfaction and reduced to passive instruments of
male pleasure and power. In "The Princess" a more dubiously
wilful heroine, Dolly Urquhart, is repeatedly violated by her moun-
tain guide when she calls for his warmth, mistakes it for male conquest, and—just as repeatedly—refuses to admire it. The envious,
murderous Lawrence knows in his bones he can't win this way. He
even writes wish-fulfilment tales now like "Sun" and *St Mawr*,
about willing women seeking love from the sun, from horses and/
or landscapes, in a world where men they respect no longer exist,
in reflection, perhaps, of that lapsed confidence in his own masculine selfhood which marks these postwar years.

For like Hepburn in *The Captain's Doll*, Lawrence seems to have
felt "that a hatchet had gone through the ligatures and veins that
connected him with the people of his affections, . . . and for the
time being he was conscious only of the cleavage. . . ."[11] He had
suffered a series of telling blows and changes—harassment by
the police in Cornwall during the war, suppression of *The Rainbow*
and delayed publication of *Women in Love*, self-exile and wandering across the world to Ceylon, Australia, America, Mexico, rejection by his friends in the Rananim venture, separation from
Frieda and the beginning of her intimacy with John Middleton
Murry—which help to explain his sense of isolation. In the face
of which he tried to school himself once more in separate selfhood,

his first law of life, with only fitful success. His outbursts of temper with new friends became more aimless, his self-importance burgeoned, he seems to have driven Frieda off to England for relief. It was from this weakened position that he flaunted ideas of political power and sexual dominance in his fiction.

Purgation came, I think, at the famous "Last Supper", when his wife called him back to England and he asked each of his old friends to return with him to America and was refused by all. He became violently ill, no doubt from sheer deflation, but the occasion seems thereby to have restored proportion to his life and art. Regaining some of his old lightheartedness, he soon discovered that the "militant ideal" he had pursued so strenuously was "a cold egg", and that tenderness might better define the future.[12]

2

Drugs, murder, rape, sexual cannibalism, soul-absorption, wish-fulfilment, pond-stoning argument—the ways of breaking a woman's will, or of getting her to acquiesce of her own free will, are varied in Lawrence's postwar fiction, and—quite understandably—most of them seem to fail. But at this point in his life he hit upon a solution, the beauty and simplicity of which had so far eluded him: if you wait long enough, the world will do it for you. It took him three versions of *Lady Chatterley's Lover* to reach that solution, and to evolve the theme of tenderness inherent in it and the explicit sexual descriptions by which that theme proceeds. Since the three versions of the novel are now in print, we can trace the evolution of this long-delayed and rather poignant discovery— about modern women, certainly—but chiefly, I think, about modern lovers like himself.

The key to that discovery is the scene at the gamekeeper's hut in which Connie begins to cry while holding one of the pheasant chicks in her hand and the gamekeeper, moved to compassion by her tears, makes love to her. In *The First Lady Chatterley* the scene occurs in Chapter IV, about sixty pages into the novel, and takes a page in telling.[13] There is no sexual description, and no connection of Connie's tears with her generation's forlornness. In the second version of the novel, *John Thomas and Lady Jane*, the scene has been moved up to Chapter VII, 112 pages into the novel, and takes four pages in telling.[14] There is sexual description now,

and though there is still no link between her tears and her generation's forlornness, the episode is prepared for by a long disquisition (a virtual essay) on sexual and fiscal acquisitiveness in modern
life. There is also a description of how nurse Bolton acquires power
over Clifford and moves him in turn to exert power over his mines
and miners. Then, as Connie turns from Clifford's world to the
refuge of the hut, there comes a long passage on the will, half-
sermon, half-confession, which is worth quoting in full:

> The wood was like a sanctuary of life itself. Life itself! Life itself!
> That was all that one could have, all that one could yearn for. And
> yet the human will cuts off the human being from living. Alone
> of all created things, the human being cannot live.
>   Life is so soft and quiet, and cannot be seized. It will not be
> raped. Try to rape it, and it disappears. Try to seize it, and you
> have dust. Try to master it, and you see your own image grinning
> at you with the grin of an idiot.
>   Whoever wants life must go softly towards life, softly as one
> would go towards a deer and a fawn that was nestling under a
> tree. One gesture of violence, one violent assertion of self-will,
> and life is gone. You must seek again. And softly, gently, with in-
> finitely sensitive hands and feet, and a heart that is full and free
> from self-will, you must approach life again, and come at last into
> touch. Snatch even at a flower, and you have lost it for ever out
> of your life. Come with greed and the will-to-self towards another
> human being, and you clutch a thorny demon that will leave
> poisonous stings.
>   But with quietness, with an abandon of self-assertion and a ful-
> ness of the deep, true self one can approach another human be-
> ing, and know the delicate best of life, the touch. The touch of
> the feet on the earth, the touch of the fingers on a tree, on a
> creature, the touch of hands and breasts, the touch of the whole
> body to body, and the interpenetration of passionate love: it is life
> itself, and in the touch, we are all alive.
>   It is no good trying to fight life. You can only lose. The will
> is a mysterious thing, but the golden apples it wins are apples of
> Sodom and bitter, insane dust. One can fight for life, fight against
> the grey unliving armies, the armies of greedy ones and bossy
> ones, and the myriad hosts of the clutching and the self-important.
> Fight one does and must, against the enemies of life. But when
> you come to life itself, you must come as the flower does, naked
> and defenceless and infinitely in touch.

(pp. 107–8)

As this lovely, clumsy, verbose sermon shows, Lawrence has found his theme in the second version but has not yet found a way to fuse it with the lives of his characters. Indeed, these verbosities have more bearing on his own misadventures in mid-career; for, in imagination or in fact, the excesses of rape, seizure, mastery, violence, self-will, self-importance, greed and bossiness, were his own. By the third and final version of the novel he had come to better fictive terms with them. In *Lady Chatterley's Lover* the first love-scene has been moved still further along to Chapter X, 161 pages into the novel, and takes six pages in telling.[15] The sermon on the will has been dropped and material from it worked into the early lives of Connie and Mellors. The ideas on touch have been moved to a late chapter, where they emerge through conversation as a conclusion drawn *from* the lovers' experience rather than prologue to it. Clifford's new industrial activity, as inspired by Mrs Bolton, has been pushed back to the previous chapter, and the disquisition on acquisitiveness has been condensed and transferred into the gamekeeper's thoughts as he returns to his hut that night and sees the need to oppose mechanized greed with tenderness. Connie's forlornness, the gamekeeper's reluctance to become involved again in love, are newly emphasized, and there is a nice touch as Connie later sees he was kind to the female in her, where other men were kind to her person. A real sorting out and focussing has occurred, then, and the displacement of the scene at the hut by 100 pages, from 60 in version one to 161 in version three, seems to be crucial to it.

What did Lawrence want to achieve by the long postponement? Chiefly, I think, he wanted to prepare us for Connie's acquiescence, her readiness for change, her willingness to "go softly towards life", to get into touch with life itself. And to do this he had to create the grounds for the attrition of self-will, the world and way of life which so deplete her volition that by the time she reaches the gamekeeper's hut "She was to be had for the taking."

This is why the novel opens with Connie's "position", rather than Clifford's, in the tragic aftermath of World War I. The consequences of her husband's war-induced paralysis are greater for her than for Clifford, and she must learn how to cope with them. She must care for Clifford, physically and emotionally, without much chance of caring for herself. The most obvious result of that arrangement would be sexual frustration; but for this third version of the novel Lawrence endows her with sufficient sexual experience to overcome that problem. She takes a pre-war lover in her student years at Dresden, and has few qualms about taking a post-war lover, when she needs one, from the Wragby circle. Her problem then is not frustration, which she knows how to accommodate, but the cold, exploitive, depleting way of life she shares with Clifford.

Chiefly she suffers from the disconnections of the mental life at Wragby. The withdrawal to Clifford's estate, following the war, is in many ways a withdrawal from the world, including the surrouding villages; but Clifford (a Cambridge man himself) gathers around him his own circle of critics and writers, admirers of the smart, spiteful stories he has begun to publish, and Connie (who hails from Kensington) plays hostess to this provincial version of post-war Bloomsbury. She feels no real closeness, however, with these unconventional friends, who (like the original Bloomsbury set) pride themselves on sexual frankness even as they deprecate or deny "the sex connection". Thus the writer Hammond sees sex as pointless, compares it to going to the privy in importance; or the scientific writer Charley May speaks out for sexual promiscuity, an exchange of sensations instead of ideas, another form of talk. For Clifford, too, though sex perfects the intimacy of marriage (by which he means the purely mental union), it is "not really necessary", an accident rather, an obsolete organic process from which his own war accident has freed him. Olive Strangeways, looking for the day when babies will be bred in bottles and women "immunized" and able to live their own lives, is Clifford's feminine counterpart in this modern refusal of the body's importance, and Connie's ally, perhaps, in the "beautiful pure freedom" of modern womanhood she knew at Dresden. But as the Wragby life continues Connie begins to sense the negation of vital possibilities such talk entails; and in her growing restlessness she makes common cause with the outsider Michaelis, the popular playwright with the stray-dog soul.

Connie's brief affair with Michaelis is at least an attempt at human contact. She yields to his abjectness out of almost maternal compassion, prefers his unscrupulousness in pursuing success to Clifford's false pretensions. But since he finishes quickly as a lover she begins to hold herself back, as she had learned to do at Dresden, so that the expended man must hang on grimly while she comes to her own crisis. At first Michaelis prides himself in giving her satisfaction this way, but eventually he explodes in resentment at her running the sexual show, and Lawrence makes the telling point that he gave her no choice, and that he has himself smashed their affair so as to avoid having to marry her. At which point Connie's sexual feeling for him, or for any man, collapses. The game of using others, at which they have both played at different times, is exploded by his brutality.

A more chronic and perhaps more basic problem for Connie is "the ghastly burden of life-responsibility" which Clifford puts upon her. "You are the great I-am, as far as life goes," he tells her; "but for you I am absolutely nothing." The infantile nature of such dependency is revealed when her health deteriorates and he is forced to replace her with nurse Bolton—from which maternal source he now draws succour for his new career in industry. Meanwhile Connie has received some oracular clues to her own regeneration. Lawrence's Wragby spokesman, the army man Tommy Dukes, explains the spitefulness of the mental life by its denial of "the whole corpus of consciousness", belly and penis as well as brain and mind, from which "real knowledge" proceeds. Like an apple of knowledge plucked from the tree, severed from the organic connection, the purely analytic mind goes "bad" and spiteful and can only "make a deadness".

Dukes offers other oracular clues ("Give me the democracy of touch, the resurrection of the body") which help Connie to find her way; but chiefly Mellors himself begins to pull her away from Clifford and his cronies. The woods on Wragby estate, where once Robin Hood had hunted, are the gamekeeper's domain; as the lower-class keeper of life who will steal the rich landlord's lady he is plainly Robin's heir. Connie glimpses him first in Chapter V when she accompanies Clifford to the woods—which he sees as the heart of old England—and he asks her to have a son by another man so as to help him preserve this place intact. The casual sex thing is nothing, Clifford tells her, compared to the long life lived together, the weaving of the steadily-lived life. Connie agrees, but wonders about weaving her own life into his by such devices: "Life may turn quite a new face on it all," she warns him. Then, as she watches a brown spaniel running out of a side-path, the gamekeeper emerges as a swift menace, "like a sudden rush of a threat out of nowhere" (p. 84). If "nowhere" is the heart and mystery of

the old, wild England, then the gamekeeper emerges from that un-
expected source as the new face life may turn, the unpredictable
father of her oddly-sanctioned child, and the threat of all these
fateful possibilities frightens Connie. Recovering a little, she judges
him "a curious, quick, separate fellow, alone, but sure of himself",
and notices also his alertness to everything around him, including
the "strange, weary yearning" which now starts in her, "a dissatisfaction . . . older than the hills" with all that Clifford represents.

Mellors' "separateness" helps to explain her weary yearning.
When, in the next chapter, she comes upon him suddenly at the
back of his cottage, washing himself with quick, subtle, animal
motions, vulnerable and in a creaturely way beautiful, she receives
the "shock of vision in her womb" by which her own bodily consciousness is first roused. The vision is of inward aloneness, of
that "warm white flame of a single life" in Mellors, that singleness
of being which is Lawrence's equivalent for what Freudians would
probably call ego-strength but which Lawrence sees as a kind of
animal or creaturely sureness. Readers may differ as to Mellors'
plausibility as a character, or *ego*, but the novel turns on his difference from Michaelis or from Clifford and his cronies in what he
brings to love—which is just this other kind of selfhood. If, as
Lawrence believes, you must in some sense lose yourself to find
yourself in sexual love, then it takes a certain creaturely strength
to risk the hazards of self-abandonment. We have already seen
how Michaelis submits himself like a wounded child to love-making, climaxes quickly out of some unexpressed fear of giving himself up to the act with real generosity of feeling, holds on grimly
in a fake simulation of caring, all the while resenting his submission to the woman's power. The point here is certainly not that all
love-making should result in mutual climaxes, or even that some
love-making involves withholding and holding on as power ploys,
but that independent strength, sure existence as a separate being,
makes for generous abandonment to the hazards of passion, the
exposures to one another that may indeed be used for damage and
denial and denigration. Mellors' capacity for creaturely tenderness,
coming out of this creaturely sureness, is what Lawrence wants to
get across.

When Connie turns to the woods for respite, then, she is moved
as much by Mellors' promise as a separate person as by the weari-

ness which makes that promise so attractive. Her frank admission, "She was to be had for the taking", is the statement of a woman exhausted by the sterilities of purely mental life, by the hurtful ploys of wilful passion, by the deadening lust for money and success, by the industrial blight which attends it, and which joins Wragby Hall to the outside world, and by the emotional blight her crippled writer-industrialist husband puts upon her as the personal sum of all these negations. It is a convincing statement of collapsed allegiance to things gone dead, all the more persuasive for the scene which precedes it in which Connie holds in her hands the cheeky chick balancing on almost weightless feet, and cries blindly in "all the anguish of her generation's forlornness"—to which personal and cultural distress Mellors responds with creaturely compassion and a melting heart. The scene is doubly or perhaps triply touching in that it affects the heart, the sensual body on which heartfelt feelings depend, and our sympathetic understanding of these live things. The connection between body, feelings, and mind is one whole thing, the apple on the apple tree, as Mellors says softly, "You shouldn't cry."

3

Connie's acquiescence, in this first of the series of sexual communions by which she is renewed, is all that Lawrence asked for in his mid-career hostilities toward women. She responds to Mellors' directions "with a queer obedience". She lies still throughout the act "in a kind of sleep", so that "The activity, the orgasm, was his, all his." She can bear the burden of herself no more, and gives herself to the man without striving. No wonder that Kate Millett exploits the scene as indicative of the pure male mastery and female subjection which, she asserts, Lawrence really wants. But the condition defined here—based on depleted will in a strong woman and sure aloneness in a vulnerable man—is only preliminary. In the long conflict ahead Connie will wake to the restorative possibilities of creaturely selfhood and Mellors will be "broken open again" to the hurtful possibilities of personal commitment. That the man who has been kind to the female in Connie is concerned also about her person (and indeed his own) is evident when he tells her, "I don't jeer at you", or warns her to care about the risk she is taking: "Don't care when it's too late," he says with a pleading voice. And there is his anger with himself for trying to get rid of his aloneness when, at the end of Chapter X, he is drawn at night to Wragby Hall: "You've got to stick to it all your life," he thinks. . . . "Accept your aloneness and stick to it . . . and accept the times when the gap is filled, when they come . . . You can't force them." And then he adds: "There must be a coming together on both sides," and turns away to wait for it to happen (p. 197). So it is creaturely selfhood, alive in the faltering Mellors and now coming alive in Connie, which takes primacy over love and allows—rather than wills—it to happen.

Not, of course, without flare-ups of self-will on either side. Detached in the ensuing acts of love, Connie finds Mellors' butting haunches ridiculous both before and after their first mutual orgasm and her obvious impregnation. She avoids seeing him for days, dreams of using him merely as her phallic tool, and does use him for a time to get herself a child. Mellors too has his wilful occasions, as when he forces himself on Connie in the forest after her deliberate absences, or when—like Michaelis with Connie—he voices his resentment against his first wife, Bertha Coutts, for having to "grind her own coffee" in the act of love, and decries her beakish, lesbian ways. Their progress is nothing if not humanly complicated. But chiefly Connie is tired of her "hard bright female power" and Mellors is tender. When, in Chapter XII, he reassures her that she need not love him, that it can't be forced, she dies to that willed mentality which finds the sexual act ridiculous and is born to her own sensual consciousness. From which new vantage-point she finds his body beautiful and yields to the sensual adoration she has long suppressed. His similar adoration has been evident from the first; but his paean of praise to her vagina here —two chapters before her paean to his penis—confirms it. They express mutual love for the first time now, without benefit of anything like male mastery or female subjection.

Does Mellors go on to reduce his lady to phallus worship, as some feminist critics hold? If so, he is himself reduced beforehand to vagina worship. Does Lawrence then reduce both lovers to their private parts, John Thomas and Lady Jane? Mellors' paean of praise—"It's thee down theer; an' what I get when I'm i'side thee; it's a' as it is, all on't. . . . It's thee, dost see: an' tha'rt a lot besides an animal, aren't ter? . . . Eh, that's the beauty o' thee, lass," (p. 234)—speaks rather to the sensual otherness of men and women and suggests to me at least a sexual version of Martin Buber's *I and Thou*. Indeed, the independent *being* of John Thomas and Lady Jane, celebrated two chapters later, invokes by personification and synecdoche the creaturely selfhood for which these "persons" stand, "it's a' as it is, all on't," as Mellors says, an *inclusion* of love's personal dimensions which insists on their creaturely basis. Considering later quarrels over the deified phallus and the exclusive masculinity of "the phallic consciousness", it might have helped if Lawrence had dwelled on the divine vulva, as the *Tantra* calls it, and its rousings: but surely Lady Jane moves verbally in that direction and—socially at least —outranks the plebeian John Thomas until Connie grants him knighthood. By the time she does so, moreover, she *initiates* foreplay, enjoys mutual activity in arriving at mutual orgasms, dances naked in the rain. Thus, if Lawrence could never articulate the value of such mutual assertiveness, nor imagine the ranges of mutuality and trust we now accept, the fact remains that in this fearful, limited, lovely, and still unrivalled book he started us on our way.

A much more problematic flare-up of hostility occurs in Chapter XVI, the now famous night of searing passion. Mellors' recourse to anal intercourse, or buggery, has caused no end of controversy since its detection in the early 1960s. Lawrence's "cowardly reticence" here, his verbal ambiguity in this otherwise explicit novel, has been remarked upon; the use of Connie as an outlet for Mellors' homosexual urges has been suggested by at least two observers; and still others take buggery itself as the supreme heterosexual practice for Lawrence, the ultimate sexual mystery, and the grand climax accordingly of Connie's sexual initiation.[16] H. M. Daleski's approach to the scene seems to me much more plausible: he sees a reversion here in Lawrence himself "to a desire for male domination" and "a recrudescence of [his] old fear of a loss of identity, which . . . is the fundamental cause of a sexual assertiveness".[17] These are the right issues, rightly posed, though I will want to diverge from them slightly and weigh them differently in the remarks which follow.

Daleski is the only critic I have read who connects the scene with its immediate novelistic context. He points out that Mellors has just had a fierce quarrel with Connie's sister Hilda and that his sensuality that night seems to spring from and to express his anger with her, so that he extends to Connie the violence coiled within him. This seems to me an important entry to the scene; but Lawrence does more to justify that transferred anger than Daleski allows. Connie's trip to Venice with her father has been impending for several chapters, and has caused some distress between the lovers. She explains her idea of appearing to have taken a lover there, so that Clifford will think him the father of their child. But, as Mellors sees, she has made use of him: to go to Venice is to hide the real source of her pregnancy and quite possibly to by-pass him altogether. So, whatever her protestations about returning to him, about keeping the tenderness between them alive, she is in fact ashamed of him and will not publicly acknowledge him as the father of her child. The problem is raised again in this chapter as Connie ponders her own behaviour: "After all, was she not giving her man the go-by, if only for a short time? And he knew it. That's why he was so queer and sarcastic" (p. 300). When her sister Hilda appears to take her off to Venice, moreover, Connie flushes vividly "like a shamed child" after naming the gamekeeper as her lover, then tries to apologize for him as a man who "really understands tenderness". Thus she shares in some measure in the disapproval and disgust which Hilda brings to the argument with Mellors. In Hilda too the wilfulness of the Dresden years and of the postwar period is writ large: so that Mellors' clash with her is a kind of focussing of related problems— a flare-up of old wilfulness linked with unpurged shame—and his sensual ferocity is designed to burn out both in Connie. Though she feels he is not angry with her, he has good reason to be angry.

Still, his anger runs in excess of the situation. His boorishness with Hilda as they vie for dominance is as ugly as her snobbery with him: they are equally spiteful and self-willed, equally obnoxious. Yet even this excess has been provided for, earlier in the chapter, by Connie's conversation with Mrs Bolton. They have been talking about having to manage and manipulate men, babies who must be flattered and deceived as to having their own way. Mrs Bolton's dead husband was an exception to all this: he was never "lord and master", nor was she; and though they had their determined moments, each knew when to yield to the other:

> Even when he was in the wrong, if he was fixed, I gave in. You see, I never wanted to break what was between us. And if you really set your will against a man, that finishes it. If you care for a man, you have to give in to him once he's really determined; whether

you're in the right or not, you have to give in. Else you break something. But I must say, Ted 'ud give in to me sometimes, when I was set on a thing and in the wrong. So I suppose it cuts both ways.

(p. 300)

As Connie ponders this she begins to have doubts, already indicated, about her trip to Venice. She sees that men as well as women are easily wounded in their pride, but as Mrs Bolton implies and now actually spells out, the "two prides are a bit different": something breaks when a determined if wrongheaded man is, in effect, outwilled—and a strong woman can always outwill him. But, if she is a caring woman who wants to keep their love intact, she can also yield more easily—presumably from her position of greater strength. There is, at any rate, more to love for either sex than winning arguments (including this one about different prides and greater strengths), if yielding cuts both ways.

It looks, then, as if Mellors' excessive anger, his renewed uneasiness about his masculine rôle, has been cast by Lawrence as an instance of wrongheaded wilfulness which can be accommodated by Connie's yielding love. She can afford to "let him have his way and his will of her . . . to be a passive, consenting thing, like a slave, a physical slave", as he proceeds that night with his "phallic hunting out" of the deepest recesses of organic shame. The trouble is, her shame, so far as we know it, has been socially conditioned and Lawrence (who elsewhere sees the connection between money and filth) fails to connect organic purging with that issue; still more importantly, he conveniently forgets that Mellors needs to be purged of excessive fear and anger and of the self-doubt that implies, and assigns him instead the fearless rôle of phallic hunter. The buggering scene is doctrinally insistent, at the expense of honesty and dramatic context, about the value of purging Connie of organic shame. Its meaning for both characters is lost in an outburst of righteous rhetoric and misplaced pride. But it might have come across as a much-needed purging of Mellors' sexual hostility and self-doubt and of Connie's social shame.

Daleski is right, then, about the resurgence of Lawrence's "desire for male dominance", via Mellors, but wrong about its irreconcilability with tenderness. The burning out of hostility and self-doubt through "sheer fiery sensuality" *is* relevant to Mellors' progress. He has his own difficulties with renewal and badly needs such purging. Lawrence comes closer to this issue when, in a later chapter, he allows Connie to credit Mellors with the "courage" of his own tenderness. It takes courage, for a man who fears being overwhelmed by strong-willed women, to risk the exposure of his own tender feelings. The risk is to his maleness, to his identity as a separate sexual being.

It follows from all this that Mellors' concern with male identity, as opposed to male dominance, is crucial to his capacity for tenderness, and the purging scene ought to have made that distinction too. As many critics have observed, Mellors shares a number of traits—his dialect speech, his work and bathing habits, his creaturely sureness—with Lawrence's father. Lawrence's deliberate investment of these traits suggests that his own choice of sexual identity had by this time become a great deal more secure, and by the same token, that his need for sexual cannibalism was nearly exhausted. He had the courage now to offer nurturing love, and in that healthier sense to compete with a woman's powers, without losing his maleness.

In insisting on such maleness Lawrence runs counter to much current thought about personhood. He seems to assert a biological basis for identity at this time, as if our choice of who we are is in one way or another a creaturely disposition, a choice of maleness or femaleness. Norman Mailer's depiction of Lawrence as a man with the soul of a "beautiful, imperious, and passionate woman" who wanted desperately all his life to be a man, speaks eloquently to this point.[18] In *Lady Chatterley's Lover* he seems to have endowed Mellors with the vulnerable but decidedly male identity he sought, and to have endowed Clifford with the egotism, self-importance, and self-will he wanted to discard—and which he elsewhere saw as the maternally-imposed traits of early childhood. These were the terms, I think, of his own struggle for self-renewal, of his own need to recover from the sexual impotence from which he then apparently suffered and which he projected also onto the hapless Clifford. Significantly, in *The Man Who Died*, written in the same period, he invests these conflicting aspects of himself serially into a single figure, who moves as it were from his maternal to his paternal heritage through the tender ministrations of a devoted priestess. The resurrection of this fallible man, the restoration of his potency by a divinely-inspired woman, was made possible, I think, by the Chatterley solution. Having waited long enough for life to do it for him, Lawrence could finally imagine the purging of his own self-importance and self-will. His maleness, if not his potency, was finally secure, and on that rich paradox he could build his ship of death.

NOTES

1   (London, 1977), p. 155.
2   *Ibid.*, p. 156. See pp. 152–60 for the full discussion.
3   *Women in Love* (New York, 1960), p. 42. Page references in the text are to this edition.
4   See Mark Schorer's venerable arguments for this position, circa 1950, in "*Women in Love* and Death", *D. H. Lawrence: A Collection of Critical Essays*, ed, Mark Spilka (Englewood Cliffs, N.J., 1963), pp. 50–60.
5   "Lessing and Lawrence: The Battle of the Sexes", *Contemporary Literature*, XVI (Spring 1975), pp. 218–40.
6   For a fuller discussion of these points see my essay, "Lawrence's Quarrel with Tenderness", *Critical Quarterly*, IX, (Winter 1967), pp. 363–77.
7   (New York, 1970), p. 263.
8   See Janice Harris's excellent account, in this regard, of Lawrence's reliance on such female antagonists for "loyal and effective opposition" to his visionary views, in "Sexual Antagonism in D. H. Lawrence's Early Leadership Fiction", *Modern Language Studies*, VII (Spring 1977), pp. 43–52.
9   *Four Short Novels of D. H. Lawrence* (New York, 1965), p. 169.
10 Millett, p. 292.
11 *Four Short Novels*, p. 224.
12 *The Letters of D. H. Lawrence*, ed. Aldous Huxley (New York, 1932), p. 719.
13 (Paris, 1944), pp. 60–61.
14 (New York, 1972), pp. 112–15. Page references in the text are to this edition.
15 (New York, 1962), pp. 161–6. Page references in the text are to this edition.
16 Andrew Shonfield and John Sparrow score Lawrence's reticence as cowardly and dishonest in their *Encounter* essays (XVII, September 1961, pp. 63–4; XVIII, February 1962, pp. 35–43); Kate Millett speaks of Mellors' "sodomous urges", here indulged, and posits an earlier homosexual love affair with his colonel, in *Sexual Politics*, p. 241; Jeffrey Meyers seems to believe that all such acts are substitutions of anal marriage for homosexual love in "D. H. Lawrence and Homosexuality", *D. H. Lawrence: Novelist, Poet, Prophet*, ed. Stephen Spender (New York, 1973), pp. 135–46; and Colin Clarke and Frank Kermode take the

grand climactic view, as discussed in my review of such matters, "Lawrence Up-Tight, or the Anal Phase Once Over", and the critical exchange which follows, in *Novel: A Forum on Fiction*, IV (Spring 1971), pp. 252–67, and V (Fall 1971), pp. 54–70.

17 *The Forked Flame: A Study of D. H. Lawrence* (London, 1968), p. 309.
18 *The Prisoner of Sex* (New York, 1971), p. 110.

Notes on Contributors

T. E. APTER is a graduate of Edinburgh University and Newnham College, Cambridge. She is author of various articles on music and literary criticism, and has contributed to such journals as *Tempo*, *Musical Opinion*, *Forum for Modern Language Studies*, and *The Human World*. She is the author of two novels, *Silken Lines and Silver Hooks* and *Adonis's Garden* (Heinemann, 1976, 1977), and of a study of *Thomas Mann* (Macmillan, 1978).

LYDIA BLANCHARD is Assistant Professor of English at Mount Vernon College in Washington, D.C. She is the author of several articles and papers on D. H. Lawrence, and is currently writing a book on the vision of history in Lawrence, George Orwell, and Norman Mailer (Vision Critical Studies, 1979).

MARK KINKEAD-WEEKES is Professor of English Literature at the University of Kent at Canterbury, and has recently finished a term of office as Pro Vice-Chancellor. He has published books on Samuel Richardson and William Golding; a number of articles, mainly on fiction; and edited *Twentieth Century Interpretations of 'The Rainbow'*. He is working on a new edition of *The Rainbow* and a book on *Lawrence at Work 1912–1921*.

HARRY T. MOORE is Research Professor Emeritus (but still teaching) at Southern Illinois University (Carbondale), and is a Fellow of the Royal Society of Literature. He is the author and editor of many books on Lawrence, and has also published books on Steinbeck, Forster, modern French and German Literature. He is the Honorary President of the D. H. Lawrence Society of America.

JULIAN MOYNAHAN holds the rank of Distinguished Professor in the English Department at Rutgers—the State University of New Jersey, where he has taught since 1964. His teaching and research interests centre on late Victorian and early modern English Literature and on

Anglo-Irish studies. He is the author of three novels: *Garden State* (1973), *Pairing Off* (1969), and *Sisters and Brothers* (1960); critical studies of D. H. Lawrence (1963) and of Vladimir Nabokov (1970); and of editions of Lawrence's short stories and of *Sons and Lovers* (Viking Critical Library, 1968). Recently published is his edition of the selected prose and poetry of Thomas Hardy as a Viking Portable (March 1977), and he has just finished a new novel.

FAITH PULLIN lectures in English and American Literature in Edinburgh University. She is the author of several essays and reviews, has edited a book of essays on *Melville* (Edinburgh University Press, 1978), and has prepared, with an introduction, an edition of Brooke's *The Fool of Quality*.

MARK SPILKA is Professor of English and Comparative Literature at Brown University in America, where he also helps to edit the journal *Novel: A Forum on Fiction*. He is the author of *The Love Ethic of D. H. Lawrence* (1955) and *Dickens and Kafka: A Mutual Interpretation* (1936), and has edited two critical anthologies: *D. H. Lawrence: A Collection of Critical Essays* (1963) and *Towards a Poetics of Fiction* (1977). He is currently working on a study of shifting taboos in modern fiction to be called *New Literary Quarrels with Tenderness*.

PHILIPPA TRISTRAM is a graduate of Lady Margaret Hall, Oxford, and lectures in Medieval English Literature at the University of York. She is the author of several articles, and of *Figures of Life and Death in Medieval Literature* (Elek, 1976).

Index